AS LEEDS GO MARCHING ON

AS LEEDS GO MARCHING ON

A History of Leeds United through Stories, Stats and Trivia

Jonny Cooper

SEVEN DIALS

First published in Great Britain in 2025 by Seven Dials,
an imprint of The Orion Publishing Group Ltd
Carmelite House, 50 Victoria Embankment
London EC4Y 0DZ

An Hachette UK Company

The authorised representative in the EEA is Hachette Ireland, 8 Castlecourt
Centre, Dublin 15, D15 XTP3, Ireland (email: info@hbgi.ie)

1 3 5 7 9 10 8 6 4 2

A CIP catalogue record for this book is
available from the British Library.

ISBN (Hardback) 978 1 3996 3679 7
ISBN (Ebook) 978 1 3996 3681 0
ISBN (Audio) 978 1 3996 3682 7

Typeset by Input Data Services Ltd, Bridgwater, Somerset

Printed in Great Britain by Clays Ltd, Elcograf, S.p.A.

MIX
Paper | Supporting
responsible forestry
FSC   FSC® C104740
www.fsc.org

www.orionbooks.co.uk

CONTENTS

FOREWORD

Sometimes in life you meet someone who has a unique way of interpreting the sphere in which you work. To me, Jonny Cooper is that person. Two colleagues at the BBC, Ian Woodcock and Ronan Sully, introduced me to Jonny many seasons ago as a prospective guest on BBC Radio Leeds. He sat down in front of the microphone and immediately made data and statistics accessible and entertaining to me. Now, bearing in mind I'm a lad who failed his maths O level back in the 1980s at the first time of asking, this was no mean feat.

Jonny's info is often amusing but it's also incredibly useful to me as a broadcaster. He digs out those hidden gems and will throw in a stat so unexpected – covering anything from Steve Morison's cheese wedge-bound shot to the percentage of vowels in Ao Tanaka's name – that you can hardly believe it's true. That's Jonny's brilliance. He combines his love for Leeds United, football and analysis with being entertaining and informative. His work is worth talking about – and now, it's worth reading.

With this book Jonny has dissected the miracle of Marcelo and the Farke phenomenon to explore the club's two recent returns to the Premier League, but he's also gone much further than that. The previous golden eras, the heartbreaks, the legendary players and goals, and all the bits in between. It's a celebration of all things Leeds – even of the bits some fans might rather forget . . .

And the Bielsa era is the perfect case in point of why Jonny's work is so useful. Somewhere amid the swirling, spellbinding magic of Marcelo, someone needed to draw those straight lines to help us all understand why Bielsaball was so effective for three years. Jonny did just that, not by the obvious goals for and against columns or simple possession stats, but – for example – by showing that a former Yeovil Town right-back eclipsed the Ballon d'Or holder into second place for progressing the ball upfield across Europe's top five divisions in 2020–21. Leeds United's Luke Ayling carried the ball for almost four miles that season, more than Barcelona's Lionel Messi. These nuggets are relevant to me because they tell a story through statistics, illuminating further what fans are seeing on the pitch and creating discussion.

Jonny's research is also brilliant for a juicy quiz question, or just a nibble of history, especially on a long journey for an awayer at Plymouth or Norwich. Look at the glittering Revie era for example. We all know about Jack Charlton's appearance record or who scored the winner in 1972, but Jonny can tell you the only player whose surname began with the letter A who made an appearance during the legendary manager's 741-game tenure. That will keep you going until Leicester Forest services at least.

One of my other favourites is how Jonny likes to bewitch us every year with this classic: which player is the only one to have played in a Premier League game on 31 October whose name contains every letter of the word 'Halloween'? No clues, but I used to work with him. Get in, Jonny, for mining that gold within the pages of this book.

Although I do keep a record of appearances, goals, cautions and contracts, I would not class myself as particularly driven by data. Conveying what I witness into a mental picture is often all about the moment and having to be a bit off the cuff – I'd like to think I'm a bit like if Pablo Hernández was on commentary, right? As such, it is an interpretation; it is prone to an element of subjectivity rather than being definitive. Cooper and his Opta cohort are far more accurate than any commentator, but Jonny stands out as he mixes figures with fascination. It is an addictive elixir he concocts, judging by how much his offerings are retweeted or shared across social media. A geek maybe to some, but he is a genius to me – and more than that, he's also a fine gentleman.

Oh, and there is one statistic I would be absolutely cast-iron sure of reiterating on the mic and that is: 'One Jonny Cooper, there's only one Jonny Cooper.'

Adam Pope

INTRODUCTION

I was fortunate to start supporting Leeds United when they were one of the best clubs in the country. They finished third in the first season I can remember in 1999–00 and reached the semi-finals of the UEFA Cup, when I was only five years old. It is strange how vividly things stick in your head as a kid, but my first Leeds memory is watching highlights on *Match of the Day* of us beating Tottenham in February 2000 and then visiting my grandpa's house in Swillington to watch us on Sky Sports a few times towards the end of that season. The one game that I particularly remember was away at Bradford City, when Neville Southall made his comeback aged forty-one. Michael Bridges scored the winner for Leeds and became my first favourite player, although – hopefully just a coincidence – he got injured almost as soon as I got his name printed on the back of my first shirt (the classic 2000–01 Strongbow home number).

At the start of the following season, my parents secretly entered a *Yorkshire Evening Post* competition to win a guided tour of Elland Road, with tickets to that evening's game against a newly promoted Manchester City. We won the competition, and a couple of weeks before my dad took a detour to go past Elland Road to show me where we'd be going for the tour. I could not believe the size of it, and counted down the days until the day came. Leeds lost the game 2–1, with Lee Bowyer scoring our goal. Eleven days later, I got to go to my second game against newly promoted Ipswich Town. Leeds lost the game 2–1, with Lee Bowyer scoring our goal. Looking back years later I thought this was an odd statistical anomaly and, with the benefit of the research I'd done on Leeds United's history, I could work out that this is the only time Leeds have lost consecutive home games by the same score with the same player scoring our goal. It will mean nothing to anyone else, but as they were my first two games it's nice to know they had some small statistical relevance.

And that's where the obsession started. After that, it was down to Garforth Library to repeatedly borrow *Leeds United: A Complete Record (1919–1989)* by Martin Jarred and Malcolm MacDonald, and pore over the statistics on all the managers, players and seasons the book offered. I remember being struck by the moustaches of Leeds City managers Gilbert Gillies and Frank Scott-Walford, and the lovely front cover with a great drawing of John Charles in the old gold and blue kit from the 1950s. I never actually owned a copy of this book until many years later I found it in the enormous Westwood bookshop in Sedbergh – and could hardly turn it down for £2.50.

VHS tapes (remember them?) of the great old Leeds teams were also watched on a weekly basis. *The Glory Years* narrated by John Motson looking at the team Don Revie built is a classic among Leeds fans and was one of my favourites, as was *Leeds United's 180 Goals,* with all the goals scored between 1969 and 1990. At the start of that video, photos of the players flash up on screen (I can still see them now: Clarke, Lorimer, Giles, Gray, Charlton, Currie, Jordan, McKenzie, Sheridan). I remember watching that at my friend's house and reeling them all off one by one and his mum being amazed at my knowledge. I suppose an eight-year-old seeing a photo of Arthur Graham (in a Bradford shirt) and being able to name him is quite odd looking back. The video that really stood out, however, was *The Pain and the Glory*, which featured footage of various eras or games of Leeds between the 1960s and early 90s, split up by a particular theme (the 1972 FA Cup final, Allan Clarke scoring goals, goalkeepers making great saves) with music played over the top. I almost wore that tape out, and years later our VHS machine chewed it up. It had never appeared on YouTube or the internet, so I was indebted to a fellow Leeds fan on Twitter who had a copy and sent it to me, allowing me to relive some childhood nostalgia. The section with clips of Billy Bremner and David Batty (generally just getting stuck in) is shown to the sounds of 'Achy Breaky Heart' by Billy Ray Cyrus, which is now my karaoke song, while the section with Colchester knocking Leeds out of the FA Cup in 1971 has 'Lessons in Love' by

Level 42 playing, who are one of my favourite bands. Leeds influencing my life everywhere.

Fast-forward to 2012, my last year of sixth form. I'd had a season ticket at Leeds since 2004–05, in which time I'd seen precisely zero seasons of Premier League football, one relegation to League One and one promotion from League One. And yet, Leeds United were still my passion. So, too, were the stats behind the team. In summer 2012, an opportunity arose for someone to take over as the researcher for Leeds on *Football Manager*, a game I'd played religiously since 2005. It was an unpaid role but you got the game free at the end of it (and your name in the credits). I went for it and got it, and for three years I was in charge of rating the players and their potential (remember Monty Gimpel? I got that one wrong), as well as trying to track the general chaos in the ownership at Leeds at that time as Ken Bates handed over to GFH Sports. There was also a slightly bizarre situation in early 2014 where allegedly the Leeds board refused to sanction the signing of Ashley Barnes because his stats on the game were worse than the ones that I'd rated for our own Luke Varney, and so apparently they believed the signing made no sense. So, in some ways I was partially responsible for Barnes never playing for Leeds – you can either blame or thank me for that, whichever you feel is applicable.

In June 2013, the head researcher at *Football Manager* sent round an email to all the club researchers flagging a job we might be interested in, while stressing he had no links to it himself. It was for a role at Opta Sports to be a data editor, and they had just opened an office in Leeds. Reading the application form, I realised it was the dream job for me. After turning down offers from universities to study sports journalism, I was now working at my local Tesco, and a few days after applying – with a cover letter in which I mentioned as many niche 1990s footballers as possible (hello Hamilton Ricard) – I was invited to an interview. I arrived twenty minutes early wearing an orange tie because a lady I'd seen in Next said she worked for a recruiter and 'orange ties stand out'. If they do, it didn't help me this time, as I missed out on the job. At nineteen, I'd probably have been the youngest data editor in Opta history (there's a stat for you), and I'd have to wait for the next opening.

Finally, two years later (after badgering them asking about jobs for most of that time), they had a vacancy and needed someone to start within a week. I was ready. I handed in my notice at Tesco and worked my last shift on 7 August, finishing at midnight. I started at Opta the following morning, which was also the opening day of the 2015–16 season, working alongside the person who had got the job ahead of me two years beforehand (we got on very well – no hard feelings, Chris). Ten years later, I'm still there and love it.

It has been fascinating to see the change in football in the decade I've been with Opta. To give you an overview of what our department does, we provide the data and statistics that a broadcaster such as Sky use in their analysis, finding the interesting pieces of information you hear a commentator share when a player breaks a record, or when a team has had an astonishing number of shots in a game. Our job is not only to keep on top of the trends but to identify the trends ourselves: are teams scoring more goals from set pieces? Why is the goals-per-game in the top-flight at its highest since the mid-1960s? Are managers getting younger? Are goalkeepers passing the ball more, and at shorter distances? These are just a small number of questions we will be asked on a weekly basis by our clients, including journalists, broadcasters, leagues, organisations, clubs themselves and even the betting industry. The beautiful thing about football is every day there is something new – you never know if a player will assist five goals in a game, a team will receive four red cards, or a manager will return to the Premier League out of the blue after a long exile. No two days in this job are ever the same.

Behind all that information is the Opta data insights team. Over the years, we have built an enormous database which is ready to answer any and all questions, helped along the way by our Opta Query Tool, Opta Search and Opta Live, extremely powerful tools we use every day. Hours, days and sometimes months of painstaking research will go into crafting specialist files which may only be used a couple of times a season but will provide the answer to a very specific query. Some of the files created and work produced over the years has been truly extraordinary and I've been so fortunate to work alongside fantastic people in my decade at Opta, many of whom are now not only colleagues (or ex-colleagues) but very good friends. I always say that we share the same common interest of football, so there's never any shortage of conversation. It really is true – you can just sit around and name ex-footballers and never get bored.

It was this inspiration from files that were being created at Opta (and learning how to proficiently use Microsoft Excel) that led me to expand my own Leeds United database. In late 2016 I started to compile a file which had every player to play in every game in the club's history, including whether they started the game, were substituted on or off, scored a goal or were an unused sub. Once I had the basics in there, I built it out further. I got hold of every player's date of birth. I amalgamated other information I had in other files – which stadium each game was played at, who was the manager for each game, which position in the table were Leeds and their opponents on the day of the game. In a bigger project, I watched back every goal Leeds had scored from 1989–90 onwards and found who had assisted them. I'd love to go back further but unfortunately not every goal has been recorded before then, so it's tricky to be completist. Given I spent dozens of hours of my childhood watching old season review tapes, this was not even in the slightest a chore, and it's nice to have a couple of seasons' worth of First Division assists before the Premier League started (Gordon Strachan had the most in 1990–91 and 1991–92 combined by the way, with 16).

It was great to then be able to use the files and apply them to the current team. In August 2017, Samuel Saiz scored a hat-trick on his debut, and it was fairly widely known that Carl Shutt was the last player to do this back in 1989. But he wasn't the only one before Saiz – a chap called Percy Whipp had scored a hat-trick on his 1922 debut, and Don Weston managed it as well in 1962. Keeping the names of these players alive, many long forgotten, is really important to me. They all played a role in Leeds United's history, and 103 years on from Whipp's hat-trick, I doubt he thought someone with an Excel spreadsheet would be keeping his name in the mind of Leeds United supporters.

The arrival of Marcelo Bielsa in the summer of 2018 and the drastic improvement in the team also proved a huge inspiration in looking deeper into the data for just how on earth he had managed to do it, but it also inspired me to keep more on top of records being broken and highlight players doing particularly well across different metrics – of which there were numerous during the period. It is much easier – and more enjoyable – to find stats on Leeds when they are doing well, and the form of Pablo Hernández, Mateusz Klich, Luke Ayling, Kalvin Phillips and the vast majority of that promotion-winning team provided no end of statistical opportunities. Being able to compare against other Premier League teams after promotion – especially as we did so well that first season – was one of the great joys of my job so far. I became far more active on Twitter (I'll always call it that) and started picking up more and more followers, and that led to more eyes being on the facts I produced. Without Bielsa transforming the football club and providing a resurgence when he did, I doubt very much I would be sat here right now writing this book.

So this book you're now reading will look at some of the key eras in the club's history from a statistical angle, offering new insight and trivia around some of the club's most important figures, and then following the club's 2024–25 title-winning season with all the best facts about the current band of heroes. It will be a chronological look at the many periods of the club, from the incredible Revie era, the resurgence under Howard Wilkinson and David O'Leary's young team, to the many painful years outside of the top-flight until Bielsa came along and gave us a magical ride; and interspersed will be chapters on some of the club's greatest ever goalscorers and a delve into our often laughably bad FA Cup record.

Whether you're reading from cover to cover or dipping in and out into your favourite eras, my main aim is for everyone who reads this to learn something new in each chapter, or relive some of the brilliant, crazy or sometimes infuriating things that have happened in the vast history of our beloved Leeds United. I hope you enjoy reading it as much as I enjoyed writing it.

Marching on together.

1

THE REVIE ERA

All Leeds fans are brought up on the stories and video clips of the great Revie team. 'And poor Southampton just don't know what day it is,' says legendary commentator Barry Davies as Leeds, 7–0 up, stroke the ball around at Elland Road with Saints players chasing shadows (in truth, some of the efforts of the Southampton players to get the ball back are half-hearted at best). Every time I watch that clip, I am always awaiting the sad moment when Paul Madeley ends the long sequence by giving it away with a loose pass – though he does win it back immediately.

There's no escaping the era on any trip to Elland Road. The statues of Bremner and Revie are regular meeting spots outside the ground. The four stands at the stadium are named after Revie, John Charles, Norman Hunter and Jack Charlton. The road leading to the park-and-ride is named Bobby Collins Way. If you're lucky enough to be in the hospitality section, you'll more than likely bump into Paul Reaney. For many years, my dad and I would go to the Pavilion opposite the East Stand before a game and on the stage would be Peter Lorimer speaking to an old teammate, usually Allan Clarke, Mick Jones or Terry Yorath. Clarke's passion for Leeds had never dimmed, and barely a week would go by without him asserting that the great Revie side would beat whoever the top side in the country was in the present day. This would always be greeted with rapturous applause.

Clarke's claim can be disputed but what can't be is that, for the ten years they spent in the English top-flight under Revie, Leeds United were the best side, statistically, in the country and Europe. The excellent John Motson-narrated VHS *The Glory Years* looks at the ten years of Leeds from 1965 to 1975, culminating in reaching the European Cup final the year after Revie left. This chapter (sadly, without the lovely

Glory Years soundtrack) will look at the period between 1964 and 1974 and examine how Revie's Leeds can claim they were the best side of the era and one of the finest teams English football has ever seen.

What came before

It is hard to now imagine Leeds United without Don Revie, but the club did have some top-flight pedigree before he joined – albeit in much different circumstances. They'd featured in eighteen seasons at England's top table between 1924 and 1960, but in four of those they'd been relegated and had only managed to finish higher than eighth once. This fifth-place finish in 1929–30 was the club's high point up to Revie's appointment. They'd led the division after fourteen games in 1929 but then lost five games in a row to slide down the table, and they wouldn't go top of the top-flight again until 1965. Their only other brief foray with a title challenge before Revie had been in 1937–38, when the goals of Gordon Hodgson fired them to second spot on New Year's Eve. From New Year's Day until the end of the season, Leeds had the fourth worst form in the division and finished ninth. They simply weren't a side who were ever likely to win the league title, and spent more days (fifty-five) top of the table in their first season in the First Division under Revie in 1964–65 than they managed in all eighteen seasons beforehand (fifty-one).

Between 1924–25 and 1959–60, the club's average finish in the top-flight had been fifteenth, and in that time they'd conceded 188 goals more than they'd scored themselves, the worst record of any team to play in the top-flight in that timeframe. Twenty-two teams played in as many top-flight seasons as Leeds had between 1924 and 1960, and the Whites had the lowest points-per-game (0.89) and lowest average finish (fifteenth) of those twenty-two. Leeds really weren't very good, sadly.

Revie turned all that on its head. Under his near-decade of leadership, between 1964–65 and 1973–74, Leeds won 237 top-flight games. This was only fourteen fewer than they'd managed in the thirty-six years between 1924 and 1960. There were thirty-one more clean sheets, 739 more days top of the table and 281 days fewer spent at the foot of the First Division. Although the Football League operated on goal average in those days (until 1976, teams locked on the same points would be separated by their goal average, which was goals scored divided by goals conceded; this was scrapped as it favoured more defensive teams), looking at it through the more modern idea of goal difference, Leeds had a positive difference of 342 goals under Revie, compared to conceding 188 more previously. It took Leeds until a 4–1 win over West Ham in December 1969 to get their First Division accumulative goal difference into a positive figure, the first time they'd done so since November 1924.

Leeds United in the First Division	Before Revie	Under Revie
Games	756	420
Wins	251	237
Draws	171	110
Losses	334	73
Goals	1,145	727
Goals Conceded	1,333	385
Goal Difference	-188	+342
Points	673	584
Win %	33%	56%
Defeat %	44%	17%
Points per Game	0.89	1.39
Average Final Position	14.8	2.3
Clean Sheets	146	177
Days Top of the League	51	790
Days in Top Four	453	2,096
Days Bottom of the League	288	7

Ten-year dominance

From the start of the 1964–65 season until the end of 1973–74, Leeds United won thirty-six more points than any other side in the First Division; in the days of two points for a win, this equates to eighteen wins. Nine clubs were ever-present in that time and Leeds won 100 more games than two of those (Stoke and West Ham), winning almost 200 points more than both of those sides. Leeds' nearest challengers were Bill Shankly's Liverpool, but even his terrific side lost sixteen more games than Leeds in that era, with the Whites responsible for seven of those defeats.

Pos.	Division One – 1964–65 – 1973–74	P	W	D	L	Pts
1	Leeds United	420	237	110	73	584
2	Liverpool	420	217	114	89	548
3	Arsenal	420	184	114	122	482
4	Chelsea	420	181	118	121	480
5	Manchester United	420	178	119	123	475
6	Tottenham Hotspur	420	177	116	127	470
7	Everton	420	174	119	127	467
8	Stoke City	420	137	120	163	394
9	West Ham United	420	137	114	169	388

Even accounting for points-per-game, only Derby County came any-where near close to Leeds and Liverpool over that ten-year period, with the Rams featuring in the last five seasons in this era.

Division One – 1964–65 – 1973–74	P	W	D	L	Pts	PPG
Leeds United	420	237	110	73	584	1.39
Liverpool	420	217	114	89	548	1.30
Derby County	210	98	51	61	247	1.18

Leeds were the leading scorers across the decade, hitting 727 goals at an average of 1.73 per game. They top-scored in both 1969–70 and 1970–71 and were in the top two scorers in the First Division in each of their final five seasons under Revie. In only one season (1966–67, when they were fourteenth top scorers) were they not among the five leading scorers in a First Division season.

Division One – 1964–65 – 1973–74	Games	Goals	Goals per Game
Leeds United	420	727	1.73
Manchester United	420	685	1.63
Chelsea	420	641	1.53
Liverpool	420	639	1.52
Tottenham Hotspur	420	638	1.52
West Ham United	420	638	1.52

Defensively, Leeds once again led the way across those ten seasons, keeping 177 clean sheets and conceding just 0.92 goals per game, which was a marginally lower rate than Liverpool's in that era (0.917 versus 0.921). Across 420 games, Leeds only conceded four goals in a game on seven occasions (only once at home) and only twice did they concede five goals. In fact, Leeds conceded four goals at Elland Road more often in the space of four days in March 2014 than they did at home in the top-flight under Revie, in 4–2 and 5–1 defeats to Reading and Bolton respectively. The defence – which across the ten seasons featured Sprake (306 times), Hunter (397), Reaney (362), Charlton (314) and Cooper (237) – was the bedrock of the team.

11

Division One – 1964–65 – 1973–74	Clean Sheets
Leeds United	177
Liverpool	162
Arsenal	142
Everton	138
Tottenham Hotspur	130
Manchester United	119

Division One – 1964–65 – 1973–74	Games	Goals Conceded	Conceded per Game
Leeds United	420	385	0.92
Liverpool	420	387	0.92
Derby County	210	220	1.05
Everton	420	483	1.15
Manchester City	336	391	1.16
Arsenal	420	492	1.17

In those ten seasons, seven different clubs won the top-flight title, with three sides winning it twice – Leeds, Liverpool and Manchester United. Leeds spent the most days top of the top-flight table in that time, however, spending 153 more days at the summit than any other team (790). They never finished outside the top four at the end of any of those ten campaigns and spent 2,096 days in the top four in total, meaning Leeds were in the top four of the First Division for 78% of the time.

Division One – 1964–65 – 1973–74	Days Top
Leeds United	790
Liverpool	637
Manchester United	431
Everton	225
Chelsea	181
Manchester City	99

Division One – 1964–65 – 1973–74	Days in Top 4
Leeds United	2,096
Liverpool	1,641
Manchester United	924
Arsenal	877
Chelsea	803
Everton	697

The title-winning side of 1968–69 set many new records; they had the fewest defeats (two), most points (sixty-seven), best goal average (2.54) and fewest goals conceded (twenty-six) of any top-flight champion in a forty-two-game season at that stage. After a 5–1 defeat to Burnley in October 1968, Leeds then went the remaining twenty-eight league matches undefeated, only conceding the opening goal in two of those and conceding a measly eleven times. This unbeaten run carried over into the following season, and a 4–1 win against Nottingham Forest was their thirty-first game without losing, breaking a record that Burnley had held since 1920 (clearly Leeds had taken that 5–1 defeat personally, getting revenge with a 6–1 win in December 1968 and breaking their unbeaten record). The thirty-four-game unbeaten run ended with a 3–2 defeat at Everton, and that remained a record until 1978, when Forest – against whom Leeds had broken the record in 1969 – went forty-two games without defeat.

Ahead of 1973–74, on the back of defeats to Sunderland and AC Milan in the FA Cup and Cup Winners' Cup finals, Don Revie challenged his team to go the entire season unbeaten in the First Division. This hadn't been done since the inaugural season of 1888–89, when Preston lost none of their twenty-two matches to win the title. As discussed, only two teams had gone thirty or more matches unbeaten in top-flight history – Leeds and Burnley – and yet here was Revie convinced that his great side could remain undefeated for forty-two games. And they gave it a bloody good go. The longest unbeaten start previously was nineteen matches by Liverpool in 1949–50, but Revie's team broke that record with a 2–1 victory at Stamford Bridge in December 1973. The run continued until the twenty-ninth match of the campaign, a 2–0 win at Manchester United, before losing 3–2 to Stoke in the thirtieth game. Since then, only Arsenal – who went the entire, thirty-eight-game 2003–04 season undefeated – have had a longer run without losing from the start of the season. It kick-started a run of four defeats in seven games for Leeds, but they still recovered and lifted the title.

> Leeds only failed to win six First Division games when they led by two goals under Don Revie but three of them were against Stoke City, in January 1966 (drew 2–2), September 1972 (drew 2–2) and February 1974 (lost 3–2).

Revie's final game in charge was a 1–0 victory against Queens Park Rangers at Loftus Road in April 1974, and it was destined to be his last ever First Division match with any side. That meant that Revie had finished inside the top four of the First Division in every single season – the first club to achieve this kind of run in the English top-flight ever. It had been an unprecedented period of continued quality that would not be matched for almost twenty years and wasn't matched by another manager until Alex Ferguson did it – but even he had seasons where he finished below the top four; Revie never did.

First Season	Last Season	Team	Consecutive Seasons in Top 4
1964–65	1973–74	Leeds United	10
1981–82	1990–91	Liverpool	10
1991–92	2012–13	Manchester United	22
1996–97	2015–16	Arsenal	20
2010–11	Ongoing	Manchester City	15

European adventures

Much as Leeds dominated English football in their ten seasons under Revie, their totals in Europe were similarly impressive. Leeds were in Europe every season from 1965–66 – by virtue of their runners-up finish in the 1964–65 season – until Revie's departure and reached at least the last sixteen in all but one season. They reached six semi-finals, more than any other club in all of Europe, and four finals, winning two and losing two. Leeds were statistically the best team in European football under Don Revie.

Leeds United's first six seasons in European football make for remarkable reading: semi-finalists, finalists, winners, quarter-finalists, semi-finalists and winners. Leeds played sixty-one games and only lost ten, with only Real Zaragoza, Ujpest Dozsa and Celtic winning at Elland Road. They had no less than two 16–0 aggregate victories, over Spora Luxembourg in 1967 and Lyn Oslo in 1969, the latter of whom were dispatched 10–0 at Elland Road. The only other English side to win by sixteen goals on aggregate (admittedly, not a regular occurrence) was Chelsea in 1971 against Jeunesse Hautcharage, who beat the Luxembourg minnows 21–0 over two legs.

Biggest aggregate wins by English clubs

Team	Opponent	Competition	Season	Agg Win
Chelsea	Jeunesse Hautcharage	Cup Winners' Cup	1971–72	21–0
Leeds United	Spora Luxembourg	Inter-Cities Fairs Cup	1967–68	16–0
Leeds United	Lyn Oslo	European Cup	1969–70	16–0
Derby County	Finn Harps	UEFA Cup	1976–77	16–1
Liverpool	Dundalk	Inter-Cities Fairs Cup	1969–70	14–0
Tottenham Hotspur	Keflavík ÍF	UEFA Cup	1971–72	15–1
Tottenham Hotspur	Drogheda United	UEFA Cup	1983–84	14–0

There were also a couple of fortuitous occasions where Leeds, locked on aggregate against Italian sides Bologna in 1967 and Napoli in 1968, were forced to go to the 50/50 scenario of a referee coin toss to decide which side went through. On both occasions Billy Bremner chose correctly and Leeds progressed, the only side to do so more than once in the Fairs Cup. The coin toss 'win' (if that's the correct term) against Bologna determined which side reached that season's semi-finals – imagine travelling thousands of miles around Europe all season in a gruelling schedule to see your fate for reaching the last four decided in this way? It's hard to imagine that in today's VAR, social media sensationalism era, that any big European team could get knocked out of a major European tournament thanks to the flick of a coin.

Neither of those coin toss escapades were in seasons where Leeds would end up lifting the trophy though, so nobody could say that the 1968 and 1971 Fairs Cup wins were in any way down to luck. The 1968 final saw Leeds maintain their excellent defence across both legs of the final against Ferencvaros, with a 1-0 home win thanks to a Mick Jones goal and a 0–0 draw away from home. Eight clean sheets was a joint record by a team in a Fairs Cup campaign, while the twenty-six goals Leeds scored in total was their most ever in a single European season.

The only slip-up on the way to reaching the 1970–71 Fairs Cup final against Juventus was in a second leg defeat in the second round against Dynamo Dresden; an away goal by Mick Jones ensured Leeds progressed on the away goal rule after a 2–2 aggregate draw. Dresden, though, were exceptional on home soil in Europe, losing only three of forty-nine games between 1967 and 1991. Leeds recovered from that loss by eliminating Sparta Prague, Vitória de Setubal and, in the semi-final, Liverpool, thanks to a 1–0 win at Anfield in the first leg (and a goalless draw at Elland Road). It was one of only two defeats Liverpool suffered over a period of eighty-one games between March 1970 and February 1973 – the other was also against Leeds in Division One on New Year's Day 1972.

The 1971 Fairs Cup final was the last before the competition ended to be replaced by the UEFA Cup. Leeds United were the last winners of the trophy, beating Juventus thanks to a 2–2 draw in Turin in the first leg and a 1–1 draw back at Elland Road to give Leeds the victory on away goals – the only time the trophy was decided that way. It was the second and last European title won by Leeds (so far, of course). A few months after the Fairs Cup final, there was a play-off between Barcelona (first winners) and Leeds (last winners) to decide who kept the trophy. Played, *somewhat* beneficially to Barcelona, at the Camp Nou, the Catalan giants won 2–1 and got to keep the trophy.

Following their 1969 title win, Leeds qualified for the European Cup for the first time in their history. They could hardly have started it any better, annihilating Norwegian side Lyn Oslo 10–0 at Elland Road with Mike O'Grady giving Leeds the lead after just thirty-five seconds. It remains the biggest ever victory by a team in their first game in the European Cup and one of only five times a club has scored in the opening minute of their first game in the competition.

Biggest debut wins in the European Cup

Date	Team	For	Against	Opponent
17/09/1969	Leeds United	10	0	Lyn Oslo
17/09/1958	Atlético de Madrid	8	0	Drumcondra
20/09/1966	TSV 1860 Munich	8	0	Omonia Nicosia
19/09/1973	Club Brugge	8	0	Floriana

Leeds won their first six games in the European Cup, scoring twenty-four goals and conceding none, becoming both the first and only side in European Cup history to win their first six games in the competition, and the only team to keep a clean sheet in each of their first six matches as well. It was an incredible introduction to European football's most prestigious competition, and Leeds faced Scottish giants Celtic in the semi-final. Celtic had won the European Cup as recently as 1967 and, having conceded none on their way to the semi-final, George Connelly gave Celtic the lead inside the opening minute at Elland Road. The score remained 1-0 on the night, one of only three games in European Cup history to be decided by a goal in the opening minute.

In the second leg – played in front of a crowd of 136,505 (not only a record for a game involving Leeds but a record involving a British team) – Leeds went 1-0 ahead through a Bremner goal early on. Sadly Celtic hit back with two goals to win 2-1, which was the only time Leeds ever scored first and lost in Europe under Revie's management.

The only time Leeds were eliminated in the first round of any European competition under Revie was in 1971-72 in the UEFA Cup, when Belgian side Lierse knocked them out 4-2 on aggregate. It is made even more surprising by the fact Leeds had a 2-0 first leg lead away from home going into the reverse fixture at Elland Road; it was only the second time a team had won the first leg by two or more goals away from home and then been eliminated in any European competition and remains the only time an English team has done so. Revie fielded many reserve players for the second leg, resting the likes of Bremner, Charlton and Giles, with Hunter on the bench in case he was needed – and he would be. John Faulkner made his fourth and final Leeds appearance, eighteen-year-old Jimmy Mann was making his first start, and nineteen-year-old Chris Galvin was making just his twelfth appearance. But the standout was the choice of goalkeeper John Shaw, who made his debut at the age of just 17 years and 237 days. It was not a happy one, as Leeds found themselves 3-0 down at half-time and Shaw was subbed off at the break to be replaced by Gary Sprake. The Welshman was the only goalkeeper younger than Shaw to have played for Leeds at that time; Shaw would later be bumped down to third youngest goalkeeper by Glan Letheren, whose debut was in November 1973 against Hibernian as a substitute for none other than John Shaw, making his second and final appearance for the club.

> Goalkeeper John Shaw is one of only four players to be substituted off in every Leeds appearance they made (2) – the others are Mickey Thomas (3 games), Eoghan Stokes (1 game) and Billy Whitehouse (1 game).

The young Leeds side – average age of just 23 years and 142 days – were beaten 4-0 by Lierse, not only the heaviest home defeat during Revie's time at the club but also only the third time they'd been beaten at Elland Road by four goals, and the others had been in 1925 (0-4 vs Huddersfield) and 1959 (0-4 vs Man City, a game in which Revie played). It is the club's joint heaviest European defeat and wouldn't be matched until losing 4-0 to Barcelona in the Champions League in 2000.

Leeds also had an early exit in their final European campaign under Revie, going out in the UEFA Cup third round in 1973-74 against Portuguese side Vitória de Setubal. Leeds went into the second leg 1-0 ahead on aggregate, but Revie was far more interested in winning the First Division title and fielded the likes of Jimmy Mann (his fifth and final game), Roy Ellam (only his fourteenth start in two seasons) and Peter Hampton (his third appearance). Leeds were beaten 3-1, with the goal scored by substitute Gary Liddell, making just his fourth appearance for the club. But Revie's decision was arguably justified three days later; with Bremner, Hunter, Jones and Madeley restored to the line-up, Leeds beat Chelsea 2-1 to break the record for the longest unbeaten start to a First Division season.

In between those exits to Lierse and Vitória de Setubal, Leeds enjoyed their only campaign in the Cup Winners' Cup, entering the competition by virtue of winning the 1972 FA Cup. Leeds didn't lose a single game on the way to reaching the final, dispatching Ankaragücü, Carl Zeiss Jena, Rapid Bucharest and Hajduk Split and winning all four matches at Elland Road without conceding a single goal. It set up a first ever meeting with AC Milan and was the club's fourth European final, the joint most of any side in the Revie era, along with Ajax and Milan themselves. Luciano Chiarugi's early free-kick gave Milan the 1-0 victory and rounded off a miserable May for Leeds, with the defeat coming only eleven days after losing 1-0 to Sunderland in the FA Cup final. The final, played in Greece, was further overshadowed by Christos Michas' refereeing (which saw him banned by UEFA) and a late red card for Norman Hunter, who retaliated following a series of bad challenges in the final minute of the match. He remains the only Englishman to be sent off in a European final. (Despite his reputation – or perhaps because of the more liberal refereeing style in that era – that was one of only two red cards shown to Hunter as a Leeds player, the other coming memorably against Derby County in November 1975, when he and Franny Lee put their football to one side and took up pugilism in front of the Baseball Ground crowd.)

There can be no argument that Leeds were the dominant side in Europe between 1965 and 1974. They played the most games (seventy-eight), won the most games (forty-two), scored the most goals (141), kept the most clean sheets (thirty-nine), reached the most semi-finals (seven) and the joint most finals (four). The only shame is that Leeds did not record more than their two titles during their period of dominance.

European football – 1965–66 – 1973–74	Games Played
Leeds United	78
Celtic	60
Milan	58
Juventus	58
Liverpool	56

European football – 1965–66 – 1973–74	Games Won
Leeds United	42
Celtic	36
Ajax	35
Milan	32
Juventus	32

European football – 1965–66 – 1973–74	Goals
Leeds United	141
Celtic	119
RSC Anderlecht	111
FC Bayern Munich	109
Ajax	106

Leeds United 2–0 Mansfield Town, 7 February 1970

Sprake, Reaney, Cooper, Bremner, Charlton, Hunter, Lorimer, Clarke, Jones, Giles, Gray.

It is the starting XI that everyone remembers about Don Revie's Leeds, each with their customary number in the days before squad numbers. Sprake wore number 1 more often than any other player in the club's history, likewise Reaney with number 2, Bremner with 4, Charlton with 5, Hunter with 6, Lorimer with 7, Clarke with 8, Jones with 9 and Giles with 10. Terry Cooper wore the number 3 shirt 282 times, placing him behind Grenville Hair for outings in the 3, while Eddie Gray's 272 games in his iconic 11 shirt were later eclipsed by the similarly iconic Gary Speed, who wore 11 on 289 occasions.

Yet unbelievably, this most famous Leeds United starting XI appeared together just once – in a February 1970 FA Cup tie against Mansfield Town, won 2-0 with goals from Giles and Clarke. It is remarkable they only started together once, given that between 1969-70 (when Clarke joined the club) and the end of 1972-73 (Charlton's retirement) they started 1,989 matches between them – yet only all together for one game.

There are other explanations for it, however. Paul Reaney suffered a broken leg in 1970, missing the 1970 FA Cup final because of it, while Terry Cooper missed the 1972 final after breaking his leg against Stoke a month beforehand, and didn't play again until early 1974. By that time, Charlton had retired and Sprake had been sold to Birmingham. Between August 1969 and May 1973, the player with the second most starts for Leeds was Paul Madeley, who was in the XI for 223 of the 242 games in those seasons, leaving just nineteen games for the XI to feature together. Of the seventy-two occasions where ten of the XI started alongside one another, seventy-one of them had Madeley as the other player. And if anyone is going to break up the dream Leeds XI, you'd want it to be a player like Paul Madeley, nicknamed 'Rolls Royce' for very good reason. Eddie Gray's injuries also meant he only started 51% of Leeds' games in that timeframe, while Sprake made his final appearance as first-choice goalkeeper in April 1972 and only made one more league appearance afterwards, starting alongside just one of the classic XI that day (Peter Lorimer, against Birmingham in April 1973).

The most used Leeds United XI of all time started together twenty-three times in the space of two years between April 1970 and April 1972. The first time was the 1970 FA Cup final against Chelsea at Wembley and across that and the following twenty-two games together they only lost twice. Paul Reaney, whose broken leg meant Madeley started in his place, is the player from the 'classic' XI who doesn't feature in this most used team. The XI is:

Sprake, Madeley, Cooper, Bremner, Charlton, Hunter, Lorimer, Clarke, Jones, Giles, Gray.

Perhaps the most iconic game this line-up featured in was in February 1972, when they defeated Manchester United 5-1 with Mick Jones scoring a hat-trick (a fortnight later, in the 7-0 win over Southampton, Reaney was in as number two, with Madeley playing left-back in place of Cooper, the first time that particular XI had played together for two years). Ten games after the demolition of Man Utd, the XI made their final appearances together in a victory against Huddersfield.

The second most used XI of the Revie era did have Reaney within it and featured eighteen times between 1969 and 1972, perhaps most memorably in both legs of the 1971 Fairs Cup final against Juventus: Sprake, Reaney, Cooper, Bremner, Charlton, Hunter, Lorimer, Clarke, Jones, Giles, Madeley. The last game they all started together was in March 1972 in a win over Arsenal, with that XI having a combined total of 4,588 appearances between them, the second most for a Leeds starting team in the club's history.

A far cry from the experienced and iconic Leeds sides of the Revie era – 44 starting XIs in that time had 4,000+ appearances between them – the Leeds line-up for their game against Bury in the Johnstone's Paint Trophy in November 2007 had just 142 appearances for the club within it, with Seb Carole (thirty-six) and Rui Marques (thirty-seven) making up seventy-three of those, and Jonny Howson (nineteen) and captain for the night David Prutton (seventeen) were the only others in double figures. Seven players had fewer than ten games under their belts: Leon Constantine (three), Filipe Da Costa (seven), Mark De Vries (six), Paul Huntington (seven), David Lucas (two), Simon Madden (one) and Ben Parker (seven). The inexperienced side, not helped by a red card to Da Costa in the first half, lost 2-1

The Revie players

In his Leeds managerial career which spanned 741 games and thirteen years, only seventy-six different players made an appearance under Don Revie, one of which was Revie himself when he was player-manager. Twenty-three of those played over one hundred games under him, many of whom are club legends. But there are others, particularly from his early years in charge, who have been long forgotten. So in alphabetical order, here's a stat for all seventy-six players to make a Leeds appearance under Revie . . .

> On 29 March 1952, Major Frank Buckley named his starting XI for Leeds United for a game against Notts County: Scott, Dunn, Hughes, Kerfoot, McCabe, Burden, Harrison, Mills, Barritt, Iggleden, Williams. Little did Major Buckley know it then, but he'd done something that no other Leeds manager would do for another thirty-three years: he had named a Leeds line-up that didn't feature a single player who played under Don Revie. The Revie era wouldn't begin in earnest until he was appointed in March 1961, but until Peter Lorimer's last appearance on 27 October 1985 at least one player who'd played under Revie was in every starting XI, a run of a frankly remarkable 1,696 games. The manager who picked the team to end this run in 1985 was Billy Bremner, who had played more times under Revie than any other player.

Mike Addy

Mike Addy was the only player whose surname begins with A to make an appearance under Don Revie, playing his fourth and final game on 29 September 1962 against Southampton, in the same game that Peter Lorimer made the first of his 707 appearances. There wouldn't be another 'A' player for nineteen years, until Tony Arins played against Ipswich in September 1981.

24

Mick Bates

Bates was the unused sub in the 1972 FA Cup final victory over Arsenal, and sitting on the bench was something he got used to under Revie – he was a substitute eighty-three times, ten more than any other player. He was the most used sub (thirty-seven appearances) and only David Harvey (forty-nine) was an unused substitute more often than Bates (forty-six) in Revie's time in charge.

Rod Belfitt

Rod Belfitt is the only player to score a hat-trick in a semi-final for Leeds United, doing so in May 1967 against Kilmarnock in the Fairs Cup. That hat-trick was also the club's first Friday hat-trick, something emulated only by Patrick Bamford in October 2020 against Aston Villa since then.

Willie Bell

In his third game for the club – and Don Revie's seventh game in charge – Willie Bell scored the second goal in a 7–0 win over Lincoln City in April 1961. He's one of three players to get their first goal for the club in a victory by seven or more goals, along with Peter McConnell (also in that 7–0 vs Lincoln) and Mick Jones (9–0 vs Spora Luxembourg in October 1967).

Billy Bremner

Billy Bremner made more appearances (649) and started more games (648) under Don Revie than any other player for Leeds United. His only substitute appearance was in May 1967 against Sheffield Wednesday, coming on for Eddie Gray in a 1–0 win.

Bobby Cameron

While Bremner is the most synonymous player with the Leeds United number 4 shirt, the player to wear the 4 under Revie in his first game in charge was Bobby Cameron against Portsmouth in March 1961.

Terry Carling

Terry Carling – the second goalkeeper used by Don Revie – is one of only eight Leeds United players whose surname ends in 'ing' to make an appearance for the club. The others are Wilf Copping, Len Browning, Matthew Spring, Marlon King, Dan Harding, Anthony Elding and Luke Ayling.

Terry Casey

Terry Casey's first two Leeds appearances were both away at Rotherham United (one in the League Cup, one in the Second Division). He's one of four players to play their first two games away at the same opponent, along with Paul Rachubka at Doncaster in 2011 and Leo Hjelde and Lewis Bate, both at West Ham in 2022.

John Charles

Charles made eleven appearances under Revie early in the 1962-63 season, with Revie captaining the Sunderland side when Charles made his last appearance for Leeds in his first spell in 1957. Charles only scored three goals in those eleven games but they all came in Yorkshire derbies, failing to score in his other eight non-Yorkshire derby games.

Jack Charlton

Charlton was the sixth highest scorer under Revie, netting 89 goals in 554 games, including scoring the very first goal of his time in charge in a defeat at Portsmouth in March 1961. It was one of twenty-five games where Charlton wore the number 9 shirt under Revie, scoring a more than respectable fifteen goals during these forays up front.

Trevor Cherry

Cherry's first four goals for Leeds United were all scored at Elland Road but in a different competition each time (League Cup vs Burnley, Cup Winners' Cup vs Carl Zeiss Jena, Division One vs Man City, UEFA Cup vs Vitória de Setubal). He is one of only two players to score his first four goals in different competitions, along with Gary McAllister (Division One, League Cup, Full Members' Cup, FA Cup).

Allan Clarke

As well as scoring the winning goal in the 1972 FA Cup final, Clarke is also the club's all-time leading scorer in the FA Cup with twenty-five goals and the only player to score more than one hat-trick in the FA Cup, scoring four versus Sutton United in 1970 and three against Norwich in 1973.

Bobby Collins

Leeds United only lost 27 of the 168 appearances Bobby Collins made for the club between 1962 and 1967; among all players to play one hundred or more games for the club, only Mick Jones (15%) has lost a lower percentage than Collins (16%).

Terry Cooper

Terry Cooper ended on the winning side in ten of his first eleven appearances for the club, the fewest games played by a Leeds player to win ten matches until Josuha Guilavogui equalled his record in January 2025. To be fair though, the Frenchman had made ten of his first eleven appearances as a substitute, while Cooper started all eleven.

Nigel Davey

There was a gap of 2 years and 207 days between Davey's first two starts for Leeds United: a 4–2 defeat to West Brom in the League Cup in October 1965 and a 4–3 loss to Arsenal in Division One in May 1968. This is the biggest gap between a player's first two starts for Leeds in the club's history. It was a similar story for his last two appearances, which were separated by 2 years and 53 days between October 1971 and November 1973 – not helped by a broken leg in April 1972 - the third biggest gap for a player's final two games for Leeds.

Keith M. Edwards

Edwards is one of three players to play exactly once under Revie, making his one appearance in September 1971 in a 2–1 defeat to Huddersfield. His nineteen-minute sub cameo makes his the shortest career of all players to play in the Revie era.

Roy Ellam

Among the players who played in the top-flight under Revie, central defender Roy Ellam has the lowest win ratio in the Revie era, winning only 28% of his matches (six out of twenty-one) across the 1972-73 and 1973-74 campaigns.

John Faulkner

John Faulkner played four games for Leeds, and his first two games and final two games were both separated by fourteen days, though they were played seventeen months apart. His first two games were in April 1970 against Burnley and Manchester City, and his final two games were in September 1971, both against Lierse in the UEFA Cup.

Peter Fitzgerald

Twenty-nine different players wore the number 8 shirt under Don Revie but the first of those was Peter Fitzgerald in March 1961 against Portsmouth. He was the only player with the letter Z in his name to play under Revie, and made his last appearance four games into Revie's reign. The next player with Z in his name to play for Leeds came in the first game after Revie departed: Duncan McKenzie in the 1974 Charity Shield.

Gerry Francis

Francis – who became the first player of colour to play for Leeds when he made his debut in 1957 – played in Revie's first game in charge and made eight appearances under him but never ended on the winning side – the most games without tasting victory of any player under Revie.

Chris Galvin

Galvin made his debut for Leeds in November 1969 in a European Cup match against Ferencvaros at the age of 18 years and 2 days old, making him the youngest player to play for Leeds in the European Cup. The second youngest is Carl Harris in 1974 against Ujpest Dozsa, who was a mere one day older than Galvin was.

Johnny Giles

Only two players – Peter Lorimer and Allan Clarke – have scored in more matches at Elland Road for Leeds United than Johnny Giles (sixty-five). But while Lorimer and Clarke lost some of those games, Giles never ended on the losing side in any of his sixty-five, winning fifty-nine and drawing six – comfortably a club record for scoring and not losing at Elland Road.

Freddie Goodwin

Goodwin was Don Revie's first captain in his first game in charge, and he captained Leeds on seventy-four occasions under Revie. Only Billy Bremner (402) and Bobby Collins (92) started more games as skipper.

Colin Grainger

Colin Grainger, who was nicknamed the 'Singing Winger' as he had a singing career alongside his football career, once played on the same bill as the Beatles in 1963 in Stockport. He made his debut for Leeds playing alongside Revie in August 1960, at Anfield, in the same week as the Beatles played their first ever gig in Liverpool.

Eddie Gray

Eddie Gray is the second youngest player to score on his top-flight debut for Leeds, aged 17 years and 349 days on New Year's Day in 1966 against Sheffield Wednesday, with only Terry Connor eclipsing that in 1979 aged 17 years and 8 days. The first time Gray scored two goals in a game was his famous brace against Burnley in April 1970, while wearing the unfamiliar number 6 shirt; it was the last brace by a Leeds player wearing number 6 for forty years, until Richard Naylor scored two against Yeovil in April 2010.

Frank Gray

With an appearance against AC Milan in the 1973 Cup Winners' Cup final, Frank Gray became the youngest player to play in a final for Leeds (18 years and 201 days). Since then, that record has been broken twice: by Frank's son Andy in the 1996 League Cup final against Aston Villa (aged 18 years and 130 days) and by Andy's son – and Frank's grandson – Archie in the 2024 Championship play-off final (18 years and 75 days). Some family, those Grays.

Jimmy Greenhoff

Jimmy Greenhoff's first four appearances for Leeds were against Southampton, Swansea, Swansea and Southampton, while his first three goals were against Stoke, Southport and Stoke. His two braces in Europe were both against Spora Luxembourg. His last goal was against Stoke in April 1968 and his last appearance was against Stoke in August 1968. Sensational.

Grenville Hair

Grenville Hair took until his 428th appearance to score his first goal for Leeds, the longest wait for a goal by any player in the club's history (the second longest is 166 games by Gary Kelly). This strike, against Middlesbrough in April 1962, came 11 years and 7 days after his debut in March 1951. He only had to wait twenty games for his next goal, scoring in the 3–1 win over Stoke in the FA Cup, the game which ended an eleven-year wait for a Leeds FA Cup victory.

Tom Hallett

Tom Hallett only made one appearance for Leeds, in a 4-0 defeat to Blackburn in the League Cup in October 1962. He is one of five players to make his only Leeds appearance in the League Cup, along with Geoff Martin (1960 vs Chesterfield), Danny Cadamarteri (2004 vs Swindon), Ross Turnbull (2015 vs Doncaster) and Eoghan Stokes (2017 vs Newport).

Peter Hampton

Hampton – an unused sub in the 1975 European Cup final – made three appearances under Don Revie, all in 1973 and Leeds lost each game, against Birmingham, Stoke and Vitória de Setubal. He was the only player to make as many as three appearances under Revie and lose every game.

David Harvey

In his second spell with the club in 1983, Eddie Gray – now player-manager – made goalkeeper Harvey captain shortly after his return. He would captain the club seventy-one times until his final appearance in December 1984 and was the first goalkeeper to captain Leeds; since then, only Nigel Martyn (once), Andy Lonergan (eight times) and Kiko Casilla (once) have captained Leeds in a match among goalkeepers.

Dennis Hawkins

Dennis Hawkins was aged just 17 years and 356 days on his first appearance for Leeds in the League Cup against West Brom in October 1965. He is the second youngest player from Wales to start a game for Leeds, behind only John Charles, who was 239 days younger than Hawkins on his debut in 1949.

John Hawksby

John Hawksby didn't score in thirty-nine appearances under Don Revie but he did score in his first two games for Leeds early in 1960-61 under Revie's predecessor Jack Taylor. Aged 18 years and 78 days, at the time he was the youngest Leeds player to score in his first two games, until Alan Smith broke that record by fifty-four days in 1998.

Tommy Henderson

Leeds won nine of the first ten games that Tommy Henderson played at Elland Road – those results were: 6-1, 3-3, 3-1, 3-1, 3-1, 3-0, 4-1, 4-1, 3-0 and 3-0. Overall, there were sixty-six goals in his sixteen games at Elland Road, the most goals per game in a player's games on home soil in the club's history (4.1 per game).

Terry Hibbitt

Terry Hibbitt – who won 63% of his matches as a Leeds player, the best ratio of any player in the Revie era – was the club's first ever substitute scorer, netting against Nottingham Forest in February 1966.

Alan Humphreys

Humphreys was in goal for Don Revie's first game in charge, a 3-1 defeat to Portsmouth. His debut was in a 5-0 defeat to Fulham in February 1960, becoming the first goalkeeper to concede five goals on his debut since Jim Twomey in 1938 against Blackpool; no Leeds keeper has done so since.

Norman Hunter

Hunter made his Leeds debut on 8 September 1962 against Swansea and then appeared in every one of the club's league matches up to 3 April 1965, a run of 113 consecutive starts. It is the most recent occasion an outfield player has started one hundred or more league games in a row for Leeds.

Albert Johanneson

Johanneson scored hat-tricks in Europe for Leeds against both DWS Amsterdam and Spora Luxembourg, making him the only Leeds player to score multiple hat-tricks in Europe. He is also the only South African player to score two hat-tricks in all major European competitions in history.

Rod Johnson

Rod Johnson scored on his Leeds United debut in September 1962 aged 17 years and 243 days and, at the time, was the youngest player to score on his Leeds debut until Terry Connor broke that record in 1979 against West Brom. Johnson was, however, the youngest player to score a goal in the Revie era.

Alf Jones

Jones made his twenty-ninth and final appearance for Leeds United on 3 March 1962 against Huddersfield Town, one of two players to play their last game for the club that day. The other? Don Revie.

Mick Jones

Mick Jones is the most recent Leeds United player to score a hat-trick against Manchester United, doing so in a 5-1 rout in February 1972.

Jones is also the club's all-time leading scorer against Man Utd, with seven goals in total, and has the most goals for Leeds at Old Trafford with four.

Joe Jordan

Joe Jordan scored 48 goals in 222 matches for Leeds United; he has both the second most appearances and second most goals of any player with an alliterative name in the club's history, behind Billy Bremner (772 games, 115 goals).

David Kennedy

Kennedy made a scoring debut for Leeds, aged nineteen, in March 1970 against Derby, a game for which Leeds made eleven changes to their starting XI for the first time ever. He was nicknamed Jack, after the US President, and later moved to Lincoln City where he played alongside a goalkeeper named John Kennedy.

John Kilford

Kilford wore the number 3 shirt in Revie's first game in charge away at Portsmouth, which was his first away appearance for Leeds United – his first six games beforehand were all at Elland Road. He's one of only two players to do that in the club's history, along with striker Anthony Elding in 2008.

Ian Lawson

In 1963–64, Ian Lawson was the club's joint top scorer with fifteen goals in twenty-nine games. He made his debut in March 1962 against Huddersfield Town, the same game in which Revie made his final appearance for the club.

Glan Letheren

Goalkeeper Glan Letheren – who was born four days before Don Revie won the FA Cup with Man City as a player in May 1956 – only played twice for Leeds United and those games were separated by 528 days between November 1973 and April 1975. Letheren is the last goalkeeper under the age of eighteen to make an appearance for the club, doing so as sub for John Shaw in a 1973 UEFA Cup match against Hibernian aged 17 years and 190 days.

Gary Liddell

Gary Liddell's three league appearances for Leeds United were all in a different season – in 1972-73 vs Birmingham, 1973-74 vs Newcastle and 1974-75 vs Sheffield United. He is one of only two players in the club's history to make three league appearances and each be in a different season, along with Tony Ingham (one each in 1947-48, 1948-49 and 1949-50).

Peter Lorimer

The club's all-time leading scorer with 238 goals, Lorimer's first and last goals for the club in September 1965 and October 1985 respectively were separated by twenty years and forty days. The last goalkeeper he scored against, Eric Nixon of Manchester City, was born five days after Lorimer's debut in 1962. Another sign of Lorimer's incredible longevity across two spells is that he played alongside Cliff Mason, born in 1929 and before the first FIFA World Cup had even been staged, and then later with four different players who were all born after England had won the World Cup in 1966 – Nigel Thompson (b. March 1967), Lyndon Simmonds (b. November 1966), Peter Swan (b. September 1966) and Terry Phelan (b. March 1967), the latter of whom was still playing in the Football League in 2001.

Jimmy Lumsden

Lumsden made four appearances for Leeds. His first two appearances were separated by 362 days (May 1967 – May 1968), his second and third appearances were separated by 686 days (May 1968 – March 1970) and his last two appearances were separated by two days, defeats to Southampton and Derby. He was also named captain against Derby aged just twenty-two, making him the youngest captain of the Revie era.

Paul Madeley

Madeley, the 'Rolls Royce' of the Revie team known for his ability to play in any position, is one of three players to start a match wearing ten different shirt numbers, along with Trevor Cherry and Terry Yorath (all 2 – 11). Madeley scored a goal wearing the most different numbers, however, finding the net wearing numbers 2, 3, 4, 5, 6, 8, 9, 10 and 11 – bizarrely it was just his fourteen games wearing number 7 where he wasn't lucky enough find the net.

Jimmy Mann

Jimmy Mann's two league starts for Leeds were separated by 576 days. He started against West Ham in October 1971 then had to wait until April 1973 for his next – and final – start against Birmingham. It's the fourth biggest gap between a player's only two league starts for Leeds and two of the other three also made their second start against Birmingham: Charlie Cresswell (686 days) and Ian Poveda (1,119 days) both in August 2023; the other is Gary Liddell (701 days), whose first start was against none other than – you've guessed it – Birmingham City.

Cliff Mason

Cliff Mason (born in 1929) was the only player – other than Don Revie himself – born in the 1920s to play under Revie, making him the last player born in that decade to play for the club. Incidentally, the last player born in the 1930s to play for Leeds was Jack Charlton, who was the only 1930s representative from 1968 until his retirement in 1973.

Derek Mayers

Mayers scored five goals in twenty-four appearances for Leeds United and found the net in each of his final two games for the club in defeats to Scunthorpe and Plymouth in February 1962, making him the most recent player to score in his last two games for Leeds. The other two players to achieve this are Willie Bennett in 1932 and Billy Furness in 1937.

Billy McAdams

A former teammate of Revie's from his time at Manchester City, McAdams scored four goals in thirteen games in the 1961-62 season and was the only Northern Irishman to play a league game under Revie and the last to do so for Leeds until John McClelland debuted in August 1989.

John McCole

Although only eleven of his fifty-three goals for Leeds were scored under Revie's management, John McCole had the best goals-per-game ratio of any player under Revie, scoring at a rate of 0.69 goals per game (eleven in sixteen games). He was also one of three players to score four goals in a game (against Brentford in the League Cup) under Revie, along with Peter Lorimer and Allan Clarke.

Peter McConnell

Wing-half McConnell made his Leeds debut in December 1958, just four games after Revie had made his own debut for the club, and wore the number 6 shirt in Revie's first game as manager. He scored just one goal in his first twenty-eight games, then had a hot streak of four goals in five games in the number 10 shirt in October 1961, before failing to score in any of his last twenty games.

Billy McGinley

Billy McGinley's only league appearance for Leeds came in April 1973 away at Birmingham City, at the age of just 18 years and 169 days. He is the second youngest player to make his only league appearance for the club in the top-flight, behind Wesley Boyle in 1996 against Newcastle, who was seventeen.

Gordon McQueen

Gordon McQueen never scored a goal in fifty-one appearances under Don Revie and actually scored more goals under caretaker manager Maurice Lindley in 1974 (one) than he did for Revie. But he still scored his fair share of goals for Leeds; his nineteen goals wearing the number 5 shirt are the fourth most of any player, behind Jack Charlton, Chris Fairclough and Paul Hart.

Mike O'Grady

O'Grady – who scored in both of his England caps separated by almost seven years between 1962 and 1969 – didn't lose any of his last thirty-one league appearances for Leeds United between October 1968 and September 1969 before he was sold to Wolves, the longest unbeaten ending to a Leeds league career.

Sean O'Neill

Sean O'Neill made three appearances for Leeds United, all as a substitute and all in October 1973. In the club's history, only Jordan Stevens (six) and Edgar Cani (four) have made more appearances without starting a game than O'Neill, who later made 442 league appearances for Chesterfield.

Alan Peacock

Only John McCole (0.69) had a better goals-per-game ratio under Revie than Alan Peacock, who netted 30 goals in 65 games (0.46 per game) between 1964 and 1967. His last game for the club came in May 1967 against Sheffield Wednesday; despite only being twenty-nine years old, he was 6 years and 257 days older than anyone else in the line-up, with Terry Cooper the closest to Peacock at 22 years and 307 days.

Paul Peterson

Paul Peterson's four games for Leeds all came within the space of twenty-two days in March and April 1970 as Leeds experienced a fixture pile-up. And particularly peculiarly, he is the only player whose first name and surname both begin with P to play for Leeds.

Noel Peyton

Noel Peyton scored 20 goals in 117 appearances for Leeds between 1958 and 1963, and is the first of only four Noels to play for Leeds; following in his footsteps were Noels Blake, Whelan and Hunt.

Paul Reaney

Only Jack Charlton and Billy Bremner have played more matches for Leeds United than Paul Reaney, who only scored 9 goals in 749 games. Reaney once scored two goals in the space of four matches in 1966 – both against Manchester United – and then only managed two in his next 516 games. His last two goals were then both against the same club, scoring against Norwich in January and April 1977.

Don Revie

His record as manager is, of course, outstanding. His record on the pitch when he was player-manager? Less so; Revie played himself in seven games during the 1961–62 season – Leeds didn't win a single one of those games. His goal against Luton in November 1961, at the age of 34 years and 117 days, makes him the second oldest player to score a goal in the Revie era, with only Jack Charlton scoring at an older age than Revie himself.

John Shaw

Goalkeeper John Shaw played just two games for Leeds and was substituted off in both. His two games were in the UEFA Cup against Lierse in September 1971 and Hibernian in October 1973 and, despite this short Leeds career, the only goalkeepers to be subbed off more often are Gary Sprake and Shane Higgs (three apiece).

Bobby Sibbald

Bobby Sibbald only played two games for Leeds, both of which were defeats. One was against Everton (as a sub) in February 1967, the other against Burnley on the last day of the season in 1968 – his only start. He's one of three players to make his only start for Leeds in the club's last league match of a campaign, along with Bobby Dawson against Hull in 1953–54 and Rob Bayly against Derby in 2006–07.

Eric Smith

Former Celtic defender Eric Smith holds the distinction of having scored the last goal before the Revie era began, netting the winner in a 1-0 win over Norwich in March 1961 in Jack Taylor's last game.

Gary Sprake

Gary Sprake was the first sixteen-year-old to make an appearance for Leeds United, doing so in March 1962 against Southampton, which also makes him the youngest goalkeeper to have ever played for the club. He also holds the record for most appearances by a goalkeeper (506) and most appearances for Leeds as a teenager (126).

David Stewart

Stewart – who was Leeds United's goalkeeper in the 1975 European Cup final against Bayern Munich – didn't end on the losing side in any of his first sixteen games for the club, the longest unbeaten start of any player in the club's history.

Jim Storrie

Centre-forward Storrie scored sixty-seven goals for Leeds United, which places him within the top twenty scorers in the club's history. He's also the only Leeds player ever to score on both his debut (1962 vs Stoke) and final appearance (1966 vs Newcastle).

Don Weston

Weston scored twenty-six goals for Leeds under Don Revie between 1962 and 1965, but it's for the first three of those, all in the same game against Stoke, that he is best known. He was the first player to score a hat-trick on his Leeds debut since Percy Whipp in 1922 against West Ham, and it has been emulated by just two players since then; Carl Shutt in 1989 against Bournemouth and Samuel Sáiz against Port Vale in 2017.

Brian Williamson

Goalkeeper Brian Williamson made eight appearances for Leeds between 1963 and 1966, with his eighth and final game coming in January 1966 against Bury in the FA Cup, a 6-0 win. He is the only player to make his final Leeds appearance in a six-goal victory.

Barrie Wright

Barrie Wright played eight games for Leeds, making his debut in April 1963 against Preston North End in the number 3 shirt, usually worn by Willie Bell who took the number 4 that day. After leaving Leeds, he joined Brighton and Hove Albion where he made his final Football League appearance in December 1969 against Leyton Orient along-side Willie Bell, who was now playing for the Seagulls. Brighton were managed by Freddie Goodwin, alongside whom Wright had made one appearance for Leeds – against Leyton Orient. Also in the Brighton side that day was a certain Howard Wilkinson.

Terry Yorath

Although he wasn't a prolific goalscorer for Leeds United, with just 12 goals in 198 games, Terry Yorath is one of only two players whose surname starts with Y to score for Leeds. The other? Tony Yeboah. He captained Leeds once, becoming the second Welshman to captain the club after John Charles.

Tommy Younger

Despite what his surname might suggest, goalkeeper Tommy Younger was the oldest player in the Leeds United starting XI when he made his debut in September 1961, aged 31 years and 173 days, and was the oldest player in the starting line-up in 50% of his appearances (twenty-one out of forty-two) for the Whites.

2

THE GREAT GOALSCORERS

As debate raged on across the 2024–25 season as to whether Leeds were more effective with Mateo Joseph or Joël Piroe playing up front – and whether Patrick Bamford would be fit enough to have a meaningful impact on the team – many fans were crying out for a striker who would score the twenty goals to get the team back into the Premier League (Piroe had a good go, but ended the season on nineteen). Scoring twenty goals in a season for Leeds is a rarity, with only twenty-six players managing it in our entire history. Some have dazzled over long periods, while others have made a big impact over a short time; some have been forgotten almost entirely. Either way, those twenty-six players have written their names into the fabric of Leeds United's history.

Tom Jennings
174 games, 117 goals
20-Goal Seasons: 26 in 1925–26, 37 in 1926–27, 21 in 1927–28

Given twenty-six players have scored twenty goals in a season for Leeds, it seems apt that the first player to do so scored twenty-six in a season that ended in 1926, scoring a hat-trick on 6 February in 1926 against Arsenal (the second month of the year, and the sixth day in it), and also scoring in the twenty-sixth league game of that season against West Ham United. Tom Jennings was Leeds United's first goalscoring hero, becoming not only the first Whites player to score twenty in a season but the first to score one hundred goals for the club. Many of his frankly extraordinary scoring records have stood the test of time, both for Leeds United and in English top-flight history.

The only Scottish player to score a treble for Leeds before Jennings arrived, Percy Whipp is the only player in Leeds United's history to score a penalty on his debut, doing so in November 1922 against Sunderland only a day after signing for the club. Brett Ormerod had the chance to emulate him in September 2004 against Sunderland but saw his penalty saved. Whipp is also the only Leeds player to score a hat-trick on Christmas Day, in 1924 against Aston Villa.

Jennings joined Leeds in 1925 from Raith Rovers, where he had been part of the side that were shipwrecked in the Canary Islands in the summer of 1923. Leeds had only scored forty-six goals in total in the 1924-25 season, with Jennings chipping in with three in the final ten games, but in 1925-26 he set about changing Leeds' low-scoring ways with twenty-six goals – none of which were penalties. This was also the season in which the offside law was changed, benefitting exceptional forwards like Jennings, with only two opposing players required to be in front of an attacker to be onside rather than three, which had been in operation since the creation of the Football League in 1888. This led to a spike in goals in the First Division with 1,703 scored in 1925-26, an increase of 43% on the previous year (1,192) – the biggest jump between seasons in the history of the English top-flight.

The 1926–27 season was Jennings' high point with thirty-seven goals, a total that only one player has bettered in Leeds United's history. After three goals in his first seven games, Jennings sparked into life with an unbelievable three consecutive hat-tricks against Arsenal, Liverpool and Blackburn – scoring four each in the latter two. This run of three consecutive hat-tricks remains a Leeds record that will possibly never be broken, especially looking at it through the prism of English top-flight history. Almost 40,000 top-flight English matches have been played since and only two players have ever emulated that – Dixie Dean for Everton in 1928 and Jack Balmer for Liverpool in 1946.

This incredible run of form saw Jennings become the first Leeds player to score in seven consecutive appearances (amazingly, before Jennings did this, Leeds United as a team had only twice managed a run of scoring in seven or more games in their history up to that point). After failing to score in a 4–2 win over West Brom, Jennings then made up for it with a hat-trick against Bury to take his total to nineteen goals in nine matches. In October 1926 alone he notched twelve goals, a club record in one month that has never been beaten.

I know what you're thinking. Leeds have found a record-breaking scorer, so they must have challenged for the league title in 1927? Well, not quite.

Jennings scored thirty-five league goals in 1926–27, which was twenty-four more than any other Leeds player that season. He only missed one league game (which Leeds lost) but even when he scored it wasn't doing much good for the team. Of the twenty-two matches Jennings found the net, Leeds managed to lose nine of them. The defence was a big problem, and Leeds were relegated in twenty-first spot, four points adrift of safety. It remains the most goals any player has ever scored in an English top-flight season for a team who were relegated. Jennings couldn't even console himself with being the league's leading scorer, either – two others scored thirty-six, and Jimmy Trotter of The Wednesday (later renamed Sheffield Wednesday) scored thirty-seven in his debut top-flight season and took the crown thanks to a goal in a 1–0 win on the final day, against – of course – Leeds.

It's impossible to imagine a player scoring twenty or more goals for a relegated team and then not getting a move back to the Premier League nowadays, but in 1927 Jennings stayed at Leeds and his twenty-one goals helped the club back into the top-flight (including four against Chelsea, the only Leeds player to ever net a hat-trick against them). Jennings was only twenty-six when the 1928–29 season began but injuries and bouts of blood poisoning were beginning to afflict him, and across the next three seasons he only played fifty games, although he still managed to net thirty goals. His final game for the club came in February 1931 against the side he'd scored the first of his 117 goals against, Liverpool.

John White
108 games, 38 goals
20-Goal Season: 21 in 1927–28

Matching Jennings's haul of twenty-one goals in 1927–28 was John White. He joined Leeds in early 1927 from Hearts with two full Scottish caps – remarkably, that's two more than Jennings ever won. And, like Jennings had done for Leeds, he had scored hat-tricks in three consecutive games against Dundee United, Alloa and Hamilton (although two of those games were in the Scottish Cup).

White's twenty-goal season for Leeds United was in the club's promotion-winning season of 1927–28, and while Jennings could only manage twenty-seven games that season, White played in all forty-two matches, netting twenty-one goals to take Leeds back to the top-flight.

Leeds had an exceptional record when John White scored – in thirty-one matches, Leeds won twenty-six of them (84%), which is the joint best win ratio by any player to score in twenty-five or more matches, along with Jack Harrison whose record is exactly the same as White's. After finding the net in a 2–2 draw with Nottingham Forest in January 1928, White then scored in seventeen further games for Leeds and they won every single one.

Scored in 25+ Games	Scored in	Won	Drawn	Lost	Win %
Jack Harrison	31	26	3	2	83.9%
John White	31	26	3	2	83.9%
Johnny Giles	102	85	11	6	83.3%
Eddie Gray	60	49	8	3	81.7%
Jimmy Greenhoff	27	22	4	1	81.5%

At Elland Road, that record was even better – Leeds won nineteen of the twenty games on home soil when White found the net, drawing the other. Often those wins were by huge margins (only once did he score in a 1–0 victory), including two at 6–0 (against Notts County and

Grimsby) and an 8–1 demolition of Crystal Palace.

If John White scored at Elland Road, fans knew the team wouldn't lose and – and even better – there was a high probability they'd see a hammering.

Charlie Keetley
169 games, 110 goals
20-Goal Seasons: 22 in 1928–29, 23 in 1931–32

With Tom Jennings struggling from injury, Leeds manager Dick Ray signed 21-year-old forward Charlie Keetley from non-league football in late 1927, Ray having managed four of Keetley's brothers during his time as Doncaster manager. As impacts go, this one wasn't bad.

Keetley became the first, and so far only, Leeds player to find the net in each of his first four games, scoring six goals, with his first hat-trick in his fourth game against Bristol City. By the end of the campaign, he'd managed eighteen in just sixteen games (including three hat-tricks) to fire Leeds to promotion back to the top-flight. This goals-per-game ratio of 1.13 is the best by a Leeds player in a season in which they've played at least five games, and Keetley had a goals-per-game scoring rate of at least one per game across his first twenty-eight games for the club. After failing to score in his twenty-ninth game, when the rate dropped to 0.97, he made amends in his thirtieth by bagging a hat-trick against Leicester.

Keetley was a serial scorer of hat-tricks, netting ten in total for Leeds – a tally that wasn't bettered until John Charles came along and scored eleven. On his first ever appearance in the First Division, Keetley scored a hat-trick against Aston Villa in August 1928, with only one other Leeds player scoring a hat-trick on his first appearance for the club in the top-flight (Harold Brook in 1956). He remains the only Leeds United player to score a hat-trick in the top-flight against a team starting the day top of the table, doing so against Sheffield Wednesday in April 1930. His record against table-topping teams was exceptional in general, with eight goals in eight games, a Leeds United record.

When we talk about strikers being prolific in front of goal, the table below shows which player has the record for the most goals in their first 10, 20, 25, 50, 75, 100 and 150 games in Leeds United's history. It is completely dominated by one man.

Player	Game No.	Goals
Charlie Keetley	10	11
Charlie Keetley	20	24
Charlie Keetley	25	27
Charlie Keetley	50	41
Charlie Keetley	75	62
Charlie Keetley	100	74
Charlie Keetley	150	103

And something should further endear Keetley to readers of this book: five of his 110 goals were scored against Manchester United, with only Mick Jones scoring more against them for Leeds. Two of them were netted in a 3–1 win in April 1930, the seventh consecutive game Keetley had scored in to emulate Jennings' record, which was broken a year later by Billy Furness, who scored in eight consecutive appearances, a Leeds record.

Although Keetley was clearly a prolific and talented scorer of goals, they tended to be spread over many seasons, with twenty-three his best scoring season in 1931–32. Keetley may have ended with even more than the 110 he scored in total (seven shy of Jennings' 117 goals) were it not for injuries; he managed just nine games in 1929–30, although he still hit ten goals in them.

One slight oddity of this era is that Jennings and Keetley each featured in every season between 1927–28 and 1930–31 but the club's first scorers of one hundred goals only played alongside one another in four games, all in February 1929, with Keetley failing to score at all and Jennings scoring twice.

Arthur Hydes
137 games, 82 goals
20-Goal Seasons: 20 in 1932–33, 25 in 1934–35

Although twelve players have scored more goals for Leeds United than Arthur Hydes, who hit eighty-two goals between 1931 and 1937, only Tom Jennings and Charlie Keetley can better Hydes' impressive 0.60 goals-per-game ratio.

Hydes was given his opportunity in January 1931 at the age of nineteen and made an immediate impact, scoring in his first two games against Huddersfield in the FA Cup and Blackburn in the First Division. Only ten games followed across the next season and a half, before Hydes finally became a regular in 1932–33. He scored a hat-trick away at St James' Park against cup holders Newcastle in the FA Cup, becoming the club's youngest ever hat-trick scorer (21 years and 51 days) – a record which wasn't broken for nineteen years until a twenty-year-old John Charles got one. He ended that season with twenty goals, becoming the first Leeds United player to achieve that at such a young age; only Charles, Peter Lorimer and Michael Bridges have ever emulated scoring twenty goals in a season aged twenty-one or younger.

Season	Player	Goals aged 21 or Under
1967–1968	Peter Lorimer	30
1952–1953	John Charles	27
1953–1954	John Charles	27
1999–2000	Michael Bridges	21
1932–1933	Arthur Hydes	20

Hydes notched twenty-five goals in 1934–35 despite not making his first appearance that season until 20 October, and scored his fiftieth goal for the club during that campaign in a 3–3 draw with Middlesbrough in just his eighty-sixth appearance for the club. Only four players have ever hit fifty goals for the club in fewer appearances. Hydes also thrived in the FA Cup, and it perhaps says something of the club's poor record in the competition that even today only four players have more FA Cup goals for Leeds than Hydes' eight.

Unfortunately, injuries later blighted Hydes and he managed just thirty games in his final two seasons for the club, scoring sixteen goals, before making his 137th and final appearance for the club in 1937 aged only twenty-five.

> Of Arthur Hydes' goals for Leeds United, 22% were scored against Middlesbrough and Blackburn (nine each). Despite this high percentage, Hydes scored against thirty-one of the thirty-eight clubs he faced with Leeds and scored against twenty-seven of the twenty-eight clubs he played more than once against, failing only in two games versus Blackpool.

George Brown
41 games, 21 goals
20-Goal Season: 20 in 1935–36

In English top-flight history, only twenty-eight players have bagged 200 goals. At the top, possibly forever unless Leeds-born Erling Haaland sticks around long enough, is Jimmy Greaves on 357. Greaves scored ten of those against Leeds United, with seven coming against Don Revie's great side, and Greaves' achievements have stood the test of time and are made even more remarkable when you consider his final top-flight game in 1971 came at the age of only thirty-one.

Three of those players with 200 goals played at some stage for Leeds United. In the post-war era, only Ian Rush has done this, playing forty-two games during 1996–97 when he was well past his Liverpool peak. He only managed three goals and left in the summer of 1997 with the lowest goals-per-game rate of any Leeds player to wear the number 9 shirt on twenty or more occasions (0.07). Sharpshooter he was not for Leeds.

The other two men in the English top-flight's 200-goal club to have played for Leeds came in the 1930s. Both had already notched 200 goals by the time they joined the club and both were aged thirty-two on their debuts. Sadly (similarly to Jennings and Keetley rarely crossing over) they didn't both feature for the club at the same time, both playing in the 1936–37 season but at different stages.

George Brown had been part of the Huddersfield side who won three consecutive titles in the mid-1920s, and his 79 goals in 116 league games for Aston Villa had helped them to two second-place finishes. But by the time he signed for Leeds in 1935, his last top-flight goal had been when he scored four in the space of seven minutes against Blackburn in April 1933. Brown had 221 top-flight goals already when he joined, and he added nineteen more for Leeds, scoring twenty goals in all competitions in 1935–36 and ending the season as top scorer as the Whites finished tenth. His twentieth goal for Leeds, in a 3–0 win over Sunderland in April 1936, came in only his thirty-sixth appearance and, at that point, only Keetley had reached twenty goals in fewer games for Leeds, with Brown now the eighth-quickest Leeds player to twenty goals.

But that was basically it for Brown; after four goalless games in 1936–37, he packed his bags and accepted the role of player-manager at Third Division North side Darlington, later retiring to pursue that classic ex-footballer pastime of the era – running a pub . . .

In his first game as Darlington's player-manager, George Brown scored away at Chester and played alongside a 35-year-old Jerry Best, who'd played for Leeds in their first ever game in 1920 at the age of nineteen. Brown then sold him to Hull where Best made his debut, as Brown had for Darlington, away at Chester. When George Brown eventually made his final career appearance in February 1938 away at Bradford, Darlington's scorer that day was one Reg Chester. It's a funny old game.

Gordon Hodgson
85 games, 53 goals
20-Goal Seasons: 26 in 1937–38, 21 in 1938–39

A man with an even greater top-flight goalscoring pedigree than Brown was Gordon Hodgson, whose record of 233 top-flight goals for Liverpool has never been beaten, with Ian Rush leaving Anfield for that glorious three-goal spell at Leeds in 1996 just four shy of his record. Hodgson sits fourth on the all-time list of top-flight scorers with only Jimmy Greaves, Steve Bloomer and Dixie Dean ahead of him, and some of his scoring records for Leeds have remained in the years since.

Hodgson had scored at least twenty top-flight goals in seven out of eight seasons between 1927–28 and 1934–35 but after joining Aston Villa in 1936 the club had been relegated to the Second Division. After seven goals in thirteen games at that level (the only league goals Hodgson scored outside of the top-flight), he joined Leeds at the age of thirty-two in March 1937 with the club struggling at the foot of the First Division. Things didn't quite go to plan on his debut – although Hodgson found the net at Goodison Park against Everton, Leeds lost 7–1.

Hodgson's six goals in thirteen games for Leeds helped them to avoid the drop in nineteenth place, and 1937–38 saw a huge improvement in Leeds' fortunes – with Hodgson's goals the catalyst. He started with one on the opening day against Charlton Athletic, and by the time they faced Charlton again on New Year's Day, Leeds were second in the league and Hodgson had bagged thirteen in seventeen matches. It took him until the end of February to notch his twentieth of the season but, having gone into the home game against Everton on seventeen goals, Hodgson scored four to take his seasonal tally to twenty-one. However Everton scored four of their own to draw 4–4, and Hodgson remains, perhaps unsurprisingly, the only Leeds player to score four in a game but not win the match. But there were better things to come.

In the club's entire history, only one player has scored five goals in a game. In an 8–2 win over Leicester City in October 1938, Gordon

50

Hodgson became that player. Even more impressively, he'd achieved it at the age of 34 years and 168 days, making him the club's fifth-oldest hat-trick scorer of all time. He was also the club's oldest player to score more than three in a game until Brian Deane's memorable four against QPR in 2004.

Date	Player	Opponent	Goals	Age
20/11/2004	Brian Deane	Queens Park Rangers	4	36 years, 287 days
10/04/1993	Gordon Strachan	Blackburn Rovers	3	36 years, 60 days
26/12/1956	Harold Brook	Blackpool	3	35 years, 72 days
20/12/1930	Bobby Turnbull	Manchester United	3	35 years, 3 days
18/08/1956	Harold Brook	Everton	3	34 years, 308 days
01/10/1938	Gordon Hodgson	Leicester City	5	34 years, 168 days

Hodgson scored twenty-one times in 1938–39 before football was halted when war broke out, ending his top-flight career. But what a career it was. Only Jennings (0.65) has a better top-flight goals-per-game ratio for Leeds than Hodgson (0.63, fifty-one in eighty-one games). He was truly one of English football's finest goalscorers and his five-goal haul against Leicester is yet to be matched by a Leeds United player.

> Although Hodgson only played three games for Leeds against Leicester, no player in the club's entire history across 131 games against them has scored more goals against the Foxes than he did (seven).

Albert Wakefield
50 games, 23 goals
20-Goal Season: 21 in 1947–48

Albert Wakefield, born in Pontefract in 1921, didn't make his league debut until 1947 due to the Second World War. When he did get his opportunity with Leeds, they were back in the Second Division after a disastrous 1946–47 Division One campaign that saw them relegated with just six wins and thirty defeats – at that stage the worst record of any top-flight side in a forty-two-game season.

Wakefield made an immediate impact by scoring in his first three appearances for Leeds, something that only Charlie Keetley achieved previously. Since then, the only other player to score in their first three Leeds games is Frank Fidler in 1951. He ended the 1947–48 campaign as the club's top scorer by a considerable margin with twenty-one goals after a hat-trick in the final game of the season against Bury. Only two other Leeds players have managed trebles in the final league game of a season, with Peter Lorimer doing so in 1972–73 against Arsenal and Rod Wallace against Coventry City in 1992–93. That season was his peak for Leeds, and he scored twice in twelve appearances the following campaign before heading to Southend United.

Len Browning
105 games, 46 goals
20-Goal Season: 20 in 1950–51

Len Browning made his Leeds United debut in a 5–0 top-flight defeat at Charlton in September 1946. When he next appeared in the first-team, two years and twenty-eight days had elapsed and Leeds were now in Division Two, Browning scoring in a 1–1 draw with Barnsley in October 1948. It was the longest gap between a player's first two games for Leeds, although it's been broken a few times since then (Andy Keogh left the club and then returned on loan between these appearances – he didn't just go missing in Thorp Arch for nearly seven years).

Player	First App	Second App	Gap
Andy Keogh	26/10/2004	16/08/2011	6 years and 294 days
Nigel Davey	13/10/1965	07/05/1968	2 years and 207 days
John Shaw	29/09/1971	07/11/1973	2 years and 39 days
Len Browning	25/09/1946	23/10/1948	2 years and 28 days
Bailey Peacock-Farrell	05/04/2016	07/03/2018	1 years and 336 days

From this point until his departure, Browning was Leeds United's regular number 9, wearing the shirt in 102 of the next 133 games (with two games in the number 8 shirt, scoring in both) until his final appearance in October 1951. Browning scored thirteen goals in his first seventeen games in 1948–49, including nine goals in his first ten matches at Elland Road, a total that only three Leeds players have bettered in their first ten appearances at Elland Road in the club's history.

Although Leeds didn't improve their league position from 1949–50 to 1950–51, finishing fifth in both seasons, Browning's goal return did increase, jumping from nine in 1949–50 to twenty in 1950–51. Of his twenty goals, Browning scored fifteen of them at Elland Road including his one hat-trick for the club against Southampton in a 5–3 victory in January 1951. The following season, after just three goals in nine games, he was transfer-listed and joined Sheffield United where he won a Second Division title-winning medal in 1953.

Ray Iggleden
181 games, 50 goals
20-Goal Season: 20 in 1951–52

Ray Iggleden – whose real name was Horatio – started his career at Leicester City, where he played alongside Don Revie. After moving to Leeds in 1948, he scored ten goals in his first three seasons before enjoying his best scoring return in 1951–52, hitting twenty in a campaign where none of his teammates made it into double figures. He scored as many goals in six consecutive appearances between September and November that campaign – eight – as any of his teammates managed all campaign long. He was the first Leeds player to score in six consecutive league appearances since Billy Furness in 1931 and it's since been emulated by just three players – John Charles, John McCole and Ross McCormack.

After that twenty-goal season, Iggleden scored twenty more goals in seventy-six appearances before his departure in 1955, including a hat-trick against former side Leicester in January 1954. The Foxes were top of the table at the time, making Iggleden one of only three Leeds players to score a hat-trick against a table-topping side, alongside Tom Jennings in 1927 versus Chelsea and Charlie Keetley in 1930 versus Sheffield Wednesday. No Leeds player has done this since then, although notable shout-outs to Max Gradel vs QPR in 2010 and Stuart Dallas vs Man City in 2021, who both scored twice.

Iggleden is also one of only three players whose surname begins with an I to play for Leeds, along with Tony Ingham in the 1940s (three games) and more notably Denis Irwin in the 1980s (eighty-two games). Goalkeeper Sasa Ilic was later an unused sub three times towards the back end of the 2004–05 season. And on that theme, Iggleden's place in Leeds United's history is safe as he leads the way for scorers whose surname starts with a vowel.

Vowel Surname	Games	Goals
Ray Iggleden	181	50
George Ainsley	94	34
Jack Armand	79	24
Ezgjan Alioski	171	22
Jack Overfield	163	20

John Charles
327 games, 157 goals
20-Goal Seasons: 27 in 1952–53, 43 in 1953–54,
29 in 1955–59, 39 in 1956–57

One of the club's greatest ever players, John Charles' achievements for Leeds United were extraordinary and many of the records he set still stand today – and are unlikely to ever be broken:

Most goals in a season (forty-three in 1953–54)
Most league goals in a season (forty-two in 1953–54)
Most top-flight goals in a season (thirty-eight in 1956–57)
Most hat-tricks for the club (eleven)
Most hat-tricks in one season (five in 1953–54)
Most goals in the Second Division (115)
Most league seasons scoring more than twenty goals (four)

His 157 goals for the club between 1949 and 1962 were also a record until Peter Lorimer surpassed that with two goals against Derby in March 1973, but this is made all the more impressive when you factor in that Charles made 115 of his first 121 appearances in central defence.

Operating in defence, Charles only scored four goals in his first 121 games for Leeds United. That is fewer than the likes of Trevor Cherry (six), Chris Whyte (five), Tony Dorigo (five) and the same amount Neil Aspin and Tom Lees scored in their first 121 games for the club. Now, no disrespect to Tom Lees, but it's hard to imagine him making the switch from centre-back and breaking goalscoring records for Leeds.

Three of those four goals had come when Charles had worn the number 9 shirt in consecutive league games late in the 1950–51 campaign in wins against Hull and Grimsby Town. His other goal had a historic significance of its own – his first for the club was a penalty scored away at Plymouth Argyle when he was just 17 years and 320 days, making him the club's youngest ever penalty scorer. Only four players have scored a penalty as a teenager since then: Chris Crowe, Billy Bremner, Peter Lorimer, and, most recently, Lyndon Simmonds in 1985. None were as young as Charles was at Home Park in 1949.

Charles moved up front for the 18 October game against Barnsley in the 1952–53 season and proceeded to knock in twenty-seven goals in twenty-eight matches until the end of the season. In his first eight games as a forward at Elland Road that season, Charles scored in all eight games, notching sixteen goals and three hat-tricks, including in back-to-back home appearances against Hull and Brentford. It was the first time a Leeds player had netted a hat-trick in consecutive Elland Road appearances since Tom Jennings back in 1926 (as part of his aforementioned three consecutive hat-tricks). It would not be the last time Charles did it.

Excluding the 1953–54 season, the most goals Leeds as a team have scored in their first two league games is seven – a feat they've managed just seven times. In 1953–54, John Charles alone scored seven goals in Leeds United's first two league games. Both were at Elland Road, with four against Notts County and three against Rotherham United. The only other Leeds player to score more than three times across Leeds' opening two games of one season was Arthur Hydes in 1933–34, who scored five.

Charles didn't stop there, and by the tenth league game of the season, he'd scored fifteen times and broken Jennings' record for goals in the opening ten league games of a season that the Scotsman had set back in 1926.

Season	Player	Goals in First 10 League Games
1953–54	John Charles	15
1926–27	Tom Jennings	14
1938–39	Gordon Hodgson	10
1928–29	Russell Wainscoat	9
1933–34	Arthur Hydes	9
1956–57	John Charles	9
1977–78	Ray Hankin	9
2008–09	Jermaine Beckford	9
2011–12	Ross McCormack	9

Charles ended the year 1953 with five hat-tricks (a joint club record in a single year along with, you guessed it, Tom Jennings) while his thirty-nine goals were the most in one year until this was equalled in 1956 – by John Charles. The man was unstoppable.

Spare a thought for poor Rotherham United, against whom Charles scored three consecutive hat-tricks in 1953 and Charles is the only Leeds player to score three hat-tricks against one opponent (overall, not just in one year). In 1976, Leeds' top scorer that year was Carl Harris with six goals; Charles scored three more goals just against Rotherham in 1953.

Top Scorer in Year	Player	Goals in Calendar Year
1953	John Charles vs Rotherham	9
2015	Chris Wood	8
2004	Mark Viduka	8
1981	Arthur Graham	7
1976	Carl Harris	6
1980	Terry Connor	6

Charles' 1953–54 season haul of forty-three goals in all competitions remains a record to this day and the only time a Leeds player has ever exceeded forty goals in a season. Of those forty-three, only one was scored outside of the league, in a 3–3 draw with Spurs in the FA Cup. Those forty-two league goals are more than Leeds scored as a team in 1980–81, 1981–82, 1995–96, 1996–97 and 2003–04. Despite this unbelievable total, it didn't fire Leeds to promotion from the Second Division – the club finished tenth, thirteen points behind the top two. Moving Charles from central defence to centre-forward had been great for the club's goals tally – up from seventy-one in 1952–53 to eighty-nine in 1953–54 – but they missed him defensively; they had conceded eighteen more goals than the previous season and only six clubs in the division had conceded more goals.

And so, manager Raich Carter had a problem. It was a nice problem, but he had both the club's best centre-half and best centre-forward and they were the same person. Charles started 1954–55 up front and scored four goals in five games before Carter moved him back to the centre of defence. It is notable that of Charles' next eighteen appearances, seventeen of them were with him playing in the centre of defence and Leeds didn't concede more than two goals in any, but in the game he was moved back up front with Jack Marsden as the number 5, Leeds lost 5–1 at Bristol Rovers. They had a fourteen-game unbeaten run with Charles at the back, and though he did still manage twelve goals that season half of those were penalties. Goals conceded dropped from eighty-one to fifty-three, while clean sheets went from five the previous season to fifteen in 1954–55. Leeds moved up from tenth to fourth, but missed out on promotion by only one point.

Early in the 1955–56 season, Jack Charlton returned from national service and Carter could finally move Charles up front permanently, with Charlton taking over the number 5 shirt for, essentially, the next eighteen years (from 24 September 1955 until the end of the 1972–73 season, Charlton wore the number 5 shirt on 743 occasions and in 80% of Leeds United's games in that time). As a centre-forward in 1955–56, Charles scored twenty-seven goals in twenty-eight appearances to fire Leeds, finally, back to the First Division in second spot. Leeds went into April in eighth position, having endured a run of just three wins in eleven games, but they won all six games in April, with Charles netting nine goals, a total only Tom Jennings in October 1926 (twelve) and Charlie Keetley in April 1930 (ten) can better in a single month for Leeds. After 275 appearances for the club, John Charles was finally a top-flight footballer.

However, the 1956–57 team was beginning to be dubbed 'John Charles United' by the press (a title that Charles himself hated), due to the overreliance on his goals. In what was his only English top-flight campaign, Charles scored thirty-eight in forty games and was the leading scorer in the division, the only time a Leeds United player has achieved this feat outright. Those thirty-eight goals were the most by a player in their debut Division One season ever (a record which still stands), breaking the thirty-seven-goal record that Jimmy Trotter had set in 1926–27, when he pipped Tom Jennings to leading scorer. Charles was producing extraordinary records and relishing playing against the country's best defences and proving himself at the top level

– only Dixie Dean has ever scored more goals for a promoted side in English top-flight history.

Most goals for a newly promoted top-flight team

Team	Season	Player	Goals
Everton	1931–32	Dixie Dean	45
Manchester City	1928–29	Tommy Johnson	38
Leeds United	1956–57	John Charles	38
Sheffield Wednesday	1926–27	Jimmy Trotter	37
Southampton	1966–67	Ron Davies	37

It was probably not unfair to describe the team as reliant on Charles' goals though. Only three others Leeds players managed five or more that season and only one, Harold Brook with eleven, reached double figures. Charles' thirty-eight goals made up 53% of Leeds United's total of seventy-two, the highest figure seen since Dixie Dean had scored a record sixty top-flight goals in 1927–28 for Everton, which was 59% of their total. In the years that have followed, only James Beattie in 2002–03 for Southampton has ever eclipsed this. Charles was too modest to admit it, but Leeds really were statistically a one-man goalscoring attack.

Team	Season	Player	Goals	% Team Goals
Everton	1927–28	Dixie Dean	60	58.8%
Birmingham City	1923–24	Joe Bradford	24	58.5%
Southampton	2002–03	James Beattie	23	53.5%
Leeds United	1956–57	John Charles	38	52.8%
Sheffield United	1930–31	Jimmy Dunne	41	52.6%
Sunderland	1999–00	Kevin Phillips	30	52.6%

With the club strapped for cash after the fire to the West Stand, they accepted a £65,000 offer from Juventus and Charles departed to win the Serie A title in three of the next four seasons, becoming a club icon for the Old Lady. Then, in 1962, Don Revie – who had been Sunderland captain in the last game of Charles' first Leeds spell in April 1957 – brought Charles home with the club once again back in the Second Division. It wasn't to be the same, however, and after three goals in eleven games (two of which were, naturally, against Rotherham to take his total to thirteen against them) he was heading back to Italy, joining Roma for £70,000.

John Charles' 327 games for Leeds were split almost evenly between defence (164) and attack (163). Had Charles played in attack for all 327 games and scored at the same rate as he did for the games he actually played up front, he would have scored 295 goals for the club. Hypothetical perhaps, but not beyond the imagination.

John Charles – Leeds record	Games	Goals	Goals per Game
In defence	164	10	0.06
In attack	163	147	0.90

Hugh Baird
45 games, 22 goals
20-Goal Season: 20 in 1957–58

With John Charles departing, Leeds replaced him with prolific Scottish striker Hugh Baird, who signed from Airdrieonians in the summer of 1957. Although Baird couldn't match Charles' goalscoring feats (in fairness, that was one hell of an ask), he did still score twenty goals in thirty-nine games in Division One in 1957–58, the same total as Jimmy Greaves managed in his debut top-flight season.

Leeds struggled for most of the season, though, and hovered around the relegation zone, including a run in which Baird scored seven goals in nine games across November and December with Leeds winning none of the games he'd scored in, and Baird ended the season having scored in seventeen matches while only being on the winning side in just eight. His twentieth goal of the campaign did come in a win, however, against Newcastle United on the final day of the season which left Leeds in seventeenth, clear of relegation, but they were the First Division's lowest scorers. Although no one referred to Leeds as Hugh Baird United, as they had done with John Charles, only Luton's Gordon Turner (48%) had scored a higher percentage of his side's goals that season than Baird for Leeds (39%).

After two goals in six games the following season, a homesick Baird returned to Scotland and joined Aberdeen.

All forty-five of Hugh Baird's appearances for Leeds United were in Division One, with Baird missing the 1957–58 FA Cup defeat to Cardiff. In the club's history, only Basil Wood (fifty-six between 1920 and 1922) and Alex Stacey (fifty-one between 1928 and 1933) made more appearances exclusively in the league.

John McCole
85 games, 53 goals
20-Goal Seasons: 23 in 1959–60, 23 in 1960–61

After scoring thirty-eight goals in forty-six games for Bradford City, John McCole joined Leeds in September 1959 with the task of scoring the goals to keep the club in Division One. He did score the goals, but sadly they didn't keep the club in the top-flight.

McCole was prolific, with twenty-three goals in thirty-four games in all competitions (twenty-two in thirty-three in the league), which was at that time the most goals scored by a Leeds player in their debut season. This was even more impressive given the fact McCole didn't debut until Leeds' ninth game of the campaign. Between Boxing Day and 6 February, McCole scored in seven consecutive matches which has only been emulated by Peter Lorimer for Leeds United since then. Despite his twenty-two league goals, Leeds finished twenty-first and were relegated since then, only two players in history have scored twenty-two goals for a top-flight team and been relegated. Leeds could point to a horrendous defensive record (ninety-two goals conceded, their joint most in a league season ever) as to why the drop was inevitable.

McCole continued his excellent scoring record in 1960–61, once again scoring twenty-three goals and becoming the first Leeds United player to score twenty goals in each of his first two seasons with the club, something only Allan Clarke and Jimmy Floyd Hasselbaink have achieved since then. Although McCole missed the historic game on 18 March 1961 against Portsmouth – Don Revie's first game in charge of the club – he did score four in five games under Revie at the back end of the season, netting back-to-back braces against Lincoln and Scunthorpe at Elland Road. The 6,975 attendance against Scunthorpe was the lowest at Elland Road for a match since May 1934. And even fewer – 4,517 – were there to see McCole create history in September 1961, when he became the first and only Leeds player to score four goals in a League Cup match, as Brentford were brushed aside 4–1.

McCole would not play in the League Cup again for Leeds, making his last appearance for the club the game before their third-round tie with Huddersfield in October 1961. He departed Leeds with the same record as Gordon Hodgson managed for the club – fifty-three goals in eighty-five games – and only Keetley and Jennings have better goals-per-game ratios than he does, while no player since McCole has scored fifty goals in as few games (eighty-two) as he managed.

> John McCole had the best goals-per-game ratio of any Leeds United player under Don Revie – he scored eleven goals in sixteen games in 1961 (0.69).

Jim Storrie
156 games, 67 goals
20-Goal Season: 27 in 1962–63

Following John McCole's departure, Don Revie experimented with five different players wearing the number 9 shirt up to the end of the 1961–62 season. Mike Addy and Revie himself both had one game, while Billy McAdams scored three goals in eight games. Late season signing Ian Lawson had seven goalless games in the 9 shirt but the most successful striking replacement that season was Jack Charlton, who Revie deployed up front. England's future World Cup-winning centre-half scored ten goals in nineteen games as striker in 1961–62 and, overall, Charlton's record when wearing the number 9 shirt was a more than respectable fifteen in twenty-six games. It wasn't quite John Charles, but he wasn't 'making such a mess of it' as Charlton would later recall in his autobiography.

Charles did then return for 1962–63 and started the season up front, but by the end of October he was back in Italy and new signing Jim Storrie took over the number 9 shirt. Similarly to Hugh Baird a few years previously, Storrie had signed for Leeds from Airdrieonians where he'd scored almost half a century of goals in just under one hundred games. Storrie scored in each of his first two games for Leeds and ended the 1962–63 campaign with twenty-seven goals in all competitions and twenty-five in the league – both records for a Leeds player in their first season with the club that still stand today.

Although his record away from home was not prolific – eighteen goals in seventy-six away games – Storrie scored a hatful at Elland Road, notching twenty goals in twenty games on home soil in the 1962–63 season and reaching twenty Elland Road goals in the second-fewest appearances of any player in the club's history, behind Charlie Keetley's fifteen games.

Injuries restricted Storrie to just fifteen league games in 1963–64, when the club earned promotion back to Division One under Revie, and Alan Peacock was an expensive late season signing from Middlesbrough to get Leeds over the line with eight goals in fourteen games. However, Peacock's own injuries allowed Storrie to return to the line-up the following season in Division One, with Storrie scoring nineteen goals as Leeds finished runners-up in both the league and the FA Cup, with Storrie playing in all eight FA Cup games that season, including the final at Wembley.

After another fifteen-goal season in 1965–66, Storrie's role became more peripheral and he only started five matches in 1966–67, scoring in his final game for the club on Boxing Day 1966 against Newcastle

United. He's one of fourteen players to make their final appearance for Leeds on 26 December – others include Matthew Kilgallon, Amdy Faye and Kenny Burns. It was also Storrie's final English top-flight appearance, later playing for Rotherham United, Portsmouth and Aldershot across the Second, Third and Fourth Divisions before returning to Scotland in 1972.

Peter Lorimer
707 games, 238 goals
20-Goal Seasons: 30 in 1967–68, 29 in 1971–72, 23 in 1972–73

Leeds United have played almost 5,000 competitive matches but only one player has played for the club before the age of sixteen. Aged 15 years and 289 days, Peter Lorimer made his Leeds United debut at home to Southampton in September 1962 alongside a thirty-year-old John Charles, making the 325th of his 327 appearances as Lorimer made the first of his 707. The fact that the pair crossed over at all is remarkable in itself, given Lorimer was two years old when Charles made his Leeds debut. He was the club's leading scorer in 1962 with 157 goals and probably doubted anyone would surpass it. By 1973, Lorimer had taken his record at the age of just twenty-six and would end his Leeds career aged thirty-eight, in a second spell in 1985, with 238 goals to his name – a record that has remained untouched.

Although Lorimer was a constant and mainstay in the greatest ever Leeds United side, making at least forty appearances in ten consecutive seasons between 1964–65 and 1974–75, the opening stages of his career were more spread out. Lorimer is the only player in Leeds United's history to make his first four appearances for the club in four different seasons, playing once in each of 1961–62, 1962–63, 1963–64, before finally breaking properly into the team in 1964–65. And he made a huge impact, scoring nineteen goals in forty-five games, a record by a teenager in a single season for the club.

Lorimer scored the first of his seven hat-tricks for the club in an FA Cup match against Bury in January 1966, the first by a Leeds player in the FA Cup since Arthur Hydes had scored one thirty-three years earlier. He was just 19 years and 39 days when he scored that treble, becoming the club's youngest ever hat-trick scorer. This was one Lorimer record that would eventually be broken, as in January 1985 Tommy Wright hit three against Notts County aged 19 years and 9 days. Playing alongside Wright that day? A 38-year-old Peter Lorimer, whose Bury hat-trick had been scored the same month Wright was born.

Date	Player	Opponent	Age
19/01/1985	Tommy Wright	Notts County	19 years, 9 days
22/01/1966	Peter Lorimer	Bury	19 years, 39 days
24/09/1955	Keith Ripley	Rotherham United	20 years, 179 days
01/11/1952	John Charles	Hull City	20 years, 310 days
11/08/1999	Michael Bridges	Southampton	21 years, 6 days

After fourteen goals in 1966–67 (although without referee Ken Burns' bizarre decision to disallow a free-kick goal against Chelsea in that season's FA Cup semi-final as the Chelsea wall hadn't retreated ten yards, it would have been fifteen), Lorimer's 1967–68 campaign was spectacular and his best scoring campaign for the club, netting thirty goals in all competitions – including eight in the Fairs Cup as Leeds won the trophy (although the final wasn't held until the start of the following season). Lorimer's four goals in a 9–0 win over Spora Luxembourg was the club's third hat-trick in Europe, following Albert Johanneson and Rod Belfitt, but it was the first time a Leeds player had scored four in a European game and it wouldn't be repeated until Alan Smith's four in a 4–1 win against Hapoel Tel Aviv in 2002. At 20 years and 293 days, Lorimer is still the youngest Leeds player to score a European hat-trick.

He also hit three in the League Cup against Luton in September 1967 and he remains the only Leeds player to score a hat-trick in that competition before turning twenty-one, making him the club's youngest hat-trick scorer in Europe, the FA Cup and League Cup. The latter competition was a favourite for Lorimer, scoring more goals in the

League Cup than any other Leeds player (nineteen), while only Paul Madeley (fifty) played more games than Lorimer (forty-two). He was also on the winning side in his first eleven games in the competition, including the 1968 final against Arsenal. It remains the only time Leeds have won it. And it says a lot about his longevity that his first goal in the competition was scored against goalkeeper Alan Kelly, born in 1936, while his last goal in the competition came in 1984, alongside teammate Denis Irwin – who was still playing in the League Cup in 2002.

Lorimer's fiftieth goal for the club came in November 1967 in a 1–1 draw against Coventry and he remains the only Leeds United player to reach fifty goals before turning twenty-one.

Date	Player	Age on 50th Goal
18/11/1967	Peter Lorimer	20 years, 339 days
24/10/1953	John Charles	21 years, 301 days
13/11/1965	Billy Bremner	22 years, 339 days
25/10/2003	Alan Smith	22 years, 362 days
29/12/1934	Arthur Hydes	23 years, 35 days

Lorimer particularly enjoyed facing the two Midlands clubs Nottingham Forest and Derby County, scoring thirteen goals against each which is the joint most by a Leeds player against a single opponent (the other with thirteen is John Charles against Rotherham United). The man synonymous with both of those clubs is Brian Clough, whose infamous forty-four-day spell in charge of Leeds in 1974 needs no introduction, or any more words written about it. Clough was booked to give a speech at a 1973 Yorkshire Television Sports Personality Awards ceremony in Leeds, with the award won by Lorimer. By the time Clough was giving his speech, Lorimer had departed to prepare for a cup replay the following day.

'I've come along to pay tribute to Peter Lorimer . . . Despite the fact that he falls as many times when he hasn't been kicked, despite the fact he protests as many times when he has nothing to protest about . . .' Clough uttered. Perhaps his antipathy was due to the fact that Lorimer so often got the better of Clough's Derby (of whom he was manager when he made these remarks) – Lorimer scored more goals against them than any other player until Clough departed later in 1973. Even though Clough's managerial career lasted until 1993, only three players scored more against his teams than Lorimer's seven, and the Scotsman never faced Forest in the top-flight when Clough was manager.

Top-Flight	Games	Goals vs Clough's Derby
Peter Lorimer	7	7
Ian Storey-Moore	7	5
Allan Clarke	6	5
Denis Law	5	4
Neil Martin	4	4

As well as hitting twenty-nine goals and winning the FA Cup in the 1971–72 season, Lorimer also played his part in two of the club's most famous (and rewatched) victories within the space of a fortnight early in 1972. After scoring in the 5–1 win over Manchester United in February, he then notched a hat-trick in the 7–0 demolition of Southampton in March, made famous by the string of passes that ended the game and Barry Davies exclaiming that 'poor Southampton don't know what day it is' on *Match of the Day*. Lorimer's third was his ninety-first strike in Division One for Leeds, equalling Tom Jennings' total, which Lorimer then broke at the end of March with a goal against Arsenal. He eventually ended on 151 top-flight goals, comfortably a club record.

Lorimer scored another twenty-three goals in 1972–73, a campaign in which he featured in sixty-three of Leeds' sixty-four matches which is the joint most appearances by a Leeds player in one season (Paul Reaney played sixty-three in 1967–68 and goalkeeper David Harvey managed the same in 1972–73). He added the Cup Winners' Cup to the list of competitions in which he'd scored, thanks to two goals against Rapid Bucharest, and also featured in the final against AC Milan. Leeds lost that 1–0, just eleven days after another final heartbreak in the FA Cup. It is odd to think that for a player who scored 238 times for Leeds, with many of them spectacular, it's for two 'goals' that weren't counted in his total that Lorimer is often remembered. In the 1973 FA Cup final, with Leeds 1–0 down to Second Division side Sunderland, Lorimer had the chance to equalise with the goal gaping and goalkeeper Jim Montgomery on the floor having saved from Trevor Cherry. On commentary, David Coleman casually said 'and Lorimer makes it one each' before realising a second later that, somehow, Montgomery had saved Lorimer's effort. Leeds lost 1–0.

Two years later, Leeds United reached the European Cup final. Lorimer scored in the first round against Zurich, the second round against Ujpest Dozsa, the third round against Anderlecht and, with a brilliant strike at the Nou Camp, in the semi-final against Barcelona. Lorimer had seven goals in fourteen European Cup appearances for Leeds at that point, one behind Mick Jones' record total of eight. Midway through the second half of the 1975 final against Bayern Munich, Lorimer struck brilliantly to give Leeds the lead. But the referee, following pressure from certain Bayern players, consulted his linesman and decided that Billy Bremner was in an offside position. It was an inexplicable decision and the score remained 0–0. Leeds lost 2–0 and it was Lorimer's last ever European appearance for the club, robbed of the chance of scoring in a final.

Lorimer ended with thirty goals in Europe, a total that only two British players – Harry Kane and Wayne Rooney – have ever beaten, while between 1965–66 and 1974–75, only some of the greats of the game – Gerd Müller, Jupp Heynckes, Eusébio and Paul Van Himst – scored more goals in Europe than Lorimer.

Lorimer's cup record up to the semi-finals of competitions is exceptional – from the first round to the quarter-finals, he scored 67 goals in 142 appearances. But in semi-finals and finals, Lorimer only scored twice in thirty games (in the 1972 FA Cup semi-final and 1975 European Cup semi-final). It probably should have been at least four in thirty-three.

Lorimer's Cup Record	Games	Goals	Goals per Game
Round 1 – QF	142	67	0.47
Semi-Finals and Finals	33	2	0.06

Sandwiched between these losing finals was the triumphant 1973–74 campaign in which Leeds won their second Division One title, with Lorimer featuring in thirty-seven of the forty-two games and scoring twelve goals. Lorimer began the season in fine form, with six goals in the opening five games of the season, but then went twenty-one consecutive games without a goal, the last of which was in the 3–2 defeat to Stoke that ended Leeds' twenty-nine-game unbeaten start. However, Lorimer hit back and was United's top scorer in the final twelve league games of the season, scoring six goals (three of them nerveless penalties) to help Leeds over the line as they brought the title back to Yorkshire.

After the departure of Don Revie, Lorimer scored the final goal of Brian Clough's short spell in charge and remained a constant presence under successor Jimmy Armfield, with no player scoring more goals during Armfield's four years in charge (thirty-five). But the appointment of Jimmy Adamson meant Lorimer's days were numbered and he joined Toronto Blizzard. At this stage, he had 219 goals in 620 appearances in all competitions, but in the league he was on 151 goals, just six shy of John Charles' league scoring record. But this wasn't to be the end of Lorimer's Leeds story.

In 1983 manager Eddie Gray re-signed a 37-year-old Lorimer to offer experience to his young team, who were now back in the Second Division. After making his second debut on New Year's Eve 1983 against Middlesbrough alongside old teammates David Harvey and Frank Gray, Lorimer added eighty-seven further appearances for the club until his final departure in October 1985. And crucially, he did eventually break Charles' league scoring record with a goal against Sheffield United early in the 1984/85 season, a penalty in a 1–1 draw.

Lorimer, who ten years previously came a questionable refereeing decision away from scoring the winner in a European Cup final, scored his 238th and final goal for the club in front of a little over 4,000 people in a 6–1 defeat at Maine Road against Manchester City in a Full Members' Cup match. At the age of 38 years and 304 days, the club's youngest ever player is also their second oldest scorer; only a forty-year-old Eddie Burbanks in 1953 has scored at an older age.

Lorimer's longevity was such that on his final ever appearance, six of the players alongside him in the matchday squad – Martin Dickinson, Ian Snodin, Ian Baird, Neil Aspin, Scott Sellars and Terry Phelan – weren't even born when he made his debut in September 1962. In Phelan's case, Lorimer had already played seventy-seven games and scored twenty-nine goals by the time he was born. Amazingly, Sellars was still making Football League appearances in the 2002–03 campaign, forty seasons after Lorimer's debut.

Allan Clarke
366 games, 151 goals
20-Goal Seasons: 26 in 1969–70, 23 in 1970–71, 26 in 1972–73

'Clarke. One-nil.'

It is a phrase etched in the memory of any Leeds fan brought up on videos of the Revie team, or anyone who has ever seen a compilation of the club's greatest ever goals. Clarke's stooping header in the 1972 FA Cup final against Arsenal – to give Leeds their first (and so far only) FA Cup trophy – is one of the most replayed Leeds United goals ever caught on camera, behind perhaps only Tony Yeboah's strikes against Liverpool and Wimbledon in 1995, or Eddie Gray weaving his way through a beleaguered Burnley defence in 1970 to score his magnificent individual goal.

Clarke had an excellent scoring record in his early years at Walsall (forty-one goals in seventy-two league games) and then Fulham (forty-five in eighty-six), and featured in Bobby Robson's first ever game as manager – a 5–0 home defeat to Leeds in January 1968. Fulham were relegated in 1967–68 despite Clarke's twenty goals and he was transferred to Leicester City for an English record £150,000. Although Clarke managed another twelve Division One goals and played his part in Leicester reaching the FA Cup final, the Foxes were also relegated. So Clarke was on the move again, this time joining league champions Leeds for £165,000 and breaking his own transfer record – the only player to do this.

Clarke, nicknamed 'Sniffer' for his qualities at finding the back of the net, made a quick start at Leeds. He reached twenty goals for the club in just his twenty-fourth appearance, the second-fastest in the club's history behind Charlie Keetley (seventeen games), and hit his twentieth goal as part of a four-goal haul against non-league Sutton United in the FA Cup in January 1970. While Sutton's team did, admittedly, contain part-time players in professions as varied as fish salesmen, a jig borer, teacher, engineer and panel beater, Clarke remains the only Leeds player to score four times in an FA Cup tie. While Leeds ended the 1969–70 season empty-handed trophy-wise, finishing runners-up in the league and the FA Cup and reaching the semi-finals of the European Cup, Clarke had scored twenty-six goals, the second most in a player's debut season behind Jim Storrie's twenty-seven in 1962–63.

The following season saw Clarke notch another twenty-three goals, becoming the second player to score twenty or more goals in his first two seasons, along with John McCole. Clarke's combined total across his first two seasons was forty-nine in ninety-nine games – the most by any player in the club's history.

First Two Seasons at Leeds	Games	Goals
Allan Clarke	99	49
John McCole	74	46
Chris Wood	85	43
Lee Chapman	76	43
Jimmy Floyd Hasselbaink	87	42

Clarke also picked up his first silverware in 1970–71, scoring in the second leg of the Fairs Cup final against Juventus at Elland Road. It was one of two final goals he scored; the other would come against Arsenal the following year. Also during the 1970–71 campaign, Clarke bagged another four goals in a game in a 4–0 win over Burnley in April, becoming the first to do so in a First Division match for the club since Gordon Hodgson's five against Leicester in 1938. In his time at

Leeds, against no side did Clarke score more First Division goals than he did against Burnley (seven) and Clarke managed to score against twenty-nine of the thirty-three teams he faced in the top-flight while at the Whites, failing only against Blackpool, Bristol City, Huddersfield and Sunderland. Extending that to his entire top-flight career, Clarke scored against thirty-one out of thirty-five teams he faced. The team he faced most without scoring? Eight games against Leeds United.

After a slow start to 1971–72 (two goals in eighteen games), Clarke hit form in the new year; from 1 January to 27 March Clarke scored twelve in fifteen games, including two in the 7–0 demolition of Southampton. Three of his other goals had come in the FA Cup – both goals in the 2–0 win over Liverpool in the third round and the equaliser against Spurs in the 2–1 quarter-final victory. Then, he went eight games without a goal before facing Arsenal in the cup final, saving his best for Wembley as his famous header secured the cup for United.

Aside from the obvious of scoring the winner against the Gunners, Clarke had an excellent FA Cup record for Leeds, and it is fitting that he is the club's all-time leading scorer in the competition with twenty-five goals. It perhaps says much for how poor the club have been in the competition outside the Revie era that no one who played outside of that time has ever scored ten in the competition for Leeds.

FA Cup	Games	Goals
Allan Clarke	45	25
Peter Lorimer	59	20
Johnny Giles	61	15
Mick Jones	36	12
Arthur Hydes	10	8
Jermaine Beckford	9	8

Clarke's partnership with Mick Jones is often cited as the club's best ever striker duo, with Jones often doing the legwork alongside the elite finisher Clarke. Jones was an excellent scorer of goals in his own right, but it is interesting to note Clarke's record in the Leeds starting XI alongside Jones and without him. It is a near identical number of games, but Clarke scored seventeen more with Jones next to him than without. There were other factors in that, with Leeds becoming a poorer side once Jones retired (they finished ninth twice and tenth once in three of Clarke's last four seasons), but Clarke certainly found the back of the net more frequently with Jones.

Allan Clarke – Starts for Leeds	Starts	Goals	Goals per Game
With Jones	181	84	0.46
Without Jones	180	67	0.37

Clarke picked up his first league championship medal in 1973–74, scoring a crucial goal in the penultimate game against Ipswich Town; from 2–0 ahead, Leeds had been pegged back at 2–2 and – having only won three of their previous twelve games – really needed a winner. Cue Clarke, twenty minutes from the end, controlling the ball and firing past Paul Cooper. In the era of VAR, it may have been ruled out for a handball, but thankfully there was none of that in 1974.

Brian Clough, who was indisputably one of the greatest goalscorers in Football League history himself (scorer of 251 goals in 274 matches before a knee injury ended his career), arrived in the summer of 1974. While he managed to upset the vast majority of the squad, Clarke wasn't necessarily among them, scoring 75% of the league goals Leeds managed under Clough. The ifs and buts of Clough at Leeds can be debated elsewhere but perhaps Clarke would have flourished under him.

Clarke's last high-scoring season at Leeds was 1974–75, in which he netted twenty-two in all competitions, his fourth twenty-goal season (level with John Charles' tally of twenty-goal-seasons). He scored four times for Leeds in the European Cup that season, including a crucial goal in the semi-final home leg against Barcelona, and anyone with working eyes can tell you he should have had a penalty in the final against Bayern Munich after being fouled by Franz Beckenbauer. His European goal total for Leeds stands at fourteen in thirty-three games, the fourth most in the club's history.

While he should've had a penalty in the 1975 final, penalties weren't something Clarke was known for scoring for Leeds. In fact, none of Clarke's first 146 goals were penalties (with Giles and Lorimer on penalty duties, he rarely got a look in), until he scored penalties in back-to-back games against Ipswich and Manchester United in April 1977; they were his only two penalty goals for Leeds. It didn't stop him for England, though – he's one of only two players in England's history to score a penalty on his debut, doing so at the 1970 World Cup against Czechoslovakia. The other was Tommy Lawton back in 1938.

Clarke's one hundredth top-flight goal for Leeds was scored in December 1975 against Aston Villa, becoming the second player to hit that total along with Peter Lorimer. He remains the most recent player to score one hundred top-flight goals for the club. He eventually departed at the end of the 1977–78 campaign, having netted 151 goals in all competitions – the third most in the club's history.

Between his time at Leeds from August 1969 to May 1978, only two players scored more English top-flight goals than Allan Clarke (110 in 273 games). It was £165,000 well spent.

> Clarke was one of five brothers who all played in the Football League. In 1973–74, Leeds went a record twenty-nine games unbeaten from the start of the Division One season. Clarke made it 2–0 in the thirtieth game against Stoke, but Leeds lost 3–2. In 1987–88, Liverpool went unbeaten in their first twenty-nine games and then faced rivals Everton looking to break Leeds' record. They lost the game 1–0. The scorer of the Everton goal? Wayne Clarke, Allan's younger brother.

Mick Jones
312 games, 111 goals
20-Goal Season: 26 in 1969–70

In a similar scenario to Allan Clarke, Mick Jones joined Leeds having already spent a few seasons playing Division One football. Jones had scored 63 goals in 149 games for Sheffield United and across the three seasons before joining Leeds he had scored fifty times, which was twenty more than any Leeds player had managed in that time. After Jim Storrie had departed, Don Revie had tried Jimmy Greenhoff, Rod Belfitt, Eddie Gray, Paul Madeley and even Terry Cooper at number 9 before deciding he needed a proper striker. He splashed out and spent £100,000 on Jones in September 1967.

Jones scored his first goal for Leeds in the Fairs Cup in a 9–0 win over Spora Luxembourg in October 1967 and while he only scored three more goals in the competition afterwards across twenty-four games, one of those was in the home leg of the 1968 final against Ferencvaros; after an inspired goalkeeping performance by Gary Sprake in the second leg, Jones' goal meant Leeds won 1–0 on aggregate and lifted the trophy.

Leeds then won the 1968–69 league championship with Jones top scoring on fourteen goals. This title success led to Leeds featuring in the European Cup for the first time and Jones had a superb season in Europe's premier competition, scoring eight goals in eight appearances, all of which came in his first four games. He remains the only Leeds United player to score a hat-trick in the European Cup, netting three in the 10–0 win over Lyn Oslo in September 1969, while those eight goals weren't matched by an English player in a European Cup season until Harry Kane scored eight in 2023–24.

Helped by those goals, 1969–70 was Jones' best-scoring season with Leeds, notching twenty-six goals in fifty-three appearances. Two of his twenty-six goals were scored against Chelsea in the FA Cup, twice giving Leeds a lead that would've won them the trophy. At Wembley, Jones made it 2–1 with six minutes remaining until a late equaliser sent the final to extra-time and a replay. In the replay at Old Trafford, Jones' superb individual goal put Leeds ahead on the night but two Chelsea goals won them the cup. Jones scored in nine matches in the FA Cup and won seven of them – the two he didn't were those Chelsea matches.

Jones was scoring again at Old Trafford a few months later but this time in happier circumstances, netting the winner against Manchester United on the opening day of the 1970–71 campaign, only the club's fourth ever win away at Man Utd. In his next fifty-one Division One appearances, Jones only scored seven goals but then Leeds faced Manchester United at Elland Road in February 1972 and Jones became only the second ever Leeds player to score a hat-trick against them, along with Bobby Turnbull in 1930, and it is a feat that hasn't been achieved since. Jones loved facing Manchester United – he only netted more goals against Southampton (eight) than he did against Man Utd (seven) and he has the most goals against them of any Leeds player in the club's history.

Leeds vs Manchester United	Games	Goals
Mick Jones	13	7
Tom Jennings	6	5
Charlie Keetley	6	5
Allan Clarke	16	5
Billy Bremner	25	5

The hat-trick against Manchester United inspired a run of goals for Jones, scoring eleven in the final fifteen games of that season. His last match of the season was the 1972 FA Cup final against Arsenal, providing the cross for Allan Clarke's winning goal. Jones dislocated his elbow at the end of the game, and the image of Norman Hunter helping Jones up the Wembley steps to receive his medal from Queen Elizabeth II – clearly in agony with his arm in a sling – is one of the most famous of the day, and summed up his stoicism.

Jones scored his one hundredth goal for the club in October 1973 against Stoke City, the sixth player to reach that tally. Injuries were beginning to creep up on Jones, but he still managed twenty-seven league games in 1972–73 and twenty-eight in 1973–74. In the latter, Jones played a key role in the club's long, unbeaten early season run, starting twenty-five of those twenty-nine games. In fact, Jones didn't start a single one of the four league defeats that season, winning nineteen and drawing nine of his twenty-eight starts. It is the most games started by a player without losing in a season in the club's history.

Season	Player	League Starts	Won	Drawn
1973–74	Mick Jones	28	19	9
2000–01	David Batty	13	9	4
1921–22	Wallace Clark	10	5	5
1965–66	Jimmy Greenhoff	10	8	2

Between his debut in 1967 and the end of the 1973–74 season, Leeds won 61% of their Division One matches with Jones starting (131 out of 215), compared to only 44% without him (32 out of 72), while they lost only 11% of games with him in the XI compared to 29% without. Jones was an integral cog in the Don Revie machine, and the team – particularly Clarke – missed him greatly when he was forced to retire in 1975.

None of Mick Jones' 111 goals for Leeds United were scored from the penalty spot, the most goals of any player for the club without scoring a penalty.

Ray Hankin
103 games, 36 goals
20-Goal Season: 21 in 1977–78

Ray Hankin joined Leeds from Burnley in September 1976, but after four goalless matches in 1976–77 an injury meant he didn't play for the club again until the opening game of 1977–78. He scored in that game (a 3–2 defeat to Newcastle United), and went on to fire in twenty top-flight goals that season. Since Leeds had rejoined the top-flight in 1964, Hankin was only the second Leeds player to hit the twenty goal mark, following Peter Lorimer's twenty-three in 1971–72.

In all competitions, Hankin started nineteen games alongside Joe Jordan in that season and fired in fourteen goals. In January, Jordan – and teammate Gordon McQueen – controversially joined Manchester United and Hankin only scored seven goals in twenty-one games without the Scot alongside him.

Ray Hankin in 1977–78	Starts	Goals	Goals per Game
With Jordan	19	14	0.74
Without Jordan	21	7	0.33

The following season Jimmy Adamson, Hankin's old manager at Burnley, got the Leeds job. Hankin had scored plenty under Adamson in Division One when he was Clarets' manager (twenty-nine in ninety-two games) but he only managed fifteen more goals in fifty-nine appearances for Leeds and handed in numerous transfer requests before leaving the club in early 1980. Hankin never played in the top-flight again.

Lee Chapman
175 games, 82 goals
20-Goal Seasons: 31 in 1990–91, 20 in 1991–92

Needing goals to get Leeds United over the line and back into the top-flight, Howard Wilkinson turned to a trusted face. While playing for Wilkinson's Sheffield Wednesday side in Division One, Lee Chapman had scored 62 goals in 149 games, comfortably the most of any player under Wilkinson. During the 1980s, only Ian Rush had scored more goals in Division One than he had. Chapman had moved around a lot, from Arsenal to Stoke to Sunderland to Wednesday to Brian Clough's Nottingham Forest, and Clough was happy to let Chapman leave and he signed for Leeds in January 1990 for £400,000.

Chapman hadn't played outside of the top-flight since December 1978 for Plymouth in the Third Division, and he hit the ground running at Leeds with eight goals in his first ten games. It was the best start by a player since Bob Forrest had scored eight in ten back in 1954, and despite not making his league debut until 13 January only Gordon Strachan (sixteen) scored more Division Two goals for Leeds that campaign. Chapman finished with twelve in twenty-one games, with his most crucial goal coming on the final day against Bournemouth at Dean Court to give Leeds a 1–0 win and guarantee promotion.

78

With Leeds and Chapman back in the top-flight for 1990–91, both enjoyed phenomenal seasons; a fourth-place finish for Leeds was fuelled by thirty-one goals in all competitions from Chapman (the most by a Division One player that season), as he became only the third player after Tom Jennings and John Charles to break the thirty-goal barrier in a campaign for the club. To go alongside his twenty-one league goals, Chapman scored ten across the FA Cup (three), League Cup (four) and Full Members' Cup (three), easily the most domestic cup goals ever in a season for Leeds.

Season	Player	Domestic Cup Goals
1990–91	Lee Chapman	10
1969–70	Allan Clarke	7
2008–09	Jermaine Beckford	7
1967–68	Peter Lorimer	6
1972–73	Peter Lorimer	6
1972–73	Allan Clarke	6
1997–98	Jimmy Floyd Hasselbaink	6
2009–10	Jermaine Beckford	6

Chapman ended the 1990–91 season in fine form, with ten goals in April and May – more than anyone else in the division managed. Half of those goals came in defeats, however, and in just two games – in April 1991, Leeds found themselves 4–0 down at half-time in a home game for the first time in the club's history as Liverpool ran riot at Elland Road. At full-time, Leeds were somewhat unfortunate to have lost, having rallied to score four goals in a 5–4 defeat. This made Chapman the first and, so far, only Leeds player to net a hat-trick and end on the losing side. In truth, he could have had four had one of his goals not been ruled out for a foul on goalkeeper Mike Hooper. Then on the final day of the season Chapman scored a brace against his old side Forest but again Leeds lost, this time 4–3.

Mick Jones and Lee Chapman are the only two players to be leading scorers in a top-flight title-winning season for Leeds, Jones doing so in both 1968–69 and 1973–74 and Chapman scoring sixteen in 1991–92. Chapman only scored five times between August and December, the same number as Mel Sterland managed and two fewer than Steve Hodge, but he exploded into life in January, scoring two goals on New Year's Day against West Ham United; he then hit a superb hat-trick away at former side Sheffield Wednesday. It was the club's first ever hat-trick on a Sunday – something only Jack Harrison has emulated since at West Ham in January 2022. It completed a Leeds hat-trick on all seven days of the week, and three of the first hat-tricks scored on those days had come against Sheffield Wednesday, including the first on a Wednesday back in 1930 by Charlie Keetley.

First Leeds hat-tricks on each day of the week

Date	Player	Opponent	Day of Week
11/12/1920	Bob Thompson	Notts County	Saturday
20/02/1922	Bill Poyntz	Leicester City	Monday
25/12/1924	Percy Whipp	Aston Villa	Thursday
09/04/1930	Charlie Keetley	Sheffield Wednesday	Wednesday
26/03/1957	John Charles	Sheffield Wednesday	Tuesday
19/05/1967	Rod Belfitt	Kilmarnock	Friday
12/01/1992	Lee Chapman	Sheffield Wednesday	Sunday

Chapman scored another hat-trick in March against Wimbledon, the first Leeds player with two top-flight hat-tricks in a season since Alan Shackleton in 1958–59, and ended the season with another twenty in all competitions (adding four in the League Cup to his sixteen league goals). His goals were undoubtedly a crucial factor as Leeds became the 'Last Champions' of the old First Division.

The Premier League arrived in 1992–93 and Chapman wrote his name into the history books by becoming Leeds United's first scorer in it, netting a brace on 15 August 1992 against Wimbledon (in total he scored seven league goals against the Dons, more than he did against anyone else). Chapman scored fifteen Premier League goals, playing in all but two of the forty-two games, with twelve of them coming at Elland Road and just three on the road as the club failed to win a single away game all season. Chapman also featured for Leeds in the UEFA Champions League first and second rounds, starting all five games and scoring his one goal in the 4–1 win over Stuttgart. Chapman's only previous European games had come in 1982 for Arsenal, two UEFA Cup games against Spartak Moscow in which he scored in both and started alongside Chris Whyte, with whom he started all five European games with Leeds in 1992–93.

Chapman then departed the club in the summer of 1993 for West Ham United but returned, briefly, on loan from Ipswich for two games in January 1996. On his return game, incidentally against West Ham, he had a mixed day; he got an assist for Tomas Brolin's goal but was then sent off for an elbow on Marc Rieper, his only red card for Leeds. His last appearance, a 5–0 hammering away at Liverpool, was his 508th and final top-flight appearance. Only forty-one players have ever scored more top-flight goals in history than Chapman's haul of 177.

Chapman joined Leeds aged thirty and his total of eighty-two goals for the club is comfortably the most any player has scored after turning thirty. He proved his best years weren't behind him, and his goals that helped secure the top-flight title in 1992 mean his place in Leeds United history is assured.

Leeds United	Games aged 30+	Goals aged 30+
Lee Chapman	175	82
Jack Charlton	388	55
Gordon Hodgson	85	53
Russell Wainscoat	123	52
Harold Brook	106	47

Jimmy Floyd Hasselbaink
87 games, 42 goals
20-Goal Seasons: 22 in 1997–98, 20 in 1998–99

The 1996–97 campaign will go down as one of the dullest in the club's history. Twenty-eight Premier League goals were scored and only thirty-eight conceded, meaning any fan who attended all thirty-eight games had seen just 1.74 goals per game, the second lowest in a team's games in top-flight history. George Graham had made Leeds hard to beat, which benefitted the defence but with just five league goals, both Lee Sharpe and Brian Deane ended as the club's joint top Premier League scorers – the lowest top scorers in a season in the club's history. Bizarrely, Gary Kelly, who'd gone 121 league games without scoring between 1993–94 and 1995–96, scored 7% of Leeds' league goals that campaign (two of twenty-eight). He played another 308 league games for the club afterwards and didn't score in any of them. Kelly was the exception to the rule of 1996–97.

In 1996–97, Jerrel Floyd Hasselbaink, more commonly known as Jimmy, had scored twenty goals in the Portuguese top-flight for Boavista, second only to Porto's Mario Jardel in the leading scorers. Although Boavista had finished seventh, only Porto had scored more goals than they had, meaning Jimmy was swapping one of Portugal's most attacking teams for the Premier League's lowest scorers.

Hasselbaink scored on his Leeds debut against eventual champions Arsenal, playing with 'Jimmy' on his back (which was later banned by the FA and he changed to the more conventional option of Hasselbaink). After three goals and a red card (away at Bristol City in the League Cup) in his first ten appearances, the Dutchman was instrumental as a substitute in the 4–3 comeback victory over Derby County in November 1997, scoring the equaliser from the penalty spot and setting up Lee Bowyer for the 90th minute winner. From here, Hasselbaink had a hand in twenty-three goals in thirty games in all competitions, scoring nineteen and assisting four to end the season with twenty-two goals – the best debut scoring season since Allan Clarke hit twenty-six in 1969–70. Hasselbaink also managed four in the FA Cup as Leeds reached the quarter-final, hosting Wolves who were a league below. After going 1–0

82

down late on to a Don Goodman goal, Hasselbaink won Leeds a penalty with only minutes to go. He stepped up to take it and was foiled by keeper Hans Segers. Leeds haven't hosted a quarter-final since.

After featuring for the Netherlands at the 1998 World Cup, Hasselbaink's form took some time to pick up in 1998–99, managing just three goals in his first fifteen games. But after scoring in a 2–1 win over Sheffield Wednesday on 8 November, Jimmy's form was outstanding: he was involved in thirty-two goals in thirty-two matches in all competitions (seventeen goals, fifteen assists), scoring and assisting a goal in six different games. Hasselbaink ended the season with eighteen Premier League goals, the joint most along with Michael Owen and Dion Dublin, making it the first time since John Charles' thirty-eight goals in 1956–57 that a Leeds player had been top or joint top of the top-flight scoring charts. In the Premier League alone, he was involved in more goals than any other player, and only Dennis Bergkamp matched his thirteen assists.

Premier League – 1998–99	Goals	Assists	Goals & Assists
Jimmy Floyd Hasselbaink	18	13	31
Dwight Yorke	18	11	29
Dennis Bergkamp	12	13	25
Michael Owen	18	5	23
Nicolas Anelka	17	5	22
Andrew Cole	17	3	20

In the summer of 1999, Hasselbaink chose to join Atletico Madrid in Spain. The move left a sour taste for many fans, but he departed with a fine record of forty-two goals and twenty-two assists in eighty-seven appearances. Across his two Premier League seasons at Leeds only Michael Owen for Liverpool scored more goals, while Hasselbaink ranked top for goals and assists combined across the entire league. He continued his good form in Spain, but his twenty-four La Liga goals weren't enough to stop Atletico from being relegated in nineteenth spot in 1999–00. He returned to the Premier League with Chelsea early the following season, but in all his years back in the English game he never found the net against Leeds.

Michael Bridges
82 games, 21 goals
20-Goal Season: 21 in 1999–00

Hasselbaink's replacement was Michael Bridges, who turned twenty-one just two days before the start of the 1999–00 campaign. Bridges had just twenty-five Premier League appearances and ten starts to his name before signing for £5m from Sunderland, and those had been in 1996–97 when the Black Cats were relegated. Bridges had been part of Sunderland's 105-point Division Two-winning team in 1998–99, making thirty appearances and scoring eight goals, but he had been behind Niall Quinn and Kevin Phillips in the pecking order and hadn't started a single game after Boxing Day. He was now joining a side who'd finished fourth in the Premier League and replacing forty-two-goal Hasselbaink.

Bridges eclipsed Hasselbaink's best Premier League seasonal total of eighteen in 1998–99, scoring nineteen goals for Leeds and helping the club to a third place Premier League finish. Only three players – former teammate Kevin Phillips, Alan Shearer and Dwight Yorke – scored more Premier League goals in 1999–00 than Bridges. He set the tone for the season with a hat-trick in his first away appearance against Southampton, becoming the first and only Leeds United player to score a hat-trick in their first ever away game. He was much more than just a poacher, with many of his goals showcasing his technical ability – including a superb winner against Newcastle in September, a dipping finish over Everton goalkeeper Paul Gerrard in a 4–4 draw in October and a 90th minute half-volley winner against Southampton in November. Bridges was scoring all kinds of goals, and, for a while, Leeds were top of the Premier League.

Bridges scored in four of Leeds' final five Premier League matches of 1999–00, taking his league tally for the season to nineteen, the best debut season since Jim Storrie scored twenty-five in the Second Division in 1962–63. His twenty-one goals in all competitions mean Bridges is one of only four Leeds players with twenty in a season aged twenty-one or younger.

Sadly, that was to be Bridges' peak at Leeds. After a ten-game goalless start to 2000–01, an injury sustained in an away game at Besiktas in the UEFA Champions League was his last appearance until September 2002. After nine appearances in 2002–03 another injury ruled him out until the following campaign, but he did make one major contribution – his cross against Swindon Town was headed in by goalkeeper Paul Robinson. In the end, it was a case of what might've been for Bridges; were it not for those debilitating injuries, he may have been one of the club's key players during the run to the Champions League semi-finals. He left the club at the end of the 2003–04 season and is the only player in the club's history to score as many as twenty-one goals but score all of them within the same season.

Mark Viduka
166 games, 72 goals
20-Goal Seasons: 22 in 2000–01, 22 in 2002–03

Mark Viduka signed for Leeds in the summer of 2000, fresh from winning the Scottish Player of the Year after scoring twenty-seven goals for Celtic. Leeds hadn't awarded any player the number 9 shirt in 1999–00 after Hasselbaink's departure, with twenty-one-goal Michael Bridges wearing the number 8, and Viduka took the shirt for the 2000–01 campaign with the club in the UEFA Champions League group stage for the first time. He did not disappoint, scoring twenty-two goals in fifty-three games, and only three players scored more Premier League goals than the Australian.

After five games without a goal, Viduka then scored five in his next three games, including back-to-back braces against Spurs and Charlton at Elland Road. Undoubtedly Viduka's most memorable afternoon in a Leeds shirt was on 4 November 2000 against Liverpool. With a depleted Leeds 2–0 down – with the lesser-spotted Jacob Burns starting in midfield and the even lesser-spotted Danny Hay replacing Jonathan Woodgate after an early injury – Viduka took the game by the scruff of the neck. He scored all four of Leeds' goals in the 4–3 victory, becoming the first Leeds player with four goals in a game since Allan Clarke in 1971, and the game showcased all of Viduka's finishing quality – two chips over Sander Westerveld, a superb header, and twisting and turning to shake off a beleaguered Patrik Berger before firing under the keeper.

Also in November 2000, Viduka scored a header in a 1–1 draw against Chelsea at Stamford Bridge, his tenth Premier League goal in just his ninth appearance. At the time, it was the second-fewest appearances by a player to reach ten goals in the competition, behind Mick Quinn's six. Erling Haaland has since matched Quinn, and Papiss Cisse and Diego Costa have equalled Viduka's nine.

Premier League	Appearances to 10 Premier League Goals
Erling Haaland	6
Mick Quinn	6
Mark Viduka	9
Diego Costa	9
Papiss Cisse	9

Leeds were struggling in the league – fourteenth on New Year's Day – but in the Champions League they were flying, with Viduka scoring in group games against Besiktas, Anderlecht, Real Madrid and Lazio as the club eventually reached the semi-final before losing on aggregate to Valencia. Viduka also registered four assists that campaign and was one of only two players with four goals and four assists – the other was Luís Figo for Real Madrid.

Across December to February in 2000–01, Viduka only managed four goals in nineteen appearances but in March he scored in all five games, against Man Utd, Real Madrid, Lazio, Charlton and Sunderland. His goal against Charlton was scored after just 11.9 seconds, the seventh-fastest Premier League strike of all time. He also became the first player to play five games in a month and score in all five for Leeds since Lee Chapman in November 1990.

Month	Player	Games Played and Scored
April 1930	Charlie Keetley	7
October 1926	Tom Jennings	5
September 1972	Mick Jones	5
November 1990	Lee Chapman	5
March 2001	Mark Viduka	5

Viduka got one goal in his first ten games in 2001–02 but really hit form in October, scoring against Leicester, Troyes and Manchester United, and after scoring against West Ham United on New Year's Day he had eleven goals and eight assists in twenty-five appearances as Leeds sat top of the Premier League, dreaming of their first title since 1992. Although Viduka scored in Leeds' next game, it was in the infamous 2–1 defeat at Third Division side Cardiff in the FA Cup and the Australian then endured a drought of eleven games as Leeds slipped down the table, eventually finishing fifth and missing out on Champions League qualification. This would soon have serious ramifications for the club.

Under new manager Terry Venables – who'd managed Viduka in the Australian national team previously – Viduka scored in three of Leeds' first five games in 2002–03 but the club struggled and by early March they were in serious danger of relegation. Venables was sacked and replaced by Peter Reid and, while Reid and Viduka did not see eye to eye in the end, the Australian enjoyed his finest period of form in a Leeds United shirt, scoring in seven of his eight games under Reid between his first game on 23 March and the end of the season. As well as a hat-trick away at Charlton Athletic in April, he scored the winning goal away at Arsenal in May, when he picked up a long ball from Dom Matteo, well onside of course, and fired into the top corner past David Seaman to ensure Leeds survived relegation. From March until the end of the season, Viduka scored fourteen Premier League goals, more than any other player, while his eight Premier League goals in April were the most by a Leeds player in one month since John Charles scored eight in March 1957.

Viduka started the following season with a goal against Newcastle United, meaning he'd scored in ten of his previous eleven Premier League appearances with fifteen goals, failing only in a defeat at Southampton in April. But as the club deteriorated further the following season – both on and off the field – Viduka's scoring dried up somewhat, although he once again ended the season in great form, hitting seven goals in ten games as Leeds scrambled to avoid the drop. However, a red card against Leicester on 5 April meant he missed a crucial relegation decider against Portsmouth, which Leeds lost 2–1, and they were in last-chance saloon the following week at Bolton. After giving Leeds the lead, Viduka was sent off again for two yellow cards and it was his final appearance in a Leeds shirt (Leeds lost 4–1 and were relegated). He is the only player to be sent off and score in his last game for the club – a sad way for Viduka's time at Leeds to end, but thankfully not the abiding memory most have of his Leeds United career.

Jermaine Beckford
152 games, 85 goals
20-Goal Seasons: 20 in 2007–08, 34 in 2008–09, 31 in 2009–10

Jermaine Beckford is one of the greatest goalscorers in the modern era of Leeds United. Although he played for the club during their lowest ebb in the three years spent desperately trying to escape League One, his goal ratio is the fourth best of any player in the club's history to play one hundred games and Beckford was a ray of light during a dark time. Without him and his goals, it would surely have taken the club even longer to get back into the Championship.

Given he's best remembered for playing for the club in League One, it's odd to think that Beckford made his debut, after his move from non-league Wealdstone in 2006, alongside Eirik Bakke in a 1–0 defeat to Crystal Palace in the Championship. Before the club was relegated to League One, Beckford only played eleven games and just two were starts – against Chester in the League Cup and Sunderland on Boxing Day in 2006–07. But loan spells at Carlisle and particularly Scunthorpe (both in League One) during that season convinced Dennis Wise that

Beckford would be the man to lead Leeds' attack as the club tried to eliminate a fifteen-point deduction and win promotion in the 2007–08 campaign.

Beckford's first goal for the club came in the first home game in League One against Southend United, while his last was in the club's last home game in League One against Bristol Rovers, neatly bookending the club's time in the third tier. After netting against Southend, Beckford had a spree of six goals in six games, including a last-minute winner at Nottingham Forest, a delicate chip against Hartlepool and an improvised overhead kick away at Bristol Rovers (a team he would enjoy scoring against). By the New Year, Leeds were in the promotion picture and Beckford had fifteen goals, five more than any other player in League One. Then, speculation about his future followed, and Beckford only scored once in the next eight games, though it came away at Crewe Alexandra with Beckford memorably replying to a reporter's question about his future at the club with: 'What shirt am I wearing, bruv? Are you being serious?' which the club then had printed on T-shirts and sold in the club shop (along with ones bearing the slightly derogatory question 'Where's Yeovil?' in response to facing them for the first time in 2007). Beckford only managed four goals in the final eighteen games of that season and failed to score during the play-offs; Carlisle goalkeeper Keiran Westwood, who'd been Beckford's teammate during his loan spell the previous season, made a string of incredible saves to keep him out. He couldn't stop Jonny Howson though, thankfully.

With Leeds enduring another season in League One, Beckford made an incredible start to the 2008–09 season, scoring eleven in all competitions by mid-September, including a superb first-half hat-trick against Chester in the League Cup – his first for the club. Another treble followed away at Northampton Town in an FA Cup replay a few weeks later, which was followed by a brace against Hartlepool and another at Sixfields in the league meeting with Northampton, taking his tally to six in three games. But Beckford sustained a hamstring injury in that game and it would be his final appearance under Gary McAllister – Leeds were knocked out of the FA Cup by non-league Histon without Beckford, and McAllister left after losing 3–1 to MK Dons just before Christmas. Enter new manager Simon Grayson.

Beckford scored fifteen goals in fourteen League One games from January until the end of the season, despite missing nine games due to injury in that time. Fourteen of those fifteen goals were scored at Elland Road as Leeds won every game in that run, and his seven consecutive scoring games at home were the best since Mark Viduka in 2003. One of those games saw Beckford score a hat-trick against Yeovil Town, which made Beckford only the second player in Leeds United's history to score a hat-trick in the league, League Cup and FA Cup, along with Peter Lorimer, and the only one to do this in the same season (incredibly he's the only player to achieve this for any team this century). This scoring run came to an end against Millwall in a 1–1 draw in the play-offs, with Beckford missing a penalty early in the second half. Only two of his fifty-four goals at this stage had been penalties, and the result condemned the Whites to another season of League One football. Beckford had scored thirty-four goals in all competitions in 2008–09, the most by a Leeds player since John Charles in 1956–57, and fans feared he'd leave in the summer.

But he stayed, and in the following season would score two of the most iconic goals in the club's recent history. He picked up where he left off, scoring nineteen goals between August and the end of the year to take his 2009 yearly tally to thirty-four goals. Only John Charles and Tom Jennings have ever scored more in a calendar year.

Year	Player	Games	Goals
1956	John Charles	41	39
1953	John Charles	40	39
1926	Tom Jennings	43	38
2009	Jermaine Beckford	43	34

3 January is a date etched into the memory of all Leeds United fans. Bobby Collins, Mick Jones, Peter Lorimer, Allan Clarke and Brian Flynn were the six men to have scored the only goal in a 1–0 win at Old Trafford for Leeds United, and on that date Beckford joined them. He chased down Jonny Howson's long ball to slide home in the 19th minute, sending Leeds into the fourth round of the FA Cup and writing

his name into the history books. Beckford then scored a brace away at Tottenham Hotspur in the fourth round to earn Leeds a replay which Spurs won 3–1 at Elland Road. It was Beckford's last FA Cup appearance for Leeds and his goals-per-game ratio in the competition is the best of any player to make at least three appearances, fittingly for a man who scored one of the club's most famous goals in the competition.

FA Cup	Games	Goals	Goals per Game
Jermaine Beckford	9	8	0.89
Arthur Hydes	10	8	0.80
Phil Masinga	5	4	0.80
Ian Baird	8	6	0.75
Mike Grella	4	3	0.75
Tommy Wright	4	3	0.75

A dip in form followed, with Beckford scoring three goals in his next thirteen League One appearances as Leeds began to wobble. From 6 February until 3 April, only four sides picked up fewer points than Leeds, and Beckford found himself substituted early in the second half against Southend on 10 April with the score at 0–0. They eventually won 2–0, and Beckford was benched for the next four matches before the final game against Bristol Rovers. It was simple: a win would guarantee promotion.

With Richard Naylor out injured, Simon Grayson made Beckford captain for the first time in his 152nd and final appearance for the club. In a manic game, with Max Gradel sent off in the first half and Leeds going 1–0 down early in the second half, Jonny Howson's equaliser was followed up four minutes later with Beckford's greatest moment. In front of the Kop, his eighty-fifth and final goal for the club secured promotion back to the Championship. It was his seventh league goal versus Bristol Rovers, his joint most against any opponent, and his thirty-first in total in the 2009–10 campaign, with Beckford the only player in the club's history to score thirty goals in consecutive seasons.

Beckford had repaid Grayson's faith in restoring him to the XI and giving him the captaincy. With forty-six goals in seventy games under Grayson, only two players have a better goals-per-game ratio under a manager in the club's history, with Beckford and Grayson's partnership the best of the modern era.

Player	Manager	Games	Goals	Goals per Game
John Charles	Raich Carter	166	123	0.74
Tom Jennings	Arthur Fairclough	97	66	0.68
Tom Jennings	Dick Ray	77	51	0.66
Jermaine Beckford	Simon Grayson	70	46	0.66
Charlie Keetley	Dick Ray	169	110	0.65

Beckford left in the summer of 2010 to join Premier League side Everton, where he scored eight Premier League goals in 2010–11 before dropping back down into the EFL. Beckford scored against fifty-five league teams during his career but the side he faced most without scoring against was Leeds United (eight games). He's Leeds, and he knows he is.

Luciano Becchio
221 games, 86 goals
20-Goal Season: 20 in 2010–11

Not many – if any, given it was the early days of social media – Leeds fans would've heard of Luciano Becchio when he arrived on trial from Spanish side Mérida UD ahead of the 2008–09 campaign but 221 games, eighty-six goals, one promotion and a place in the club's top ten league scorers later, Becchio remains a Leeds United cult hero to this day – he cost less than Berbatov and scored more goals, didn't you know?

Becchio's first league start saw him score inside thirty seconds away at Yeovil in August 2008 – the club's quickest goal in League One – and by the end of the campaign the Argentinian had nineteen goals, the best by a player in their debut season since Mark Viduka in 2000–01.

Of those nineteen, the most memorable came in the play-offs at home to Millwall in front of 37,000 fans, with his sliding finish from a Ben Parker cross making it 1–1 on aggregate. Hope then turned to despair when Millwall equalised and knocked Leeds out, but that goal – and the noise of the accompanying celebrations – remains iconic.

Forming a terrific partnership with Jermaine Beckford up front, Becchio scored another nineteen goals in the 2009–10 promotion campaign to go alongside Beckford's thirty-one to give the Leeds strikers a combined total of fifty. When the pair started together in fifty-nine games across the 2008–09 and 2009–10 seasons, they scored a combined total of seventy goals (forty-three for Beckford, twenty-seven for Becchio), with at least one of the duo scoring in 75% of those games. It was a formidable partnership.

With Beckford departing, Becchio took up the mantle of main striker, and scored the club's first goal back in the Championship on the opening day of the 2010–11 season in a 2–1 loss to Derby County. By the time Christmas arrived, Becchio had scored eleven, the third most of any player. Three of those came in the same game against Bristol City and their goalkeeper David James, made more significant by the fact Becchio came on as a substitute. This made him just the second Leeds United player to score a substitute hat-trick, along with Phil Masinga in a 1995 FA Cup replay against Walsall. As it was for Masinga, it was the only hat-trick Becchio scored for Leeds. He ended the 2010–11 campaign with twenty goals, and his injury late in the season hampered the club's play-off hopes as they finished seventh.

> Luciano Becchio scored against fifty different teams for Leeds United, with only Peter Lorimer (seventy-one) and Billy Bremner (fifty-six) scoring against more.

Injury problems hampered the next season for Becchio – although he still managed eleven goals – but 2012–13 saw him return regularly to the scoresheet, hitting seventeen goals in twenty-six appearances by Christmas. Only four players had ever scored more goals in the lead up to 25 December in a season for Leeds. He added another two goals to that total after Christmas and was then, inexplicably, sold to Norwich

City in January with Leeds gaining Steve Morison in return (the less said about that, the better). It was a move that meant Becchio played Premier League football but after thirteen goalless top-flight matches, Becchio's only other league appearances in England were seven matches at Rotherham, making his last appearance in January 2016. Had he remained at Leeds, there's little doubt that at his rate of scoring in the 2012–13 campaign, Becchio would've broken the one-hundred-goal mark for the club. As it was he left on eighty-six goals, marginally outside the club's top ten all-time scorers but forever part of club folklore.

Ross McCormack
158 games, 58 goals
20-Goal Season: 29 in 2013–14

Arguably one of the best players in recent years to have never made the step up from the Championship to playing Premier League football, Ross McCormack scored fifty-eight goals for Leeds across four seasons, with half of them coming in 2013–14 when the Scottish striker almost single-handedly kept the club away from relegation trouble and the danger of sinking back into the third tier.

It was a slow start for McCormack, who failed to find the net in any of his first nineteen games (fifteen as a sub) and he had only scored four times in his last forty league games for previous club Cardiff. But when he did finally score – against Burnley in the penultimate game of the 2010–11 campaign – it inspired a hot streak. McCormack notched twelve in his next fifteen matches, including late winners against Crystal Palace and Bristol City and a last-minute equaliser in a 3–3 draw at Brighton. He ended the campaign with nineteen goals, and his eighteen in the Championship placed him fourth on the top scorers that season.

In February 2012, Neil Warnock replaced Simon Grayson as Leeds manager and McCormack's goals total began to dip, with just five in 2012–13. His most memorable strike that campaign came in an FA Cup win over Tottenham at Elland Road, arrowing a shot into the top corner with his left foot past Brad Friedel. He did manage to score in Warnock's final game in charge in April 2013, giving Leeds the lead

94

against Derby ten minutes after coming on as a substitute and firing a few choice words in Warnock's direction. McCormack's goals per game under Warnock was his lowest under any Leeds manager.

McCormack's Leeds Managers	Games	Goals	Goals per Game
Simon Grayson	52	16	0.31
Neil Redfearn	5	2	0.40
Neil Warnock	46	10	0.22
Brian McDermott	55	30	0.55

Warnock's replacement was Brian McDermott and, as the table shows, McCormack enjoyed his best spell at Leeds under him. In 2013–14, he was not only Leeds' best and most influential player, he was the best player in the Championship full stop. McCormack was the leading scorer, had the most goals and assists combined and created the most chances of any player in the division, all while playing for a side who lost twenty-one games and finished fifteenth.

Player	Ross McCormack	Championship Rank
Goals	28	1
Assists	8	=10
Goals + Assists	36	1
Total Shots	143	3
Shots on Target	57	3
Chances Created	108	1
Chances Created from Open Play	87	1
Goals (Outside Box)	7	2
Big Chance Created	16	1

Data via Opta

Leeds won sixteen Championship matches in 2013–14 and McCormack scored in thirteen of them, and 47.5% of Leeds United's league goals that season were scored by the Scot – the highest ratio in a season since John Charles in the 1950s.

Season	League	Goals	Team Goals	%
1956–57	John Charles	38	72	52.8%
1926–27	Tom Jennings	35	69	50.7%
2013–14	Ross McCormack	28	59	47.5%
1953–54	John Charles	42	89	47.2%

In November, Leeds scored eight Championship goals and McCormack scored seven of them, all consecutively without another teammate finding the net in between. Four of those were in one match away at Charlton Athletic, where he became the first player to score four in a game since Brian Deane against QPR in November 2004. Perhaps unsurprisingly to anyone who has paid attention to Leeds' recent record in the capital, the Whites haven't scored four goals in a game in London since.

After a humiliating 6–0 defeat to Sheffield Wednesday, McDermott changed captain and gave McCormack the armband, becoming the first striker to lead the team since Jermaine Beckford against Bristol Rovers. In just his third game as skipper McCormack faced Huddersfield Town at Elland Road, a day after the bizarre sequence of events involving Massimo Cellino attempting to sack McDermott and put former Middlesbrough defender Gianluca Festa in charge, Cellino's taxi being chased around Elland Road by angry supporters and McCormack phoning Sky Sports News late on Friday night to confirm he would be staying at the club on transfer deadline day. Amid all this chaos – with assistant manager Nigel Gibbs in the dugout instead of McDermott, who was later reinstated – McCormack delivered yet again, scoring a hat-trick in a 5–1 victory.

McCormack was ever-present in 2013–14 and his twenty-eight league goals were the most by a Leeds player since Charles scored thirty-eight in 1956–57. He was sold to Fulham for £11m in the summer, scoring thirty-eight Championship goals in his two seasons there before earning another big money move to Aston Villa in 2016. He later played for Central Coast Mariners in Australia and put his creative skills to good use by assisting Usain Bolt (yes, really) for a goal in a friendly match in 2018.

Chris Wood
88 games, 44 goals
20-Goal Season: 30 in 2016–17

One of the most consistent strikers the club has had this century, Chris Wood never went more than four consecutive starts without finding the net for Leeds, achieving an impressive rate of exactly a goal every other game across his two years at the club. Wood was the quintessential poacher, scoring forty-three of his forty-four goals for Leeds from inside the box and enjoying a shot conversion rate of just under 20%.

Wood scored thirteen goals in his first season at Leeds, which began under Uwe Rosler before he was sacked and replaced by Steve Evans. The Leeds side of 2015–16 were not an attacking force by any means, having the second fewest shots on target and third fewest touches in the opposition box of any side in the Championship, so thirteen was a very respectable return in a side that struggled to create chances.

In 2016–17, under new manager Garry Monk, Leeds once again ranked lowly in attacking metrics. They had the third fewest shots and the fewest shots on target of any side, but of those 151 shots on target, Wood scored with twenty-seven of them and had a shot conversion of 25.7% – the best ratio by a Championship player in a season Opta has on record since 2013–14.

Season	Player	Goals	Shots (100+)	Shot Conversion Rate
2016–17	Chris Wood	27	105	25.7%
2020–21	Ivan Toney	31	135	23.0%
2018–19	Tammy Abraham	25	109	22.9%
2013–14	Troy Deeney	24	110	21.8%
2021–22	Aleksandar Mitrovic	43	198	21.7%

Wood spread his scoring around different opponents, finding the net against nineteen different teams, a joint club record in a season for Leeds along with John Charles in 1953–54, and the only sides Wood didn't score against were Brentford, QPR, Preston and Wolves.

Season	Player	Opponents Faced	Scored Against
1953–54	John Charles	21	19
2016–17	Chris Wood	23	19
1926–27	Tom Jennings	21	18
1956–57	John Charles	21	18
1925–26	Tom Jennings	21	17
2013–14	Ross McCormack	23	17

He ended the campaign with thirty goals in all competitions, notching his thirtieth goal against Wigan on the final day of the season. All thirty were scored from inside the box – he only had twenty-two shots from outside the box all season long. And although sixteen of Wood's league goals in 2016–17 had come with Leeds inside the top six of the Championship, they ended the campaign in seventh, missing out on the play-offs by five points.

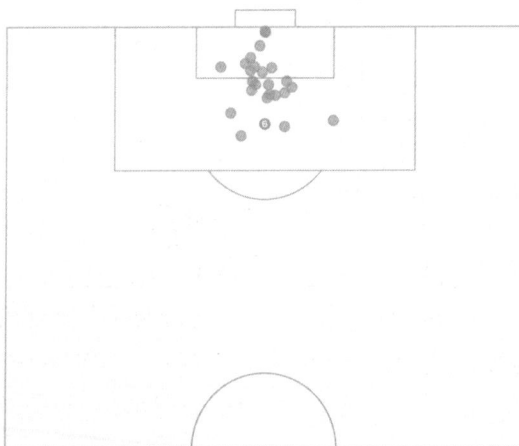

Chris Wood
Leeds United | 2016-17

Opta

30 goals

0.70 goals per 90

3,845 minutes

4 headers

2 left foot

24 right foot

Number on point indicates
the number of penalty goals

Wood started the following season with Leeds, scoring on the opening day away at Bolton Wanderers, but departed in August for Premier League side Burnley. He continued his consistent scoring and netted at least ten Premier League goals in each of his four full seasons with the Clarets, and could be playing European football in 2025–26 with Nottingham Forest.

Crysencio Summerville
89 games, 25 goals
20-Goal Season: 21 in 2023–24

While it wasn't enough to earn Leeds promotion in 2023–24, Crysencio Summerville enjoyed one of the finest individual seasons of any Leeds player in modern times. Turning twenty-two during the season, Summerville scored twenty-one goals and assisted ten more, becoming the first Leeds player with twenty goals and ten assists in a campaign since fellow Dutchman Jimmy Floyd Hasselbaink in 1998–99.

Going into the 2023–24 campaign, Summerville had only managed four goals in forty appearances for Leeds and all had come in consecutive games in October and November 2022 in the Premier League before the break for the Qatar World Cup, including a late winner at Anfield against Liverpool that arguably saved Jesse March's job. After the World Cup, Summerville didn't score a goal in twenty matches under four different managers as Leeds were relegated.

The drop in division wasn't good news for Leeds but it did help Summerville establish himself, and he was named Championship Player of the Year for 2023–24 after a number of terrific performances. In an October victory over Huddersfield Town, he became the first Leeds player to both score two goals and assist two goals in a game since Lee Bowyer in October 2001 against Troyes in the UEFA Cup, with Summerville born the same month Bowyer achieved that. Between 4 October and New Year's Day, Summerville either scored or assisted in nine consecutive matches at Elland Road, scoring seven goals and assisting five

With his Thursday goal against Norwich City in the play-offs, Summerville became the first player in Leeds United's history to score a goal on all seven days of the week within the same campaign.

Summerville's twentieth goal of the season, scored in a brace against Middlesbrough in April 2024, made him the youngest player to score twenty in a season for Leeds since Michael Bridges in 1999–00, and one of the youngest ever.

Player	Season	Age on 20th goal
Peter Lorimer	1967–68	20 years, 353 days
John Charles	1952–53	21 years, 42 days
Arthur Hydes	1932–33	21 years, 144 days
Michael Bridges	1999–00	21 years, 272 days
John Charles	1953–54	21 years, 322 days
Ray Hankin	1977–78	22 years, 50 days
Crysencio Summerville	2023–24	22 years, 175 days

Following the 1–0 play-off final defeat to Southampton, Summerville left the club to join West Ham United and return to the Premier League. While he struggled for goals back in the top-flight, he did score a winner against Manchester United – never a bad way to further endear yourself to Leeds supporters.

3

THE SGT WILKO ERA

The two indisputably most successful managers in the club's history are Don Revie and Howard Wilkinson. They are the only two men to lead Leeds United to the pinnacle of the English game – the top-flight league championship. Of the eight league titles Leeds have won across the first and second tiers of English football, five were achieved by either Revie or Wilkinson. In terms of sheer numbers of games managed, no one compares to Revie's 741 or Wilkinson's 412, nor is anyone likely to in the future. They are out on their own in the annals of Leeds United history.

One of the first things Wilkinson did when he arrived at Leeds was to take down the photos around the club of the great Revie era, feeling the club needed to stop looking back and start looking forward, saying he'd put them back up when the club was back in the First Division. The club sat twenty-first in the Second Division on the day Wilkinson was appointed in October 1988, the lowest point the club had been since late in the 1961–62 campaign – Revie's first full season in charge. Back then they sat second bottom of the Second Division, before going nine games unbeaten to finish nineteenth and avoid the drop by just three points. Two seasons later, they won the league.

It didn't take Wilkinson that long.

Creating new heroes

Removing the photos of the Revie era was a drastic choice but it wasn't only the still images that reminded everyone of the club's greatest era – the previous three managers before Wilkinson had been Allan Clarke (106 goals in 237 games under Revie), Eddie Gray (276 games under Revie) and Billy Bremner, who made 649 appearances under him and had made his debut alongside Revie in January 1960. The likes of Paul Madeley, Trevor Cherry and Gray himself were still playing in the early 1980s, and Frank Gray, David Harvey and Peter Lorimer all returned for second spells. Wilkinson was arguably the first Leeds manager with no direct links to Revie since Major Frank Buckley, who served as manager between 1948 and 1953; Buckley's successor, Raich Carter, had signed Revie at Hull when Carter was player-manager, and Carter's Leeds successor, Bill Lambton, signed Revie in 1958 and he then featured fifty-two times under Jack Taylor – from whom Revie took over as manager. Even Buckley, with no direct link to Revie, gave a certain Jack Charlton his debut in his final game in charge. Perhaps it was time for a new dawn.

Wilkinson made an immediate impact, beating Peterborough 3–0 in the League Cup in front of 8,893 supporters, then went ten league matches unbeaten to record the longest ever undefeated start to a Leeds manager's league career. Leeds went bottom of the league in late October after a 1–1 draw with Swindon Town in Wilkinson's first league game in charge, but by the time they faced the Robins in the reverse fixture in February they'd moved up to sixth. The play-offs may have been out of reach but had only results from Wilkinson's first game until the end of 1988–89 counted, they'd have finished fifth.

P	Team	G	W	D	L	GF	GA	GD	Pts
1	Chelsea	35	25	8	2	80	38	42	83
2	Crystal Palace	36	20	7	9	56	37	19	67
3	Manchester City	35	17	11	7	60	40	20	62
4	Swindon Town	37	17	11	9	54	43	11	62
5	Leeds United	37	16	13	8	53	37	16	61

Of the starting XI for Wilkinson's first game – which was the same XI he played in each of his first seven games – four made their final appearances for the club across the final five league games of the season, with Neil Aspin, John Sheridan, David Rennie and Mark Aizlewood departing as Wilkinson started to shape a new team. Aizlewood's memorable sign off was with a goal and a gesture to the Kop end in a 1–0 win over Walsall in May 1989, and he was the first player to score in his final game for the club while also starting the game as captain (the only other to do this, in happier circumstances, is Jermaine Beckford in 2010). Noel Blake took the captaincy for the final two games of the season but from the start of the following campaign, Gordon Strachan made the role his own.

Strachan made his debut for Leeds in March 1989 and then started the next 104 matches in a row, not missing a game until March 1991. Leeds were eleventh in the Second Division on his first start; the next time a Leeds XI didn't feature him, they were in the top four of the First Division. It was some impact.

Date of First Game	Date of Last Game	Player	Consecutive Starts
13/10/1979	05/03/1983	John Lukic	164
28/08/1920	15/12/1923	Jim Baker	149
08/01/1955	26/04/1958	Eric Kerfoot	148
30/10/1954	18/01/1958	Roy Wood	144
30/01/1926	30/03/1929	Tom Townsley	141
21/08/1954	18/09/1957	Jimmy Dunn	138
01/05/1971	25/04/1973	Peter Lorimer	118
14/08/1993	02/12/1995	Gary Kelly	118
08/11/1986	10/12/1988	Mervyn Day	115
07/03/1953	24/09/1955	Grenville Hair	108
23/12/1990	04/11/1992	John Lukic	105
25/03/1989	24/02/1991	Gordon Strachan	104

At thirty-two on his debut, Strachan was the club's oldest outfield debutant since Frank Worthington in 1982 but he would still be playing for the club at the age of thirty-seven, making his final appearance on New Year's Eve in 1994. He is the club's fourth-oldest outfield player, behind only Eddie Burbanks, Jack Charlton and Peter Lorimer. Across 201 league appearances for Leeds, Strachan scored thirty seven goals and almost half came in the club's 1989–90 promotion-winning season, when he was on hand with sixteen. Many of them proved crucial: the winner away in a 2–1 victory at Blackburn on Lee Chapman's debut in January; a 90th minute winner in a topsy-turvy 4–3 win over Hull in February; and, perhaps most famously of all, his 85th minute, left-footed strike past Martin Hodge in the Leicester goal in a 2–1 win in April to put the club on the brink of promotion – his sixteenth and final goal of the season.

It wasn't just his goals that stood Strachan apart as the club's key player. While the term 'assist' wasn't part of English football's lexicon in that era, club season review tapes allow us to retrospectively look back on goals to see which players contributed the crucial final pass to the goals of those seasons. In the 1989–90 season, Strachan assisted eighteen goals, which is the most by any Leeds player in a league season on record since then, and meant that of the seventy-nine goals scored in that season, Strachan had either scored or assisted 43% of them.

Opta has collected assists on all goals in the Premier League era, done by painstakingly watching old VHS season reviews for every club (which were stored in a cupboard in the offices in London; opening the cupboard door for the first time was a bit like when Indiana Jones finds the Holy Grail, only while he found the Cup of Christ, I found Nottingham Forest's 1992–93 campaign). This inspired me to rewatch old Leeds season reviews to document all goals scored from 1989 onwards, to create a more rounded picture of player goal contributions; Jermaine Wright, a player not necessarily remembered too fondly by Leeds fans, was surprisingly creative in 2004–05 with ten assists.

1989–90: Division Two	Games	Goals	Assists	Goals and Assists
Gordon Strachan	46	16	18	34
Bobby Davison	29	10	3	13
Lee Chapman	21	12	1	13
John Hendrie	27	5	6	11
Ian Baird	24	5	4	9

The 1989–90 season began with a 5–2 defeat at Newcastle United – the only time Leeds lost a Division Two match under Wilkinson by three goals – but Leeds were the first side to ship five goals in their opening league match and recover from that to win a Football League division since Millwall in 1927–28. Leeds had only lost back-to-back league matches twice in their first term under Wilkinson and never did so in 1989–90, following up their nine defeats across the season with six wins and three draws. At Elland Road, there was just one loss in twenty-three league matches, and only one game in which Leeds failed to score (0–0 with Port Vale in March). Leeds pipped Sheffield United to top spot on goal difference, only the seventh time the title had been decided that way in the second tier and the most recent occasion it had happened until the 2024–25 campaign, when Leeds won it ahead of Burnley after being level on 100 points. It helped that Leeds had hammered the Blades 4–0 at Elland Road in April.

Leeds returned to the top-flight thanks to a 1–0 victory away at Bournemouth on 5 May, with the winner headed in by Lee Chapman – it was one of eighty-two goals Chapman scored for Leeds but one of only two he scored in a 1–0 win, with the other coming away at Wimbledon in April 1991. The assist for Chapman's header was provided by a cross from Chris Kamara, his second and last assist for the club. Unbelievable, Jeff.

Back in the First Division

When Howard Wilkinson departed Sheffield Wednesday in 1988, they were ninth in the First Division and Leeds were twenty-first in the Second Division. Now, Leeds were back in the top-flight and Wednesday, under Ron Atkinson, had been relegated in 1989–90. It was looking like a shrewd decision from Wilkinson. After three games in 1990–91, Leeds sat second in the table, equalling Wilkinson's highest position in the table as Wednesday boss and in the top-flight overall; he'd managed Notts County in 1982–83 and had never been higher than seventh.

Leeds United finished fourth in the First Division in 1990–91, the best performance by a newly promoted side since Watford had finished second in 1982–83. Although they never seriously mounted a title challenge, they had been only six points behind leaders Liverpool on New Year's Eve after a run of four consecutive wins – their best run in the top-flight since 1979. For 123 of the final 141 days of that season, Leeds sat in fourth position, and they ended up nineteen points behind champions Arsenal who finished on eighty-three points.

The team was starting to take shape. Of the starting XI on the opening day of 1990–91 (a 3–2 win over Everton) nine of them had 1,520 games of combined First Division experience and the other two – youngsters David Batty and Gary Speed – eventually played 957 times in the top-flight between them. John Lukic, re-signed from Arsenal in the summer, had played 340 First Division games and won the title with the Gunners in 1989, the second most of any goalkeeper between 1979–80 and 1989–90 behind only Peter Shilton. Four of the XI – Lee Chapman, Imre Varadi, Mel Sterland and Glynn Snodin – had already played under Wilkinson in the top-flight, with Chapman scoring 118 First Division goals prior to the 1990–91 season.

The victory over Everton also saw the first time the famous midfield of Strachan, Batty, McAllister and Speed all started in the same game. In total this midfield would play together 107 times for Leeds, including eighty-two in the league, with the final occasion coming over three years later in September 1993 against Sheffield United, when both McAllister and Strachan were on the scoresheet in a 2–1 win. Between their first and final appearances alongside one another, Leeds had a far higher win ratio and points-per-game in league matches when they were together, compared to games with a different combination.

25 Aug 1990 – 18 Sept 1993	G	W	D	L	Pts	PPG	Win %
Strachan, Batty, McAllister, Speed	82	41	23	18	146	1.78	50%
Other combinations	48	16	16	16	64	1.33	33%

Leeds 4–5 Liverpool

One game when all four started together was possibly the finest defeat in the club's entire history – Leeds 4–5 Liverpool in April 1991. Liverpool came into the game on a run of just four wins in twelve games and were virtually out of the title race, though one of those four wins had been in a 7–1 hammering at Derby in which they were 3–0 up at half-time. They went one better at Elland Road and were 4–0 up after twenty-seven minutes, with their slick passing producing four superb goals. It was unchartered territory for Wilkinson's Leeds; the first time they'd trailed by four goals under his management and the only time in the club's history they've been four goals behind at half-time at Elland Road. Leeds pulled two goals back through Chapman and Carl Shutt, which seemed to annoy Liverpool as Barnes made it 5–2 a minute after Shutt had halved the deficit. Undeterred, Chapman added a third and fourth goal to make it 5–4 and give him his first hat-trick for Leeds, with both goals headers and both beautifully assisted by Batty and Strachan. Chapman remains the only Leeds player to score a hat-trick in a defeat, though had he not had one ruled out for a foul on Mike Hooper with the score at 4–1 it might have ended 5–5. As well as being Chapman's first hat-trick for Leeds, it was the first against Liverpool in the top-flight since 1986.

During the 1990–91 season, Leeds played Arsenal six times (twice in Division One, and four times in the FA Cup after their fourth round tie went to three replays). David Batty played in all four cup matches but missed the two games sandwiched between Spurs and Man Utd, making Batty the only Leeds United player to make four appearances in a row all against the same opponent.

Champions of England

Only nine clubs have won the top-flight of English football within two seasons of being promoted into it. Leeds United – who'd had constant progression under Howard Wilkinson, finishing tenth in the Second Division in his first season, winning the Second Division in his second season and finishing fourth in the First Division in his third – became the eighth of these nine teams to achieve it when they lifted the 1991–92 First Division title, the last before the Premier League began. Since then, only Leicester City in 2015–16 have emulated Wilkinson's achievement, but he's the last manager to lead a side out of the second tier and then to the top division title in that space of time.

Season	Top-Flight Winners	Seasons after Promotion
1905–06	Liverpool	1
1907–08	Manchester United	2
1931–32	Everton	1
1950–51	Tottenham Hotspur	1
1961–62	Ipswich Town	1
1963–64	Liverpool	2
1967–68	Manchester City	2
1977–78	Nottingham Forest	1
1991–92	Leeds United	2
2015–16	Leicester City	2

Leeds had the most wins (twenty-two), fewest defeats (four), best goal difference (plus thirty-seven), most clean sheets (twenty) and were the only side to remain unbeaten at home all season, winning thirteen and drawing eight of twenty-one games at Elland Road. After they lost 4–0 to Manchester City, Leeds were second and had played two games more than Manchester United who were top. But after this, Leeds then had the best points-per-game tally of any side, winning four of five games and keeping four clean sheets, while Man Utd had the seventeenth worst form in the league and lost three of their final seven games. Leeds had held their nerve to overtake their rivals.

From 5 April until end of 1991–92 season

Form rank	Team	P	W	D	L	Pts	PPG
1	Leeds United	5	4	1	0	13	2.60
17	Manchester United	7	2	2	3	8	1.14

This resilience was shown throughout the season, too. In 1990–91, Leeds had fallen behind in fifteen league games and recovered just three points, all in draws, losing the other twelve. In 1991–92, Leeds went behind twelve times but this time only lost four and recovered twelve points from losing positions, with one of two wins from behind that season coming in the penultimate and, ultimately, crucial victory over Sheffield United at Bramall Lane in April 1992. Leeds' only defeat when going ahead all season had been away at QPR in March, losing 4–1 after Speed had made it 1–0, and the Hoops had also been the only team to beat Leeds from behind in 1990–91 also – Leeds had gone 2–0 ahead that day but lost 3–2 at Elland Road, with Roy Wegerle scoring twice, one a superb individual effort which was applauded by the Elland Road crowd.

Leeds started the season with ten league games unbeaten for the first time since going twenty-nine without defeat in 1973–74, and after victory over Oldham in the fourteenth match they went top of a top-flight table for the first time since their 1974 title win. It was a victory a few games earlier that had given Leeds the real hope that this season might be the one, beating Liverpool 1–0, their first win against them since October 1973 and ending a twenty-game winless run (the longest run without winning against an opponent in the club's history). The win against Liverpool was also Strachan's one hundredth league appearance and while he didn't score in that game, he had netted four penalties in the first five games of the season, and though these would be his only goals of the campaign, Strachan chipped in with nine assists, the joint most of any player with Speed.

1991–92 – Division One	Games	Assists
Gary Speed	41	9
Gordon Strachan	36	9
Mel Sterland	31	6
Gary McAllister	42	5
Rod Wallace	34	5

Much like the Revie era team had its classic starting line-up (used only once against Mansfield in the FA Cup, of course), so too this Wilkinson title-winning side had its famous XI: Lukic, Sterland, Whyte, Fairclough, Dorigo, Strachan, Batty, McAllister, Speed, Chapman, Wallace. This XI featured in seven First Division matches in 1991–92 and Leeds won six of them, failing only to beat Man Utd in a 1–1 draw in December. The final time it was used came in a 2–0 home win over Luton Town on 29 February, as Dorigo suffered an injury that would rule him out till late March, by which time Sterland's season had been ended by injury. This Luton victory also saw the emergence of a certain Frenchman, who would appear from the bench to score his first goal for the club.

Cantona

The influence – or lack of – that Eric Cantona had on the title triumph of 1992 has been debated many times before. Statistically, none of his goals that season won Leeds any points; they'd have beaten Luton, Wimbledon and Chelsea without his goals included. But there were signs of his class in the goals he created for McAllister away at Spurs and Chapman at home to Chelsea, the latter just minutes before his brilliant solo strike to make it 3–0. He only played 768 minutes across his fifteen league appearances, starting six (despite scoring against Luton, three days later Wilkinson gave the number eight shirt to Tony Agana, one of his two games for Leeds), but he still managed three goals and two assists; only Chapman and Wallace could do better for goals and assists between Cantona's debut and the end of the season.

At the start of 1992–93, Cantona scored two hat-tricks in the space of five games; against Liverpool in the Charity Shield at Wembley – only the third club hat-trick scored at the national stadium by any player – before becoming the first player to score a Premier League hat-trick with his treble in a 5–0 win over Spurs in August. He's one of only four Leeds players with two hat-tricks in a single month.

Player	Month	Scored Against
Tom Jennings	October 1926	Liverpool and Blackburn Rovers
John Charles	November 1952	Hull City and Brentford
John Charles	August 1953	Notts County and Rotherham United
Eric Cantona	August 1992	Liverpool and Tottenham Hotspur
Tony Yeboah	September 1995	Monaco and Wimbledon

Until his final Premier League appearance in a Leeds shirt on 7 November against Man City, only three Premier League players had more goals and assists in 1992–93 than Cantona had for Leeds. After his sale to Manchester United he was involved in the second most goals of any player across the league over the remainder of the season, behind only Teddy Sheringham at Spurs, continuing the form he'd started at Leeds. He still has the best minutes per goal or assist ratio (one every ninety-nine minutes) for Leeds in the Premier League era.

Only Tony Yeboah scored or assisted at a more frequent rate per game in the top-flight for Leeds under Wilkinson than Cantona. As hard as it is to now admit, Cantona shone in his brief time at Elland Road.

Wilkinson – Top-flight	Games	Goals	Assists	Goals & Assists	Per Game
Tony Yeboah	40	24	3	27	0.68
Eric Cantona	28	9	7	16	0.57
Lee Chapman	118	52	12	64	0.54
Tomas Brolin	19	4	5	9	0.47
Brian Deane	111	27	18	45	0.41

1992–93 title defence

Leeds went into the inaugural Premier League campaign of 1992–93 as reigning league champions. Each of the previous ten reigning top-flight winners had finished in the top four, though no side had retained the league since Liverpool in 1983 and 1984. In the event, Leeds only spent four days in the top four of the league all season – all in August – as they produced the English top-flight's worst title defence for thirty years, finishing seventeenth and winning just twelve games all season. The only reigning champion to be relegated was Manchester City in 1937–38 and though Leeds never spent any days in the relegation zone, on Christmas Day they were only three points above the drop zone and they ended the season on fifty-one points – two points clear of relegation, having won just one of their final ten games.

Away from home, Leeds became the first ever reigning English champions to go through an entire season without a win on the road. The best chance they had of an away victory was at Oldham early in the season, going 2–0 ahead before drawing 2–2, and in the penultimate game of the season away at Sheffield Wednesday, with Leeds leading from the 35th minute until the final minute. On the final day, away at Coventry, Leeds recovered from 3–1 down to draw 3–3 with two late Wallace goals to complete his hat-trick, but it meant they ended the season with just seven away points, fourteen defeats and forty-five goals conceded. Between October and February, Leeds lost nine away games in a row, their worst run since 1981.

It was only Leeds' home form that saved them; they had the third best home record in 1992–93 behind Man Utd and Norwich, but were comfortably the worst side on their travels.

Form	Home – 92-93	P	W	D	L	GF	GA	GD	Pts
1	Manchester United	21	14	5	2	39	14	25	47
2	Norwich City	21	13	6	2	31	19	12	45
3	Leeds United	21	12	8	1	40	17	23	44
4	Aston Villa	21	13	5	3	36	16	20	44

Form	Away – 92-93	P	W	D	L	GF	GA	GD	Pts
19	Middlesbrough	21	3	6	12	21	48	-27	15
20	Southampton	21	3	5	13	24	40	-16	14
21	Oldham Athletic	21	3	4	14	20	44	-24	13
22	Leeds United	21	0	7	14	17	45	-28	7

Ten players made their Leeds debuts during the 1992–93 season but half of those (Frank Strandli, Jamie Forrester, David Kerslake, Ray Wallace and Rob Bowman) made fewer than ten Premier League starts for the club, and none managed fifty top-flight appearances for the club, with Noel Whelan coming closest on forty-eight. Of those, only Mark Beeney – who made two appearances deputising for Nigel Martyn in 1996–97 and 1997–98 – outlasted Howard Wilkinson to make an appearance under his successor David O'Leary. After the integration over the previous couple of seasons of McAllister, Whyte, Dorigo and Rod Wallace, it's fair to say none of the signings or debutants in 1992–93 made any lasting impact on the first team.

The debuts of Forrester and Bowman were only the fourth and fifth given to a teenager under Wilkinson at that stage – of his first thirty-three debutants, only Gary Speed (aged nineteen in 1989), goalkeeper Neil Edwards (aged eighteen in 1989, his only game for Leeds) and Gary Kelly (aged seventeen in 1991) had been teenagers when Wilkinson introduced them into the first team; in the case of Kelly, he made three appearances as a winger in 1991–92 and then none in

1992–93, until his eventual integration in the team as a right-back in 1993–94.

Rob Bowman made his first start in the goalless draw with Manchester United in February 1993 aged only 17 years and 79 days, and in doing so ended a run of 174 consecutive Leeds games without a teenager in the starting XI, the longest run since going 197 games between 1925 and 1930. This marked the start of a shift towards youth. After only three teenage debutants out of his first thirty-three, fourteen of the thirty-two debuts Wilkinson awarded from February 1993 until the end of his time in charge in 1996 were teenagers. Five of these were in 1992–93, which was a celebratory time for the Leeds United youth team.

Leeds won the 1993 FA Youth Cup, triumphing in both legs against Manchester United to win 4–1 on aggregate. Bowman – who'd featured against them in the Premier League in February – started both games and was one of seven players in the XI who would go on to make a first-team appearance for Leeds, all given their debuts under Wilkinson (though they'd only play 200 times combined). It would be a few more years before Wilkinson's vision in creating the academy at Thorp Arch produced genuine first-team players such as Jonathan Woodgate, Harry Kewell and Ian Harte. Unfortunately, by that time, Wilkinson had departed.

FA Youth Cup 1993 Starting XI	First Team Appearances	Starts	Goals
Paul Pettinger	0	0	0
Andy Couzens	35	21	2
Kevin Sharp	18	11	0
Mark Tinkler	27	15	0
Kevin Daly	0	0	0
Rob Bowman	9	5	0
Matthew Smithard	0	0	0
Mark Ford	42	39	1

Noel Whelan	58	36	8
Simon Oliver	0	0	0
Jamie Forrester	11	8	2

Back-to-back 5th finishes

After a disappointing seventeenth-place finish that saw thirty-one players used in 1992–93, the following two seasons were a period of stability for Leeds, finishing fifth in both 1993–94 and 1994–95. Only thirty players were used across both seasons and of the title-winners, McAllister (eighty-three games), Speed (seventy-five), Wallace (sixty-nine), Dorigo (sixty-five), Lukic (sixty-two) all played more than fifty Premier League games for the club, while Gary Kelly emerged to play every single league game across both seasons – the only outfield Premier League player to do so. Kelly's run of consecutive league appearances was ended at ninety-nine in December 1995, when he was sent off against Liverpool. Only three players have started more consecutive league games for the club from their first start than Kelly.

Date of First Start	Date of Last Start	Player	Consecutive Games
13/10/1979	05/03/1983	John Lukic	146
28/08/1920	15/12/1923	Jim Baker	145
08/09/1962	03/04/1965	Norman Hunter	113
14/08/1993	02/12/1995	Gary Kelly	99
13/01/1990	12/01/1992	Lee Chapman	84

Gary Kelly's 44th game for Leeds was in the 4–0 win over Queens Park Rangers on 4 April – the 4th day of the 4th month in 1994.

Brian Deane, scorer of the first Premier League goal in August 1992 for Sheffield United, signed from the Blades and was directly involved in twenty-two goals in 1993–94, one of only four players in double figures for both goals (eleven) and assists (eleven) that campaign. Deane remains one of only two Leeds players to achieve that in a Premier League season, along with Jimmy Floyd Hasselbaink in 1998–99.

Deane scored the first goal of the 1993–94 campaign, a last-minute equaliser away at Manchester City in a 1–1 draw, in a match which saw the debut of a 35-year-old David O'Leary. Three defeats in four games followed but by the time Leeds faced City again in December, it was their thirteenth unbeaten game in a fourteen-game run, with Deane scoring the third in a 3–0 win. Leeds were in second spot for one month in November and December, but the closest they got to top spot was ten points off (for one day on 18 December), and after six winless games they dropped to eighth. Twenty-one points in the last eleven games took Leeds back up to a top-five finish, with that run including impressive wins away at QPR (4–0) and a final day 5–0 hammering of Swindon. Leeds' fifth goal that day was netted by Chris Fairclough and was the one hundredth conceded by Swindon in the Premier League that season.

Leeds made just thirty-seven line-up changes in the 1993–94 Premier League season, the fewest of any side, and in the following season used just twenty-one players. Only one side, Nottingham Forest, used fewer with twenty. Seventy points in 1993–94 was nineteen more than Leeds had managed the season previous, and they went three better in 1994–95, with seventy-three points, enough to finish fifth again and this time qualify for the UEFA Cup.

September 1994 saw one of the season's highlights as Leeds ended a fourteen-game winless run against Manchester United, with Wetherall and Deane on the scoresheet to secure their first victory over them since 1981. There were contrasting fortunes in the cup competitions, with Leeds failing to score in either leg of their second round League Cup tie against fourth tier side Mansfield Town, losing 1–0 on aggregate. Lucas Radebe made his Leeds debut in the 1–0 defeat at Elland Road in that tie, coming on as a substitute for Gordon Strachan, but his South African teammate Phil Masinga had better fortunes in the

FA Cup, scoring an extra-time hat-trick in a third-round replay against Walsall – the first ever treble by a Leeds player as a substitute. Leeds reached the fifth round that campaign, knocked out 3–1 by Manchester United. A disappointing result, but a notable afternoon for another reason; the Leeds goal that afternoon was the first scored by their new January signing from Eintracht Frankfurt.

Even by his standards, breathtakingly brilliant

Tony Yeboah is the only Leeds United player to score his first goal for the club at Old Trafford against Manchester United; this was the first of thirty-two goals in sixty-six games for the Ghanaian striker, who was born on the sixth day of the sixth month in 1966. Yeboah's impact on the team and the Premier League was exceptional, so much so he is one of the most fondly remembered strikers of the mid-1990s, in what was a crowded field. But then, scoring goals like the ones he did away at Liverpool and Wimbledon will ensure you're never forgotten. In 2004, Leeds released a DVD of their one hundred greatest goals and the Wimbledon strike came in at number four, while his volley against Liverpool came first.

Yeboah's first Premier League start on 22 February saw him find the net in a 1–0 win over Everton, and from then until the end of the season Yeboah scored more goals than any other Premier League player (twelve in sixteen games) – including a hat-trick against Ipswich in April which took him to ten goals in thirteen matches in all competitions, becoming just the third player in the club's history to reach ten goals that quickly, along with Charlie Keetley in 1928 (seven games) and Percy Whipp in 1923 (twelve games). This run of goalscoring also helped Leeds go from seven points behind fifth to ending in that position at the end of the campaign, with Leeds winning more points in that time than any other side (thirty-four).

PL (22 Feb – 14 May 1995)	Games	Goals
Tony Yeboah	16	12
Andrew Cole	14	10
Les Ferdinand	13	10
Stan Collymore	13	10

Yeboah started the following season with the same aplomb, and across August and September he hit eleven goals in eleven games in all competitions. After the third game, a 2–0 win over Aston Villa and a rare game where Yeboah didn't score, Leeds went top of the top-flight for the last time under Wilkinson.

In September, Yeboah was on the scoresheet eight times in seven games, the most by a player in one month since Mick Jones scored eight in November 1969. Six of those goals came in two games, hat-tricks against Wimbledon and Monaco, the latter the club's first European hat-trick since 1979 and his only European goals for Leeds. He had an exceptional record in Europe for all of his clubs, notching seventeen in twenty-seven games overall. In an alternative universe, Yeboah could've still featured for Leeds in the 2000–01 UEFA Champions League, but while Leeds' young team during that memorable semi-final run didn't feature a now 34-year-old Yeboah, he did play in the competition that season for Hamburg, scoring home and away against Juventus.

After eight goals in September, Yeboah didn't score at all in October and only managed eight more goals in thirty-five games for Leeds – all under Wilkinson in 1995–96. One of those was particularly special though, scoring a superb individual goal in a 3–1 win over Manchester United on Christmas Eve 1995. This was the only Premier League match played on 24 December until Wolves beat Chelsea 2–1 in 2023, ruining the fact that Leeds were the only side with a win on that date. Humbug.

Although Leeds' record in London in recent years has been terrible, the same could not be said of Yeboah when he turned up in the capital – he scored ten goals in eight games, with only two players scoring more for Leeds in London in the club's entire history. His eight goals in London in 1995–96 were also a record by a Leeds player in one season.

Leeds in London: Season	Player	Games	Goals
1995–96	Tony Yeboah	5	8
1969–70	Allan Clarke	5	7
2002–03	Harry Kewell	6	7
1969–70	Peter Lorimer	9	6

Sadly, he couldn't find the net in the 1996 League Cup final at Wembley against Aston Villa, which was his final game under Wilkinson. He'd scored his final goals for the club earlier that month in a win at QPR, and the Villa game was his last game until Boxing Day – by which time George Graham had taken over. In the seven games he played, in which he drew blanks under the Scotsman, Leeds only scored four times as a team. Yeboah was unable to produce his earlier form, although he did hit the crossbar from way out away at Sunderland which would have been a goal to match his 1995 peak had it been just an inch or two lower.

> Though he is best remembered for his spectacular long-range goals, Tony Yeboah scored as many Premier League goals from outside the box for Leeds (three) as Jason Wilcox, David White and Patrick Bamford managed.

End of the Wilko era

Leeds had topped the Premier League table early in the 1995–96 season and, following back-to-back fifth-place finishes and with Yeboah scoring goals aplenty, there must have been some supporters dreaming of another title. But by the time Leeds lost 6–2 at Sheffield Wednesday on 16 December, they were seventeen points behind leaders Newcastle United and had won just four out of their previous fourteen games.

After a 2–0 win over West Ham in January – with both goals scored by Tomas Brolin, his only Leeds brace and his last goals for the club

– Leeds became statistically the Premier League's worst team until the end of the season, winning just eight points in sixteen games and scoring only ten goals. In that time, they also had the worst defence in the league, conceding thirty goals, and lost the most matches of any side (twelve). Leeds suffered a six-game losing run in April and May, their worst run since losing their last six games in 1946–47 – a season in which they came bottom of the top-flight with only eighteen points, fifteen points from safety. Thankfully, things weren't quite that bad this time around, with the stronger early season form ensuring Leeds still finished in thirteenth place. The final day saw a 0–0 draw with Coventry, and this was a scoreline Leeds fans would soon become painfully familiar with.

The 1996–97 season began with a 3–3 draw away at Derby. Despite being 2–0 up after 72 minutes and then 3–2 ahead after debutant Lee Bowyer gave Leeds the lead again with just five minutes remaining, a late equaliser from Dean Sturridge earned Derby a point in what was the highest scoring Leeds opening game since the 5–2 defeat at Newcastle in Wilkinson's first full season in 1989. Amazingly, this was to be the highest scoring Leeds match all season long, with 9% of the goals in games involving Leeds in the Premier League that campaign coming in that one afternoon at the Baseball Ground.

Leeds sat sixth after a couple of 1–0 wins over Wimbledon and Blackburn, and were actually above Man Utd in the table going into their clash at Elland Road. But the 4–0 defeat, the heaviest against them since losing 6–0 in 1959, was the final game of the Wilkinson era at Leeds United. Eric Cantona had missed a penalty in the match – one of only two he missed in the Premier League – but scored the fourth goal in the 90th minute; the final goal of the Wilkinson reign was scored by a player who'd notched fourteen goals of his own for Leeds under Wilkinson in 1992. Following this crushing defeat, Wilkinson was sacked; it was a sad ending for a club legend and the manager who – Don Revie aside – arguably had the greatest positive impact on Leeds United.

Between 1990–91 and his final game on 7 September 1996, Wilkinson's Leeds had won the fourth most points in the top-flight and comfortably won more games (105) than they'd lost (69). Given they were the forty-third best team in the country at the time he took over in 1988, that was a seriously impressive achievement.

Most points won in top-flight (1990–91 until 7 September 1996)

Top-Flight	G	W	D	L	Pts
Manchester United	249	141	70	38	493
Liverpool	249	116	67	66	415
Arsenal	249	108	82	59	406
Leeds United	249	105	75	69	390
Aston Villa	249	94	71	84	353
Tottenham Hotspur	249	86	75	88	333

Wilkinson remains the last Englishman to win the English top-flight title; his immediate successor would be the manager who'd lifted the league title the year before Leeds won it, conceding a measly eighteen goals along the way. George Graham briefly brought the same miserly defending to Leeds, but something much more exciting was coming down the tracks. Under the guidance of a Wilkinson signing, David O'Leary, the full potential of the Thorp Arch academy was about to explode into life.

Although Wilkinson did give fourteen debuts to teenagers in his time at Leeds, the last player to debut under him was 34-year-old striker Mark Hateley on loan from QPR, three days after Ian Rush had made his bow at Leeds away at Derby – also aged 34. Wilkinson is the only manager in Leeds United's history to give as many as four debuts to players aged 34 or older; along with Rush and Hateley, he also gave 35-year-olds Mickey Thomas and David O'Leary a debut. Don Revie never did this in thirteen years at Leeds; the oldest player to debut under Revie was a 32-year-old Cliff Mason in 1962.

4

THE O'LEARY ERA

Leeds entered the new millennium on top of the Premier League, with a young manager leading his fledgling side to nineteen wins across twenty-three games in the final few months of 1999, scoring over forty goals in the process. With a side featuring the likes of Woodgate, Harte, Kewell, McPhail and Smith, all products of the academy, Leeds were, for a time, the second favourite team of supporters of other clubs (if it is possible to have a second favourite) and the envy of many others.

It is highly unlikely, however, that anyone had the 1996–97 Leeds United team down as their second favourite side to watch, unless someone was looking for a cure for insomnia . . .

1996–97
0-0 (x9)

I didn't get my first season ticket at Elland Road until the 2004–05 season, but had my first one been in 1996–97 it might have been a tough decision to renew. After Howard Wilkinson was replaced by George Graham five games into the 1996–97 campaign, Leeds United's thirty-three games under the Scotsman saw just fifty-two goals scored, with Leeds the lowest scorers in the entire division in that timeframe with twenty-three goals. Although Wilkinson only took charge of five matches, 18% of the goals Leeds scored in the Premier League that season came under him.

Leeds ended the 1996–97 season in eleventh place with twenty-eight goals scored, at that point the lowest by any side to survive relegation (Huddersfield Town equalled this is in 2017–18, finishing sixteenth with twenty-eight). There was also the small matter of nine goalless draws, the joint most by a team in a thirty-eight-game Premier League season. Excitement was not on the menu, but clean sheets certainly were – twenty in total, the most in the Premier League and the most ever by a team to finish as low as eleventh in a top-flight season. The previous lowest had been a Leeds United team who finished ninth in 1980–81. In a similar scenario, there'd been a decent total of goals in the opening few games of the season (seventeen in the first six under Jimmy Adamson, an average of just under three per game) but once Allan Clarke arrived as manager, only sixty-nine were scored in total by either side in his thirty-six league matches that campaign (under two per game), with six 0–0 draws.

Lowest positions by a team with more than twenty clean sheets in the English top-flight

Season	Team	Final Position	Clean Sheets
1996–97	Leeds United	11	20
1980–81	Leeds United	9	20
1922–23	West Bromwich Albion	7	20
1970–71	Liverpool	5	22
1971–72	Arsenal	5	20
1981–82	Arsenal	5	20

That Leeds were about to become the Premier League's toughest team to score against under Graham was not immediately obvious; eleven goals were conceded in his first eight games, while Third Division side Darlington arrived at Elland Road for Graham's first home match in charge and picked up a 2–2 draw in the League Cup. After eight Premier League games, Graham's Leeds had lost six and were seventeenth in the table, but they followed up this poor run with a run of five clean sheets in a row up to Christmas – the best run of clean sheets since January 1989. The first game in this clean sheet spree was in a 2–0 win away at Southampton, a game famous for Ali Dia's one Premier League appearance. It also featured another notable event – a first Leeds goal for Gary Kelly. The Whites may have been low scorers under Graham but Kelly, after 165 scoreless games, then hit two in eleven games (he followed this up with a further 193 goalless games before firing in a free-kick at Crystal Palace in the FA Cup in 2003). Only Grenville Hair has ever had a longer wait for his first Leeds goal.

Date of First Leeds Goal	Player	Opponent	Game No.
07/04/1962	Grenville Hair	Middlesbrough	428
23/11/1996	Gary Kelly	Southampton	166
25/12/1948	Tom Holley	West Ham United	156
11/04/1959	Jack Charlton	Blackburn Rovers	138
02/03/1935	George Milburn	Portsmouth	131

Thirty-five-year-old striker Ian Rush ended his run of thirteen top-flight games without a goal – the longest run of his career – by netting the second in a 2–0 win over Chelsea. After Rush's strike in the tenth minute of the match, it would be almost six hours of football until there was another goal in a Leeds United match, with three consecutive 0–0 draws following the Chelsea victory. Seven goals were then conceded across the next three games, all defeats, with former title winners Gary McAllister and Eric Cantona scoring in victories for Coventry and Manchester United. McAllister's goal would be the last league goal scored against Leeds at Elland Road for 14 hours and 9 minutes, as they then kept eight consecutive home clean sheets (with five games ending goalless), the second longest run without conceding at home in the club's history behind a nine-match stretch in 1955.

The first game in this long run of Elland Road clean sheets saw the debut of Dutch defender Robert Molenaar in a 3–0 victory over Leicester City, and Leeds didn't concede a single goal at home that season with him on the pitch, a total of 540 minutes. Only two defenders have ever played more minutes in a Premier League season at their home venue without conceding than Molenaar in 1996–97.

124

Season	Player	Venue	Minutes Played without Conceding
2013–2014	Nacho Monreal	Emirates Stadium	630
1994–1995	David May	Old Trafford	616
1996–1997	Robert Molenaar	Elland Road	540
2018–2019	Joe Gomez	Anfield	493
2005–2006	Stephen Warnock	Anfield	455

Data via Opta

Molenaar was on the scoresheet for the first time in a 1–0 win over Everton in February at Elland Road, a third consecutive 1–0 win. But this would be the last victory of the season as Leeds ended the campaign on a run of seven draws and two defeats, with four games ending – you guessed it – goalless. The 0–0 draw away at Chelsea on 3 May was the ninth goalless draw of the season to equal a Premier League record set by Sheffield United in 1993–94 (in a forty-two-game season), which has never been beaten and only Sunderland in 2014–15 have managed to match it since.

Season	Team	0–0s
1993–94	Sheffield United	9
1996–97	Leeds United	9
2014–15	Sunderland	9
1994–95	Crystal Palace	8
1994–95	Everton	8
1997–98	Wimbledon	8
1998–99	Everton	8
2001–02	Fulham	8
2008–09	Fulham	8

With just sixty-six goals scored in total in Leeds United's games in 1996–97, this is the lowest of any side in a Premier League campaign. I haven't watched back old episodes of *Match of the Day* from that season but I can't imagine Leeds were the lead game very often. Looking at it through the prism of top-flight history, only Liverpool's games during the 1970–71 campaign have ever seen fewer goals per game than Leeds in 1996–97. Anyone following these teams all over the country during these seasons deserves a medal.

Team	Season	Games	GF	GA	Total	Per Game
Liverpool	1970–71	42	42	24	66	1.57
Leeds United	1996–97	38	28	38	66	1.74
Notts County	1924–25	42	42	31	73	1.74
Birmingham City	1948–49	42	36	38	74	1.76
Coventry City	1970–71	42	37	38	75	1.79

It was at least a successful season for new goalkeeper Nigel Martyn, who'd joined in the summer for a record fee for a goalkeeper of £2.25m – a fee that now looks like the bargain of the century. His nineteen clean sheets in his debut season were the most of any goalkeeper in the Premier League that campaign, and the joint most by an English goalkeeper in Premier League history, level with Bobby Mimms and David Seaman. It still wasn't enough to get him into the Team of the Season, though (Seaman took that honour, just like he usually kept Martyn out of the England team as well).

The same success could not be said of the strikers. Rod Wallace scored five goals in his first six games under Graham in September and October 1996 – as many as in his previous sixty games combined – but then followed it up with three goals in twenty-one games for the remainder of the season. That his total of just eight still made him the leading scorer in all competitions tells its own story. In the league, the top scorer accolade (if you can call it that) was shared by Brian Deane and Lee Sharpe, who each managed five Premier League goals and between them made up 36% of the club's goals for the campaign. It remains the fewest goals netted by the leading scorers in the league for Leeds in a season.

Lowest top scorers in a league season for Leeds

Season	Players(s)	Goals
1996–97	Brian Deane/Lee Sharpe	5
2004–05	David Healy	7
1979–80	Kevin Hird	8
1983–84	George McCluskey/Tommy Wright	8
1981–82	Arthur Graham/Frank Worthington	9

Derek Lilley made his Leeds United debut in a 0–0 draw with Blackburn Rovers in April 1997 – in twenty-one league appearances, he featured in seven 0–0 draws (33% of his total games), the highest ratio of any player in the club's history. It's as many goalless draws as Luciano Becchio was involved in during his 190 league matches for the club. Five of Becchio's 0–0 draws were when he was managed by Simon Grayson, with Grayson the only player in the club's history to play in more than one league game and draw them all 0–0 (his only two league appearances for the club vs Huddersfield and Birmingham in 1987–88).

1997–98
104% increase in goals

After being the Premier League's lowest scorers in 1996–97, only the top four teams scored more than Leeds in 1997–98 – their fifty-seven goals was a touch more than double their total from the snoozefest of the previous campaign. Although it was an extremely low bar to beat, the 104% increase in goals between seasons is the biggest increase by a team in the history of the English top-flight.

Team	Season	Goals	Season	Goals	% Increase
Leeds United	1996–97	28	1997–98	57	104%
Chelsea	2022–23	38	2023–24	77	103%
Everton	1983–84	44	1984–85	88	100%
Manchester City	1966–67	43	1967–68	86	100%

Opposition own goals were the club's fourth top scorer in 1997–98, with four benefitting Leeds. One came from Derby County's Jacob Laursen, who'd netted on the opening day of 1996–97 in the 3–3 draw, and he is one of only two players to score two Premier League own goals against Leeds. The other, Mark Venus of Ipswich, did so in consecutive 2–1 wins for Leeds at Portman Road in 2000–01 and 2001–02. Laursen's own goal in 1997–98 came in a 5–0 win for Leeds at Pride Park in March, the club's biggest win under Graham. It was one of five Premier League games that season where Leeds scored four or more goals, and four of the five were home and away against Derby and Blackburn, with the 4–0 home win over Rovers coming in the game directly before the 5–0 win at Derby.

The 4–3 win at Ewood Park in September 1997 was notable for seeing all seven goals scored within the first 33 minutes of the game, the earliest that seven goals have ever been scored in a Premier League match. Leeds' fourth of the afternoon was from David Hopkin in just the 23rd minute, and at that point it was the second earliest into a Premier League game a team had scored four times. Bizarrely, the earliest had been Blackburn in their previous home game, when they went 4–1 up against Sheffield Wednesday in the 20th minute (they eventually won 7–2).

There was another memorable game with a glut of scoring in the opening 33 minutes in 1997–98 but none of them were scored by Leeds, as they found themselves 3–0 down to Derby County in November. By half-time, goals from Wallace and Kewell had given Leeds a fighting chance but it took them until the 82nd minute to equalise via a Jimmy Floyd Hasselbaink penalty. He then turned provider in the 90th minute to pull the ball back for Lee Bowyer to rifle it into the back of Mart Poom's net and give Leeds a superb 4–3 win, the first ever comeback in the Premier League by a side three goals down and something that has only been emulated four times since.

Date	Score
08/11/1997	Leeds United 4–3 Derby County
09/09/1998	West Ham United 3–4 Wimbledon
29/09/2001	Tottenham Hotspur 3–5 Manchester United
25/10/2003	Wolves 4–3 Leicester City
13/03/2024	Bournemouth 4–3 Luton Town

The victory over Derby was the start of a run of three consecutive wins when conceding first in the Premier League, coming back to beat West Ham 3–1 and Barnsley 3–2 – with Leeds going 2–0 down in the latter. These were very much exceptions to the rule under Graham; in the other twenty-five Premier League games in which Leeds conceded first under the Scotsman, they lost twenty-three of them, and drew two, failing to score in twenty.

Leeds finished fifth in 1997–98 to get back into the UEFA Cup for the 1998–99 campaign, though Graham would only be in charge for the first round against Maritimo, and the second leg of that tie would prove to be his final game as Leeds manager. After a seven-game unbeaten start in the Premier League – the club's best unbeaten start to a league campaign since 1991–92 – which left Leeds in fifth spot, Graham departed for Tottenham Hotspur after overseeing the 1–0 second leg defeat (Leeds progressed via a penalty shootout after a 1–1 aggregate draw). Spurs had been Graham's last league opponents, an uncharacteristically high scoring draw of 3–3 which followed three goalless draws in six games. In all, 19% of Graham's Premier League games as Leeds manager had been goalless, the highest percentage for any manager at a club in the history of the competition. Graham features twice on the list, with 16.1% of his Arsenal games also ending 0–0.

Team	Manager	Games	0–0s	% 0–0
Leeds United	George Graham	78	15	19.2%
Sunderland	Gustavo Poyet	60	11	18.3%
Coventry City	Ron Atkinson	64	11	17.2%
Arsenal	George Graham	112	18	16.1%
Blackburn Rovers	Sam Allardyce	76	12	15.8%

Graham's departure saw David O'Leary take over as caretaker manager for four games before he was given the job full-time after a goalless draw with Chelsea on 25 October. This match saw the Leeds starting XI have an average age of just 23 years and 296 days, the club's youngest for a top-flight game since 1973. It was a sign of things to come.

O'Leary's Babies

Norwegian right-back Gunnar Halle scored the opening goal in George Graham's last league game in charge, and he was also on hand to score the opening goal of the O'Leary reign. It came away at Nottingham Forest and was the first of Leeds United's 229 Premier League goals under the Irishman. It was Halle's fourth goal in his last thirteen league games and it was notable for not only being the first goal of the O'Leary reign but also the last time something happened under him; Halle was thirty-three years old and this was the last time any player over the age of thirty scored a league goal with O'Leary in charge. Leeds would not have another scorer of that vintage until December 2002, when a 31-year-old Jason Wilcox (a player signed by O'Leary in 1999 and the oldest player to make a Leeds debut under him) scored a superb goal in a 3–0 win away at Bolton under Terry Venables. This run of 246 Premier League goals scored by players under the age of thirty is the longest run by any side in Premier League history.

Start of Run	End of Run	Team	Consecutive Goals by Players under 30
17/10/1998	16/12/2002	Leeds United	246
13/09/2014	26/12/2017	Tottenham Hotspur	234
24/08/1993	28/10/1995	Blackburn Rovers	151
03/12/2005	09/03/2008	Tottenham Hotspur	143
09/03/2008	13/03/2010	Tottenham Hotspur	109

Data via Opta

There was a notable shift in the average age of starting XIs in 1998–99 between Graham's seven games and O'Leary's thirty-one, a drop from 26 years and 6 days under Graham to 25 years and 33 days under O'Leary. The only players under the age of twenty-one to appear in a Graham starting XI early in 1998–99 were Harry Kewell and Ian Harte; in O'Leary's second game at Forest, he gave eighteen-year-olds Stephen McPhail and Jonathan Woodgate their first Premier League starts, only the second time two players that young had made their first starts in the same top-flight game (the other was Mark Tinkler and Jamie Forrester in 1993 against Sheffield United). O'Leary had worked with the youth team during his time as coach under George Graham and was now given the opportunity to blood them in the first team, and he was taking it; by the end of January 1999, he'd already given more debuts to teenagers from the academy (five) than Graham had (four).

In the space of six games in October and November 1998, O'Leary gave debuts to Woodgate, Paul Robinson and Alan Smith who would play a combined 489 games for Leeds and win sixty-eight England caps. Howard Wilkinson's vision for the future of Leeds was bearing fruit and O'Leary was definitely the beneficiary, but he still had to have the courage to put the players in the first-team of a club who were in the race to qualify for a European spot in the Premier League.

Nineteen-year-old Robinson stepped up to deputise for an injured Nigel Martyn in a 0–0 draw with Chelsea and became the youngest Leeds goalkeeper to keep a clean sheet in a top-flight match since John Lukic in December 1979. He remains the second youngest goalkeeper in Premier League history to keep a clean sheet on his debut (19 years and 10 days), behind Richard Wright in 1995 for Ipswich, who was eighteen.

Alan Smith's impact was even more pronounced, scoring with his first touch away at Anfield to equalise in a game Leeds went on to win 3–1. At 18 years and 17 days old, Smith was the youngest Leeds debutant scorer since Tommy Wright in 1983, and he then followed it up with a goal at home to Charlton a week later to become the youngest ever Leeds United player to score in his first two games. In the Premier League, he is the youngest English player to achieve this and only Federico Macheda has done so at a younger age. In his first start – a 4–0 home win over West Ham in December – he assisted goals by Molenaar and Hasselbaink, making him the second youngest player (18 years and 38 days) with two assists in a Premier League game, behind only a seventeen-year-old Theo Walcott for Arsenal in 2006. Smith ended the 1998–99 season with nine goals in all competitions, with only four Leeds players scoring more in a season as a teenager. Not a bad start for the young lad from Rothwell.

Season	Player	Goals as Teenager
1965–66	Peter Lorimer	19
1984–85	Tommy Wright	15
1958–59	Chris Crowe	12
1961–62	Billy Bremner	12
1983–84	Tommy Wright	11
1960–61	Billy Bremner	10
1998–99	Alan Smith	9

Leeds and their young team were in superb form, and between 17 February and 3 April they won seven consecutive Premier League matches, with Smith scoring three goals in those victories and Hasselbaink on hand with five. From O'Leary's first permanent match on Halloween until the seventh victory in a row over Nottingham Forest in April, only Manchester United had picked up more points and scored more goals than Leeds. O'Leary had Leeds just two points off a UEFA Champions League spot (which was just the top three sides then, of course) but sadly the young side ran out of steam somewhat; two wins in the last seven games, including a defeat to Chelsea that secured third place for the Blues, meant Leeds finished fourth. It had still been a fantastic season, with their highest position since the 1991–92 title win and something hugely exciting to build on for next season.

1999–00

Leeds had the youngest average starting XI age of any side in the 1998–99 season and it got even younger in 1999–00 – the second youngest in a season in Premier League history in fact, at 24 years and 162 days. Making their final appearances in the previous season had been David Wetherall (aged twenty-eight), Gunnar Halle (thirty-three), Robert Molenaar (twenty-nine) and, departing for Atletico Madrid, Jimmy Floyd Hasselbaink (twenty-seven). Early in 1999–00, Leeds gave debuts to Danny Mills (aged twenty-two), Michael Bridges (twenty-one), Michael Duberry (twenty-three), Eirik Bakke (twenty-one) and Darren Huckerby (twenty-three) and only used twenty players all season long, the fewest of any Premier League side.

David Batty had returned to the club in late 1998 from Newcastle United and he started the first sixteen league games of 1999–00 (and Leeds won eleven of them, a 69% success rate), but injury meant his next game wouldn't be until the seventeenth match of 2000–01. Leeds' win ratio dropped to 46% without him in the side. Given Batty had played a major role in the 1991–92 title win, was an established England international and, on a lesser level, featured in Blackburn's 1994–95 title triumph (albeit in only five games), his experience in the team would've been valuable in the second half of the campaign. Without 31-year-old Batty, the only appearances in the last twenty-one league games of that season by players over the age of thirty were by Nigel Martyn and Lucas Radebe.

The season started and ended with a goalless draw, something O'Leary's predecessor may have been proud of, but in between there were ten consecutive victories to set a new club record, eighty-eight goals scored in all competitions and the club's most successful European season since reaching the 1975 European Cup final. Leeds spent ninety-four days on top of the Premier League table, including being in first spot at the turn of the Millennium, and were still leading the table as late as 28 January. They ultimately settled for third spot and a place in next season's UEFA Champions League.

Of the eighty-eight goals Leeds scored in 1999–00, over half (forty-eight) of them were by players aged twenty-one or younger, with only the 1967–68 season seeing more when the likes of Lorimer, Greenhoff, Gray, Hibbitt and Belfitt were on the scoresheet on sixty-one occasions. Leeds gave 255 appearances to players aged twenty-one or younger, with only two seasons in the mid-1980s seeing more awarded in a single campaign, one of which – 260 in 1984–85 – was Eddie Gray's last full season in charge. Gray was now assistant to O'Leary, and was also responsible for forty-six of the appearances below across the 1965–66 and 1966–67 seasons. His presence runs deeply throughout the history of Leeds United.

Leeds United All Comps	Apps (21 or under)
1985–86	269
1984–85	260
1999–00	255
1965–66	253
1966–67	246

In the Premier League, the 154 starts given to players aged twenty-one or younger in 1999–00 is the third most in the history of the competition in a season, with only Manchester City in 2007–08 and Arsenal in 2008–09 handing out more. O'Leary may have christened them his 'babies', but he was happy to give them the opportunities to flourish, and Leeds reaped the rewards. Thirty-seven Premier League goals were scored by these players, a competition record, with twenty-nine of them coming from Bridges (nineteen) and Kewell (ten).

Season	Team	Goals (21 or under)
1999–00	Leeds United	37
2022–23	Arsenal	31
2006–07	Manchester United	30

Teenager Matthew Jones played eighteen times for Leeds in the 1999–00 season. Jones, who debuted away at Portsmouth in a 5–1 win in the FA Cup in January 1999, didn't end on the losing side until featuring in a 2–0 defeat at Arsenal in December 1999, his sixteenth game for the club. This run of fifteen unbeaten games is the longest ever unbeaten start by an outfield player in the club's history.

After losing 2–1 to Liverpool in August, Leeds then enjoyed a run of ten wins in a row to set a new club record, with the old record of nine consecutive wins standing since 1931. The victories came across the Premier League (six), UEFA Cup (three) and League Cup (one), and Leeds conceded the opener in the first three against Spurs, Coventry and Partizan Belgrade before recovering to win. At this stage, the only other Premier League side to have won ten games in a row in all competitions were Manchester United in 1996 and, having started the winning run in tenth spot, Leeds went top of the table after victory at Watford in early October. Tireless, all-action midfielder Lee Bowyer was in particularly good form; despite missing two of the wins, he was the leading scorer across the ten victories with six goals.

The winning run was halted by a 4–4 draw with Everton, the club's highest scoring top flight draw since 1938, also 4–4 with Everton. Strangely, of the four 4–4 draws Leeds have had in the top-flight, three of them have been against Everton, with David Weir's 90th minute header earning the Toffees a draw in the 1999 fixture.

Opponents	Date	GF	GA	Leeds Scorers
Leicester City	01/09/1928	4	4	Keetley 2, Turnbull, Armand
Everton	06/03/1935	4	4	Hydes 2, Stephenson 2
Everton	26/02/1938	4	4	Hodgson 4
Everton	24/10/1999	4	4	Bridges 2, Kewell, Woodgate

Leeds followed up the high-scoring affair at Everton with a further eight wins in eleven games and, following a 2–0 away win at Chelsea on 19 December with a brace of second half Stephen McPhail goals (McPhail got one goal in his other 106 games for Leeds), Leeds United went top of the Premier League for Christmas Day. Historically, this was not the place to be if you wanted to win the title – only two of the first eight sides top of the Premier League on 25 December had maintained that and won the league. Sadly, Leeds would fall away to make it two out of nine.

Harry Kewell scored Leeds' first goal of the new Millennium in a 2–1 defeat to Aston Villa at Elland Road, with Gareth Southgate scoring the only brace of his 426-game Premier League career (he only scored one more away goal in ninety-nine appearances after this, and that was also at Elland Road in a 2–1 win in December 2000). Kewell's goal was the twenty-fifth consecutive Premier League goal scored by Leeds players aged twenty-two or younger, the longest run by any team in the competition's history. The run began with an Ian Harte penalty away at Coventry in September and only ended when Jason Wilcox – a seasoned veteran at twenty-eight years old – scored his first goal for the club in the 2–1 win over Sunderland in late January. The only other player over the age of twenty-five to score for Leeds in the league that campaign was a 29-year-old David Hopkin (who at this stage was a peripheral figure in the team) away at Sheffield Wednesday in a 3–0 win in April.

Start of Run	End of Run	Team	Consecutive Goals by Players Aged 22 or Under
11/09/1999	03/01/2000	Leeds United	25
04/12/2019	21/01/2020	Everton	12
18/08/2019	14/09/2019	Chelsea	11

Leeds went into a game with Manchester United on 20 February just three points behind them and with the chance to go level at the top. Bakke, Kewell and Smith all hit the woodwork, and Bowyer missed an open goal as the Whites lost 1–0, but Leeds did recover to go seven unbeaten afterwards, winning five games in a row – including a memorable 1–0 win over Roma in the UEFA Cup to knock them out and reach the quarter-finals. After the fifth game in that winning run, a 4–1 home win over Wimbledon, Leeds had closed the gap at the top of the Premier League to four points and were still dreaming of a title.

A run of six consecutive defeats followed, the worst losing run since May 1996, though Leeds being out of the title race and the UEFA Cup paled into insignificance after the deaths of supporters Kevin Speight and Christopher Loftus on 5 April 2000 ahead of the semi-final first leg, sending shockwaves through both the club and footballing world. It was a tragic moment in the history of Leeds United, and Chris and Kev will never be forgotten.

That Leeds were able to rally following this harrowing loss to remain unbeaten in their final five Premier League matches – to take nine points and pip Liverpool to third – is of great credit to the young squad at the time. Goals in four consecutive games by Bridges against New-castle, Sheffield Wednesday, Watford and Everton helped get Leeds over the line, although it was an old face from the 1990s Leeds team who deserves the most credit on the final day. David Wetherall, who played 250 games for Leeds and was the scorer of two goals against Man Utd in 1994 and 1997, had left in the summer of 1999 to join

Bradford City, and his header in a 1–0 win over Liverpool meant that Leeds' place in the UEFA Champions League was assured whatever the result. It was only Wetherall's second goal of the season, and not only did it book Leeds' place in Europe's premier competition, but it also ensured Bradford stayed in the Premier League. Leeds may have freshened up their squad with younger players, but it was nice that, inadvertently or not, one of the old guard was on hand to help the new generation.

> Thirteen of David Wetherall's fifteen Premier League goals were headers (87%), the second highest percentage of any player to score more than fifteen Premier League goals in its history.

2000–01 and 2001–02
Fourteenth for Auld Lang Syne

Leeds made a strong start to the 2000–01 campaign, winning all four games in August; two victories over 1860 Munich in the third qualifying round of the UEFA Champions League were complemented by wins against Everton and Middlesbrough in the Premier League to put Leeds in second spot. All four wins had the same theme: Alan Smith. He scored in every game, becoming the first and, so far, only Leeds United player to score in each of the first four matches of a season. He was something of a lucky charm when he found the net for Leeds – he had scored in seventeen matches so far and Leeds had won all seventeen (with Smith wearing No. 17 on his shirt). He extended this to twenty-one wins during the season before scoring in the 3–2 defeat to Real Madrid at the Bernabeu – not the worst place to see the run come to an end. This remains the longest run of wins when a player has scored in the club's history.

First Game in Run	Final Game in Run	Scorer	Consecutive Games Won
14/11/1998	21/02/2001	Alan Smith	21
07/08/1968	19/04/1969	Mick Jones	18
07/10/2023	21/12/2024	Daniel James	17
25/02/1928	11/01/1930	John White	17
15/09/1965	13/12/1967	Billy Bremner	16

After five in his first four games of the season, Smith then followed it up with only four goals in his next thirty-five. Leeds could've used his magic winning touch when finding the net as they suffered consecutive home defeats to newly promoted sides Manchester City (unthinkable today, but they were relegated at the end of the season) and Ipswich Town. In 1999–00, while Leeds had a poor record against the sides around them, losing all six games against Man Utd, Arsenal and Liverpool, they had an unblemished record against the promoted clubs, winning every game. But between September and December 2000, Leeds dropped points in draws with Coventry (finished nineteenth), Derby (seventeenth), Bradford (twentieth) and defeats to West Ham (fifteenth) and Leicester (thirteenth) to end the year 2000 – a year they started top of the league, of course – in fourteenth place and only six points clear of relegation.

Nigel Martyn picked up an injury in a 3–1 win over Charlton in October 2000, with backup goalkeeper Paul Robinson coming into the side as his replacement, starting the next league match at Old Trafford against Man Utd. The oldest player in the team that day was Dom Matteo at just 26 years and 176 days and the XI had an average age of just 22 years and 341 days, at that point the youngest ever fielded in the Premier League (it is now fifth youngest) and the youngest Leeds XI named in a top-flight match since April 1970 against Ipswich Town.

The main high point of the first half of the Premier League campaign came on 4 November, the 4–3 victory over Liverpool with Mark Viduka scoring all four goals to cement it as a Premier League classic. It was Leeds' only victory over a run of ten games in all competitions and came immediately following a 3–2 defeat against Tranmere Rovers in the League Cup, having been 2–0 up at half-time (Tranmere would later finish bottom of the First Division that season). The subs bench for the Liverpool game told its own story about the injury issues surrounding Leeds; only four subs were named, and Danny Hay was introduced for his fourth and final Premier League appearance within 16 minutes after Woodgate suffered an injury of his own. By contrast, the three subs Liverpool used in the game – Nick Barmby, Robbie Fowler and Steven Gerrard – had already played 510 times in the top-flight. Leeds' other subs that day were goalkeeper Danny Milosevic (zero Premier League appearances), Gareth Evans (33 minutes of Premier League football) and Matthew Jones (ten Premier League starts to his name). Viduka was almost a one-man band that day, becoming the first Leeds player with four in a game since Allan Clarke in 1971.

While things weren't going brilliantly in the Premier League, in Europe it couldn't have been more different. Leeds, in their first season in the UEFA Champions League group stages, were taking the competition by storm.

Dom Matteo, scored a lovely header, at the San Siro

Leeds United began their UEFA Champions League campaign away at Barcelona, who had reached the semi-finals of the previous campaign before they were knocked out by Valencia. Not many people would've believed you if you'd said Leeds would see their 2000–01 campaign end in exactly the same way, especially after Barcelona hammered Leeds 4–0, after going 2–0 ahead inside the opening 20 minutes. It was the club's joint heaviest European defeat, equalling the 4–0 reverse against Lierse in 1971, and every single Leeds player who featured for the club that night were making their UEFA Champions League debuts, with two players – Danny Hay and Tony Hackworth – making their first ever appearances for Leeds.

From this difficult starting point, Leeds then kept three clean sheets in a row, with a 1–0 victory over AC Milan at a rain-soaked but delirious Elland Road going down as one of the club's greatest European nights. The win was achieved thanks to an 89th minute strike from Lee Bowyer, with thanks also due to Dida for his mistake, and this was the club's latest ever winning goal in a European match. It was one of two late winners by Bowyer this campaign, who also netted in the 87th minute against Anderlecht in a 2–1 win in February, and overall Bowyer's six goals were second only to Raúl scoring seven for Real Madrid. Bowyer remains the highest scoring English player in Champions League history to have only played one season in the competition.

In the third game, Leeds hammered Besiktas 6–0, the biggest European Cup victory by an English team for nineteen years. In his sixth game for the club, Viduka scored his first Leeds goal and Bowyer (twice), Matteo, Bakke and Darren Huckerby were also on the scoresheet, giving Leeds their biggest European victory since 1970.

Date	Team	Opponent	For	Against	Competition
17/09/1969	Leeds United	Lyn Oslo	10	0	European Cup
03/10/1967	Leeds United	Spora Luxembourg	9	0	Inter-Cities Fairs Cup
17/10/1967	Leeds United	Spora Luxembourg	7	0	Inter-Cities Fairs Cup
01/10/1969	Leeds United	Lyn Oslo	6	0	European Cup
02/12/1970	Leeds United	Sparta Prague	6	0	Inter-Cities Fairs Cup
26/09/2000	Leeds United	Besiktas	6	0	UEFA Champions League

Draws against Barcelona and AC Milan were enough to take Leeds into the second group stage, with the 1–1 draw at the San Siro seeing Dom Matteo famously head home from a Bowyer corner. This was his second goal of the campaign, and in the 2000–01 season Matteo was directly involved in four goals, all against teams from different countries: goals against Besiktas (Türkiye) and Milan (Italy) and assists against Anderlecht (Belgium) and Bradford (England). But that San Siro header was without doubt the most iconic goal he scored for the club.

Leeds picked up nine points in the first group stage and went one better in the second, winning ten points to finish second in a tough group. Lazio, who'd lost just two out of thirty-six home European matches heading into their game with Leeds, were beaten 1–0 at the Stadio Olimpico thanks to a late goal by Alan Smith. It was his only goal across twenty-six games between October and February, but it couldn't have been better timed. Anderlecht were beaten both at home and away, most impressively in the latter with Leeds taking them apart in a 4–1 win in Belgium; they had been unbeaten in twenty-one home games beforehand and won their previous nine at home in Europe. Smith scored two of the four that night and, at the age of 20 years and 116 days, was the youngest player to score a brace in that season's competition, and the youngest Leeds player to ever do so in a European game.

Date	Player	Opponent	Goals	Age
21/02/2001	Alan Smith	Anderlecht	2	20 years, 116 days
03/10/1967	Peter Lorimer	Spora Luxembourg	4	20 years, 293 days
04/11/1999	Michael Bridges	Lokomotiv Moscow	2	21 years, 91 days
03/10/1967	Jimmy Greenhoff	Spora Luxembourg	2	21 years, 106 days

The victory at Anderlecht secured Leeds a place in the quarter-final with two games to spare, and both remaining group games were high-scoring – a 3–2 defeat at Real Madrid and 3–3 draw with Lazio, the club's highest-scoring draw in Europe. Next up were reigning

Spanish champions Deportivo La Coruña at Elland Road in the first leg. Possibly spurred on by pre-match comments from their opponents that Leeds were the weakest team left in the competition, Leeds demolished the Spaniards 3–0, with Ian Harte slamming in an exceptional free-kick to give Leeds the lead, his second free-kick goal of the campaign. He was one of only three players to score more than one free-kick that season and wasn't in bad company – the others were Roberto Carlos and Rivaldo.

Left-back Harte had a direct hand in more goals in the 2000–01 Champions League campaign than any other Leeds player, scoring three goals and assisting six. Only three players for any team had more goals and assists than Harte that season and it remains the joint most ever by a defender in one season.

Player	Team	Goals	Assists	Goals & Assists
Luís Figo	Real Madrid	5	7	12
Raúl	Real Madrid	7	3	10
Gaizka Mendieta	Valencia CF	2	8	10
Giovane Élber	FC Bayern Munich	6	3	9
Ian Harte	Leeds United	3	6	9

Data via Opta

Rio Ferdinand's header to make it 3–0 was the last goal scored by Leeds in the Champions League that campaign. In the second leg against Deportivo, Leeds survived an onslaught and came away with a 2–0 defeat, taking them into the semi-final to face Valencia. Leeds became the only team in UEFA Champions League history to lose their first game of the season by four goals and recover to reach the last four of the competition. After a 0–0 draw in the first leg at Elland Road, a 3–0 win for Valencia in the second leg ended Leeds' roller-coaster journey and was the fifth defeat Leeds suffered against Spanish teams that season – the most defeats suffered by a team against sides from one nation in a single European campaign ever. Leeds didn't lose against a single non-Spanish team all season; if only Leeds had avoided

Spaniards that season, maybe they'd have gone one step further. But while it was gutting to come so close yet so far, fans could console themselves thinking this was just the start. Surely there'd be plenty more Champions League campaigns to come for this swashbuckling young side?

Leeds opponents – UCL – 2000–01	Non-Spain	Spain
Games	8	8
Won	5	1
Drawn	3	2
Lost	0	5
GF	18	6
GA	6	15
GD	12	-9
Win %	62.5%	12.5%

Titles aren't won in calendar years (sadly)

The second half of the Premier League season was the polar opposite of the first. From fourteenth on New Year's Day, Leeds surged up the table with the form of a title-winning side, winning thirteen of their last nineteen Premier League matches, and from 1 January until the end of the campaign Leeds were comfortably the best side in the division.

Team	P	W	D	L	GF	GA	GD	Pts
Leeds United	19	13	4	2	38	16	22	43
Liverpool	18	10	6	2	34	14	20	36
Chelsea	18	10	4	4	31	18	13	34
Manchester United	17	10	3	4	31	16	15	33
Arsenal	17	9	4	4	25	17	8	31

Martyn, Kewell and Batty all returning from injury had a major impact on the team, the latter in particular once again offering the experience that had been lost in his full year out with injury. With Batty in the starting XI in 2000–01, Leeds were unbeaten in all thirteen matches, conceding just eight goals; contrast that with ten defeats in twenty-five games without him in the middle of the park. Had Leeds had a fully fit David Batty for an entire season, a Premier League title may have been within reach. Sadly, they got him in the first half of 1999–00, and the back end of 2000–01.

With Batty	1999–00 + 2000–01	Without Batty
32	Games	44
22	Wins	19
6	Draws	8
4	Losses	17
69%	Win %	43%
72	Points	65
2.25	Points/Game	1.48

Players returning from injury are often described as 'like new signings' (think Andrea Radrizzani and Adam Forshaw in summer 2021) and while it was true for Leeds in 2000–01, there were other actual new signings making a similar impact. Rio Ferdinand was signed in November for £18m from West Ham United, becoming in one fell swoop Leeds' record signing, the most expensive British signing and the world's most expensive defender. Although he endured a tricky start, with Leeds losing four of the first five games he started, once he settled into the team his performances saw him become a regular in the England starting XI by the end of the campaign. From January until April, the only Premier League game Leeds had lost had been the one Ferdinand had missed, falling 3–1 to Newcastle. After injury ended Lucas Radebe's season in March, Ferdinand stepped up as captain and would keep hold of the armband as Radebe missed the entirety of 2001–02 with injury.

Irish striker Robbie Keane had scored twelve Premier League goals in 1999–00 for Coventry aged just nineteen – the most of any teenager that season – before joining Inter Milan for an unhappy six-month spell and he played just six times in Serie A, all without scoring. In December 2000, Leeds took him on loan with the option to sign him for £12m at the end of the season. Keane made an immediate impact by scoring or assisting in a run of seven consecutive Premier League appearances between 1 January and 7 February, the joint best sequence by a Leeds player in the Premier League. Keane ended the season with nine goals, a total that only former Leeds striker Jimmy Floyd Hasselbaink, now playing for Chelsea, could better from New Year's Day onwards.

The 2000–01 campaign was the final Premier League season in which only the top three teams were guaranteed qualification for the following season's UEFA Champions League. Leeds had been as many as thirteen points behind third in mid-January, but starting with a win away at thirteenth-place Aston Villa on 24 January (the last league game of the season to feature number 13 Paul Robinson), Leeds then went thirteen Premier League games without defeat, including a victory over Liverpool on Friday the 13th, and they concluded this thirteen-game undefeated streak with a 2–0 win over Chelsea, which was Batty's thirteenth and final league start of the season. After this Chelsea win, Leeds were third.

> 'Triskaidekaphobia' is the fear of the number 13. Hopefully no one who read that last paragraph has that fear.

In the previous season, 1990s club stalwart David Wetherall had ensured Leeds a safe passage to the UEFA Champions League while playing for another club, but in 2000–01 the man who started more games for Leeds in the nineties than anyone else had a big impact to swing third spot away from Leeds and in Liverpool's favour. Immediately after losing 2–1 to Leeds in April, Liverpool faced Everton. On a run of just two wins in nine games, they were drawing 2–2 and had twice relinquished a lead. In the 90th minute, Gary McAllister's long-range free-kick won Liverpool the game and they ended up winning six of their remaining seven games. Those two extra points in the Merseyside derby proved pivotal; Leeds finished one point behind them in fourth on sixty-eight points. Despite losing just one of the last sixteen games, away at Arsenal on 5 May, and ending the campaign with two wins and nine goals against Bradford (6–1) and Leicester (3–1), Leeds would have to settle for the UEFA Cup in 2001–02. From that point on, the top four would qualify for the Champions League and secure you the huge riches that came with playing in the competition. Of course, Leeds would be the final fourth placed team before this change.

> Ian Harte ended the 2000–01 Premier League campaign on a run of three consecutive scoring matches. What makes these so special is that Harte scored a direct free-kick in all of them, against Arsenal, Bradford and Leicester. He's one of just two players in Premier League history to achieve that, along with Wayne Rooney in 2013.

Leeds started the 2001–02 season as they'd ended the previous one, with two wins over Southampton and Arsenal, the latter despite going down to nine men when Lee Bowyer – his only Leeds red card in 265 appearances for the club – and Danny Mills were sent off. Leeds held on to win 2–1, one of only four occasions a team has won with two red cards in Premier League history, while it ended a run of six consecutive league losses at Highbury. The season's champions had been in action that night, but unfortunately it wasn't to be Leeds.

Four consecutive clean sheets followed the victory at Highbury, and while in October Leeds took the lead at both Anfield and Old Trafford before being pegged back to 1–1 draws in both, a 2–1 victory over Spurs in early November saw Leeds go into the international break top of the table and as the only unbeaten side in the Premier League. Defensively, Leeds had been imperious, conceding only five goals in eleven games, the joint lowest by a side after eleven matches in a season in the Premier League era up to that point. With this strong defensive performance, it was no surprise to see both Martyn and Ferdinand starting that month's England friendly against Sweden, with Mills a second-half substitute.

The unbeaten run came to an end in a 2–0 loss away at Sunderland before a 1–1 draw with Aston Villa, a game in which Smith scored and was sent off. It was his third red card of 2001 to go along with red mists against Sunderland in March and Valencia in May, and he remains the only Leeds player sent off three times in a single year. His seven red cards overall looked an unassailable target until a certain Gaetano Berardi came along with eight red cards in his Leeds career.

The defence was looking solid but going forward Leeds had the same number of goals (sixteen) as sixteenth place Charlton Athletic after thirteen games, so Robbie Fowler was signed expensively from Liverpool. Up to the end of November 2001, Fowler was the fourth highest scoring player in Premier League history with 120 goals in 236 games, and though his first game was a goalless draw at Fulham, Leeds scored thirteen goals in the next five. Fowler himself hit five of them, including a superb hat-trick away at Bolton Wanderers on Boxing Day – the first by a Leeds player on 26 December since Harold Brook in 1956.

Fowler featured in a 1–0 win over Southampton on 29 December with Bowyer scoring an 89th minute winner to send Leeds third and a point off top spot. It rounded off 2001 with a victory, and Leeds had been comfortably the Premier League's best side in the calendar year as a whole, winning eight more points than anyone else and losing only four games. Sadly, Premier League titles are not handed out for being the best side in a year. '*Premier League champions of the calendar year 2001, you'll never sing that*' and so on.

Premier League in 2001

Form	Team	P	W	D	L	GF	GA	GD	Pts
1	Leeds United	39	23	12	4	68	33	35	81
2	Liverpool	37	21	10	6	63	33	30	73
3	Arsenal	37	20	10	7	66	41	25	70
4	Manchester United	37	21	6	10	79	46	33	69

Though Leeds were great in this period, against Newcastle United they were not. The final league defeat of 2000, on Boxing Day, was against Newcastle. The first league defeat of 2001 on 20 January was against Newcastle. The last league defeat of 2001, on 22 December, was against Newcastle, despite being 3–1 ahead. Then the first league defeat of 2002 was against Newcastle, on 12 January, despite taking the lead in the 1st minute.

10 games and 64 days without a win

On New Year's Day 2002, Leeds United beat West Ham United 3–0 at a snowy Elland Road to go two points clear at the top of the Premier League. Things were looking positive. But by the time they next won a Premier League match, they trailed the leaders by thirteen points and were seven points shy of a spot in the coveted UEFA Champions League. They'd also been knocked out of the FA Cup by a side from the Third Division. Not a good start to 2002, it's fair to say.

The 2–1 FA Cup defeat at Cardiff City is seen by many as the turning point of the O'Leary era. It was the first time a side top of the top-flight had been eliminated by a side from outside the top two divisions since (typically) Leeds themselves in 1971 away at Colchester. Leeds even took the lead through an early Mark Viduka goal, but Ferdinand was subbed off injured and, for the fourth time in twenty-six appearances, Alan Smith was sent off to compound a miserable afternoon in Wales. The defeat began a run of ten games without a win in all competitions, the club's worst run since 1997.

Leeds had started struggling to hold on to leads. Between mid-March and early October 2001, they'd taken the lead in sixteen games and won all sixteen matches, conceding just six goals. But after going 1–0 ahead against Liverpool on 13 October and until a 2–2 draw with Middlesbrough on 9 February, Leeds held a lead in eighteen games and failed to win in ten of them, conceding twenty-six goals.

Just scoring a goal at all became an issue at one stage in a run of six goalless games out of seven – three of them 0–0 draws in a throwback to the George Graham days – as fans took out their frustrations on first-team coach Brian Kidd after the tenth winless game, a 0–0 draw away at Everton. It was exactly one year to the day since he'd first sat on the first-team bench with O'Leary and Gray in the 1–1 draw with Manchester United in March 2001, and many fans felt Kidd had stifled some of the free-flowing attacking intent of the young Leeds team. They'd won the fourth most points in the Premier League in the year he'd been there – scoring more goals in those thirty-eight games (sixty) than they'd scored in the thirty-eight before he stepped up to first-team duties (fifty-five) – but with his prior links to Manchester United, he seemed an easy target.

It was during this winless run that Leeds were eliminated from the UEFA Cup by PSV, who'd knocked Leeds out 8–3 on aggregate in Wilkinson's last European tie. The 1–0 defeat against PSV in the fourth round at Elland Road would prove to be O'Leary's last European game as manager as well. Between the 1999–00 season and the PSV defeat, only six sides had won more matches in Europe than Leeds (sixteen) and O'Leary had led Leeds to two semi-finals, but sadly they couldn't make the next step and win a European title.

The PSV player who scored the goal to knock Leeds out of the UEFA Cup in 2001–02 was the brilliantly named Jan Vennegoor of Hesselink. His name would score you forty-four points in Scrabble, which was the same total of points Leeds had in the Premier League when he scored the goal on 28 February.

The winless run finally came to an end with a home win against Ipswich and Leeds won five of the next seven games, with Viduka – who'd gone eleven games without a goal since scoring in the Cardiff defeat – finding form with four in five games before an injury ended his season. Victory in the next game over Fulham would've given Leeds a glimmer of UEFA Champions League football but the 1–0 defeat at Elland Road – against a side who'd picked up just two points in their previous nine games – put an end to any hopes of fourth spot. Leeds ended the season with wins against Derby and Middlesbrough and had the third best form of any side over their final ten games, but their mid-season dip had proven costly – both for the season and metaphorically for the next decade.

O'Leary finished fourth, third, fourth and fifth in the Premier League with Leeds, finishes that any manager in the modern era would probably happily agree to before a ball is kicked, given they would guarantee qualification for the Champions League (in 2024–25, the fifth placed Premier League team was given a spot). Between his first game in September 1998 and the end of the 2001–02 season, only Man Utd and Arsenal picked up more points, while Leeds had the exact same record as Liverpool. The only difference was they qualified for the Champions League twice, while for Leeds it was only once, and O'Leary was sacked in the summer of 2002. As Peter Ridsdale famously declared, we'd lived the dream. But as the coming years would show, the dream was well and truly over.

3 October 1998 – end of 2001–02 season

Form	Team	P	W	D	L	Pts
1	Manchester United	146	95	31	20	316
2	Arsenal	145	88	34	23	298
3	Liverpool	145	75	34	36	259
4	Leeds United	145	75	34	36	259

5

THE FA CUP

'And travelling there is number nineteen – Leeds United, third in the Championship and four-time finalists,' announced host Seema Jaswal as former England midfielder Trevor Steven pulled Leeds out of the hat (well, it's more of a bowl) to face Peterborough United at London Road in the FA Cup third round in January 2024. Steven may not have known it then, but by randomly plucking the number nineteen ball out he'd helped make FA Cup history. For a thirteenth consecutive tie (it just had to be unlucky number thirteen), Leeds had been drawn away from home, setting a new record in a competition that had begun 152 years earlier and breaking the runs of Aston Villa between 1977 and 1983 and Brighton between 1993 and 2000.

Team	Away Ties	Between
Leeds United	13	2015–16 Fourth Round – 2023–24 Third Round
Aston Villa	12	1976–77 Quarter-Final – 1982–83 Third Round
Brighton and Hove Albion	12	1992–93 Fourth Round – 2000–01 Second Round
Stockport County	11	1996–97 Second Round – 2000–01 Fifth Round
Swansea City	11	2003–04 Fifth Round – 2007–08 Second Round

In the same time that Leeds had thirteen consecutive away ties, 102 clubs played in the Premier League and Football League and one hundred of those had at least one home tie – Leeds were joined on

152

their FA Cup travels by Barnet, whose two ties as a league club in 2016–17 and 2017–18 had seen them drawn away both times. One of those was at Shrewsbury Town who, by some stroke of luck, began a run of thirteen consecutive home draws in the same round Leeds started their thirteen away ones, the 2015–16 fourth round. While Leeds created an away record, the Salopians fashioned their own FA Cup record for consecutive home draws. Incredibly, in the same time Leeds had zero home ties, Shrewsbury played at home twenty times.

Any Leeds fan with even a brief knowledge of the club's history in the FA Cup would never have expected those fortunes to be reversed and to have an improbable run of thirteen home draws; but they probably would shrug and say 'that's Leeds, that' upon being informed thirteen away ties in a row is a record. The FA Cup has never been a particularly happy competition for Leeds United.

Early struggles

After joining the Football League in 1920, Leeds were forced to play in FA Cup qualifying rounds in the 1920–21 season as they'd been elected into the league and hadn't featured in the competition in 1919–20. These clashed with Second Division fixtures so Leeds sent a reserve team to beat a local side, Boothtown, 5–0 in the first qualifying round. Following this win, they received a £50 fine from the FA for fielding a weakened side, which Boothtown reckoned had affected the attendance and gate receipts, a share of which they were entitled to. By the time the second qualifying round match with Leeds Steelworks came around a fortnight later, Leeds had already reached an agreement with the FA and decided to withdraw from the competition to avoid the eight qualifying rounds it would take to even get to the first round, which clashed with league fixtures. They fulfilled the Steelworks fixture – and won 7–0 – and then immediately pulled out. An inauspicious start.

Seven of Leeds' first eight ties in the FA Cup proper were away from home (some things never change), which wasn't helpful as Leeds didn't win any of their first fourteen away matches in the competition – taking until 1933 to win on the road in a 3–0 win at Newcastle, with Arthur Hydes scoring a hat-trick. That was Leeds' only away win in the competition before the Second World War, and by the time war broke out fourteen of their fifteen wins had been on home soil at Elland Road. In 1930–31, top-flight Leeds visited Exeter City of the Third Division South in the fifth round and lost 3–1, with the Grecians reaching the quarter-final for the first time at the expense of Leeds. Since then, Exeter have won just one of twenty-seven other FA Cup matches against top-flight teams.

Things began to change in 1949–50. With John Charles in the team, Leeds finally made some headway in the competition, winning more away games that season than they'd managed in total up to that point; a 5–2 win at Carlisle in the third round and 3–2 in extra-time at Bolton Wanderers in a fourth round replay, setting up a home game with Cardiff in the fifth round. Leeds won 3–0 in front of a crowd of 53,099, the second largest ever for an FA Cup match at Elland Road. The average attendance for league games that season up to the Cardiff match had been just over 32,000 – the FA Cup was the magical competition of the era. Leeds had, finally, reached an FA Cup quarter-final in their forty-first tie in the competition, the fourth-longest wait for a side to get to the final eight while competing in the top two tiers of English football (it took Plymouth fifty-five attempts, while Port Vale and Rotherham have never got to an FA Cup quarter-final in the first or second tier of English football).

Leeds were knocked out by eventual winners Arsenal in the 1950 quarter-final, losing to a goal by Reg Lewis who would score both goals in the final against Liverpool. With the club finally breaking their quarter-final duck, they must've hoped for further success across the decade. But after comfortable wins over Third Division North sides Rochdale and Bradford Park Avenue put Leeds into the fifth round in 1951–52, it would be a scarcely believable 4,050 days – or 11 years and 32 days – until Leeds won another match in the FA Cup, a record-breaking bad run.

Between February 1952 and January 1962, Leeds went sixteen consecutive FA Cup matches without victory, drawing five and losing eleven, including a humiliating 4–0 defeat to Torquay United of the Third Division South. This is the longest winless run in FA Cup history by a side playing all those games while in the top two divisions of English football.

Run Start	Run End	Team	Matches without Winning (1st/2nd Tier)
23/02/1952	10/01/1962	Leeds United	16
23/01/2010	05/01/2019	Ipswich Town	14
30/01/1960	28/01/1967	Blackpool	13
10/03/1906	11/01/1913	Birmingham City	12
17/02/1968	06/01/1976	Norwich City	12

Leeds 1–2 Cardiff (x3)

Although in recent years Leeds have had cause to complain about their lack of home ties, that wasn't the case in the 1950s. Leeds were drawn at home every season in the third round between 1953–54 and 1957–58 but found themselves knocked out every time (although in the first two of those seasons elimination came in away replays). Between 1955–56 and 1957–58, they were beaten at Elland Road by the same team, in the same round and by the same scoreline. Leeds United 1–2 Cardiff City: the trilogy.

Part I: Going into their tie with Cardiff City in January 1956, Leeds United were unbeaten in thirty-two home matches and had won twenty of their previous twenty-one games at Elland Road, all in the Second Division. The largest attendance of the season piled into the stadium in the hope of eliminating a top-flight Cardiff team whose side featured future England striker Gerry Hitchens, and the history books suggested Leeds had a good chance – they'd lost none of their previous ten home games against Cardiff. But late goals in this tie by Hitchens and Johnny McSeveney were only halved by

155

Harold Brook, and Leeds were eliminated 2–1. Not to worry – Leeds focused on the league instead and were promoted from the Second Division in second place at the end of the season to join Cardiff in the top-flight.

Part II: In 1956–57, Leeds were once again drawn at home to Cardiff City in the FA Cup. Since losing 2–1 the previous January, Leeds had only lost twice at Elland Road but both had been 2–1 defeats, which was a portent of what was to come. Johnny McSeveney was once again on the scoresheet for Cardiff, scoring their second goal in the 2–1 victory as Leeds suffered their sixth consecutive FA Cup elimination. Welshman John Charles scored his tenth goal across his last five Elland Road appearances, but it wasn't enough, and this was his final FA Cup appearance for Leeds. His next FA Cup game? For Cardiff against Leeds in January 1964. He was on the losing side again (it wasn't 2–1, though – Leeds won 1–0).

Part III: A month after losing 2–1 to Cardiff in January 1957, Leeds beat Cardiff 3–0 at Elland Road in the league and the Bluebirds were relegated from Division One at the end of the season. With John Charles gone, Leeds were struggling at the foot of the top-flight when they were drawn together with Cardiff in the FA Cup third round at Elland Road for a third consecutive season. It is the only time in the history of the FA Cup a team has played the same team at the same venue in three consecutive FA Cup ties. Seven Leeds players lined up in all three games (Wood, Hair, Kerfoot, Charlton, Dunn, Gibson, Overfield) and were on hand to see Cardiff win 2–1 again and knock Leeds out. It was the first time the same team had eliminated another in three consecutive seasons since Blackburn against Derby in the early 1900s. A truly bizarre sequence of events.

Seasons	Team vs Opponent	Consec. Seasons Eliminated
2000–01 – 2003–04	Chelsea vs Arsenal	4
1901–02 – 1903–04	Blackburn Rovers vs Derby County	3
1955–56 – 1957–58	Leeds United vs Cardiff City	3
1976–77 – 1978–79	Doncaster Rovers vs Shrewsbury Town	3
2013–14 – 2015–16	Hull City vs Arsenal	3

It was Raich Carter's last ever FA Cup game as Leeds United manager and Carter, who is the only player to win the FA Cup as a player both before (in 1937 with Sunderland) and after (in 1946 with Derby) the war, left Leeds without winning a single game in the FA Cup, a club record. He was no doubt sick of the sight of Cardiff City.

FA Cup	Games	Won	Drawn	Lost
Raich Carter	7	0	2	5
Marcelo Bielsa	4	0	0	4
Dennis Wise	3	0	1	2
Kevin Blackwell	3	0	2	1
Jack Taylor	2	0	0	2

The greatest in the land

In the time between Leeds United's long, eleven-year winless run in the FA Cup, Don Revie played in two finals as a player for Manchester City. After losing the 1955 final against Newcastle, he was on the winning side in 1956 against Birmingham in which he executed what was called 'the Revie plan', playing as a deep-lying centre-forward – which wasn't common in English football at the time. He was named man of the match; no mean feat given goalkeeper Bert Trautmann had played on with a broken neck.

Revie joined Leeds as a player in 1958 and featured in one FA Cup match for the club, losing 5–1 against Luton Town in January 1959 (which extended the club's aforementioned winless run to twelve matches). After his appointment as manager in March 1961, his first FA Cup tie wasn't until his thirty-sixth game in charge but he did manage to end a seven-game losing streak in the competition; his side drew 2–2 with Derby County before losing the replay 3–1 at the Baseball Ground in January 1962, as the winless run hit sixteen. Spare a thought for Grenville Hair, who had played in all sixteen games and was in the last Leeds team that had won in the competition back in 1952.

Thankfully for Hair he was also in the Leeds team that finally ended their FA Cup winless run in 1963 against Stoke. The Whites then followed it up with a win over Middlesbrough in the fourth round to reach the heady heights of the fifth round, only to then lose 3–0 at top-flight Nottingham Forest. Leeds went out in the fourth round the following season against another top-flight side, Everton, but had more important matters to attend to in the league, winning the Second Division with sixty-three points to secure a return to the top-flight.

Having been eliminated in eleven consecutive FA Cup ties between 1952 and 1962, Leeds played forty-three ties during their time in the top-flight under Revie and were only eliminated nine times. Sadly, three of those were in the finals of 1965, 1970 and 1973, but Revie did manage to lead the club to their first and (so far) only FA Cup trophy in 1972. He won thirty-four ties in those ten seasons between 1964–65 and 1973–74, and it took Leeds until the year 2001 to be successful across thirty-four ties after he left. Over 30% of the FA Cup ties Leeds have won came during that ten-season period (34/109) and Leeds, while only lifting one trophy, were statistically the best side in the competition in that timeframe, reaching more finals than anyone else (four).

Grenville Hair's longevity at Leeds United – 474 appearances between 1951 and 1964 – was such that he played alongside a player born before the start of the First World War (Eddie Burbanks, April 1913) and one born after the Second World War had ended (Jimmy Greenhoff, June 1946).

FA Cup: 1964–65 – 1973–74	Ties Won
Leeds United	34
Chelsea	31
Liverpool	29
Everton	27
Tottenham Hotspur	23
Arsenal	23
Leicester City	23

FA Cup: 1964–65 – 1973–74	Goals
Leeds United	100
Chelsea	94
Tottenham Hotspur	87
Peterborough United	85
Liverpool	73

In 1964–65, Leeds reached their first FA Cup final after knocking out Manchester United in a semi-final replay at the City Ground thanks to a late winner from Billy Bremner (not the last time that would happen), but lost their first ever game at Wembley 2–1 to Liverpool. Leeds also came second in the top-flight that season, and remain the only newly promoted club to finish runners-up in both the league and FA Cup.

The runner-up spot in the FA Cup and the league was something Leeds were getting used to. In 1970 they made the final again thanks to a win in the semi-final (second) replay against Manchester United after another Bremner winner. Bremner scored that winner in his one and only appearance for Leeds at Bolton's Burnden Park, yet played thirteen games at Hillsborough (hosts of the initial 1965, 1970 and 1972 semi-finals) across league and cup and never scored – the joint most he played at one ground without scoring along with Highbury.

Leeds had beaten Chelsea 5–2 at Stamford Bridge in a First Division match in January 1970 and twice took the lead when they met at Wembley in the April final with goals from Jack Charlton (at 34 years and 338 days, the third-oldest FA Cup final scorer) and Mick Jones. But they were pegged back by goals from Peter Houseman and Ian Hutchinson, marking the first time an FA Cup final had gone to a replay since the month the Titanic sunk in 1912.

The replay was staged at Old Trafford on 29 April. It was the 1,999th match of the club's history, but party like it was 1999 they did not. It started well, with Jones scoring a superb solo goal to give Leeds the lead – the third time they'd gone ahead over the two games – but a late Peter Osgood header took the game to extra time. In what was the 224th minute across both games, David Webb steered a back post header into David Harvey's net to give Chelsea their first lead of the final and, unlike Leeds, they didn't surrender it. Leeds were just the second side in FA Cup history to take the lead in both the final and the replay but not win the trophy, along with Sheffield United against Spurs in 1901, who had gone ahead via a Fred Priest goal in both games. Sadly, there was no divine intervention for either the Blades or Leeds.

Leeds had also finished runners-up in Division One in 1969–70 – though a full nine points behind Everton in first – and became the first side to finish runners-up in both the FA Cup and league on more than one occasion. So close and yet so far – again.

Colchester

Up to their 1971 fifth round meeting with the Fourth Division's Colchester United, Leeds had an exceptional record against lower league sides in the FA Cup under Don Revie. They had played thirteen and progressed from all thirteen, winning eleven of those games without conceding and only needing one replay to go through (that season's third round meeting with Rotherham). The fourth tier had been created in the 1958–59 season and this would be Leeds' third tie against a Football League side that low in the pyramid, after beating Southport 3–0 in 1965 and Swansea 2–1 in 1970 and going on to reach the final both years. Good omens, then.

Although Leeds had lost the previous week in a First Division game away at Liverpool, they were top of the table going into the Colchester match and had only lost five of thirty-eight games in all competitions in the 1970–71 campaign; in December, they'd dispatched Czech side Sparta Prague 9–2 on aggregate to reach the quarter-final of the Fairs Cup, a competition they would win that season. Colchester, on the other hand, were eighth in the Fourth Division but were on a good run of form, winning five of their previous seven games with former England centre-forward Ray Crawford – who'd won the top-flight title with Ipswich in 1962 – scoring in each of his last three games at Layer Road. Although he was thirty-four by this stage, Crawford had 128 top-flight goals to his name and had scored against Leeds in the First Division as recently as their title-winning 1968–69 campaign, as well as scoring eight times in the 1962–63 European Cup.

On paper Colchester's team was not packed with the quality to seriously challenge Leeds, although five of their XI had played in the top-flight at one time or another. Aside from striker Crawford, goalkeeper Graham Smith gained a move to West Brom later in 1971 and made his debut against none other than Leeds United at Elland Road (Leeds won 3–0); Bobby Cram – uncle of athlete Steve Cram – played 141 top-flight games for West Brom in the 1960s; and John Kurila and Brian Lewis had both spent a season playing in the top-flight in the mid-1960s at Northampton and Coventry respectively. Of their starting line-up, only one player – Mick Mahon – never played higher than the Fourth Division in his career.

Captain Billy Bremner was injured but Leeds had won seven of their nine games in 1970–71 without him at that stage and the line-up who faced Colchester had a combined total of 3,538 appearances for the club, with all but two (Mick Bates and Allan Clarke) playing at least one hundred times. It had more than enough experience and might to defeat a side from the Fourth Division.

Crawford scored twice in the opening twenty-five minutes and a shell-shocked Leeds went in 2–0 down at half-time for the first time in an FA Cup tie since 1955 away at Torquay United, while it was the only time it happened under Revie. Shortly after the restart, Dave Simmons made it 3–0 and Leeds were three goals down in a match for only the second time all season. It remains one of three occasions the team top of the top-flight has conceded three times in an FA Cup match against a team from outside the top two divisions, though neither of these sides found themselves three goals down. It remains unchartered territory for a table-topping top-flight side.

Season	Team	GF	GA	Opponent	Opponent Division
1956–57	Manchester United	4	3	Hartlepool United	Third Div. North
1970–71	Leeds United	2	3	Colchester United	Fourth Division
2014–15	Chelsea	2	4	Bradford City	League One

Goals from Norman Hunter and Johnny Giles gave Leeds a fighting chance but a point-blank save from a Jones shot by Smith in Colchester's goal stopped a Leeds equaliser as a humbling defeat was confirmed.

In the quarter-final, Colchester were hammered 5–0 by Everton, while Leeds got over the shock of their FA Cup exit by winning five consecutive matches and losing just two of their remaining twenty games of the season. But in many ways the damage was done, and one of the FA Cup's most famous and replayed giant killings had been born.

Leeds didn't play at Layer Road again until April 2007 when, despite going 1–0 ahead, they lost 2–1 in a crucial match in the battle to avoid relegation from the Championship. Colchester then moved to a new ground – the Colchester Community Stadium – and with Layer Road a thing of the past, Leeds have won both games at their new stadium.

Consecutive Finals – Glory and Pain

After that defeat to Colchester United, Leeds then won their next eleven FA Cup ties (as many as the club had won in total between 1934 and 1962) to reach consecutive finals. One ended in wonderful success, the other in total disappointment.

Leeds knocked out Bristol Rovers, Liverpool, Cardiff City (it wasn't the 1950s anymore), Spurs and Birmingham City to face Arsenal in the centenary final of 1972. Although the Gunners would be tough opponents – they'd also won eleven consecutive ties up to the 1972 final and were holders of the trophy – Leeds had a good recent record against them. Going into the final, they'd won fifteen of their previous twenty-two games against the north Londoners and beaten them 3–0 in the league in March, only forty-two days before the final. Allan Clarke had scored the opening goal that day.

After two failed finals in 1965 and 1970, Leeds finally lifted the FA Cup with a 1–0 victory thanks to Allan Clarke's diving header, becoming the first team to beat the holders of the trophy in the final for sixty-one years – though it wouldn't be that long until it happened again.

The starting XI for the game trips off the tongue; Harvey, Reaney, Madeley, Bremner, Charlton, Hunter, Lorimer, Clarke, Jones, Giles, Gray. Amazingly, this was the last time that XI ever played together again for the club and it was only the third time they'd all started together, with the previous two coming in April against Birmingham in the FA Cup semi-final and in a 1–0 defeat to Newcastle in the First Division. The same team may have started the crucial league game two days later against Wolves – which Leeds lost 2–1 and conceded the title to Derby – had Mick Jones not dislocated his elbow to be replaced by the final's unused substitute, Mick Bates.

In 1972–73, Leeds continued their excellent FA Cup record and knocked out four different fellow top-flight sides (Norwich, West Brom, Derby and Wolves) as well as Third Division team Plymouth Argyle to reach another final against Second Division Sunderland. In the semi-final – a 1–0 win over Wolves at Maine Road – Billy Bremner once again scored the winning goal, meaning he'd fired Leeds to the FA Cup final in three of their four semi-finals.

A First Division side had played a Second Division team in six previous FA Cup finals and the team in the division above had only lost once, with Birmingham going down 2–1 against West Brom in 1931. Leeds went into the final on their worst run of form – four defeats in six games – since losing four in a row in 1970, which culminated in the FA Cup final replay defeat to Chelsea. The starting XI for the Sunderland game was only the third time they'd all started together (this was: Harvey, Reaney, Cherry, Bremner, Madeley, Hunter, Lorimer, Clarke, Jones, Giles, Gray), the other two of which were in the cup earlier that campaign. Leeds made ten changes for the final from their previous game, a 2–1 loss at Birmingham, with only Peter Lorimer keeping his place (though the Birmingham game saw Revie name what was essentially a reserve side, featuring the likes of Galvin, Hampton, Ellam, Liddell and Mann, who were never realistically going to start).

Like last season's final, it was decided by just one goal but this time it didn't go Leeds' way. Ian Porterfield's first-half strike proved to be the winner as Leeds lost their third final in four attempts. Although at the time it was an unprecedented victory for a Second Division side in an FA Cup final, it wasn't the only one of its era; in 1976, Manchester United lost 1–0 to Southampton and in 1980 Arsenal lost 1–0 to West Ham United, with both sides finishing those seasons in the top four of the First Division. But – of course – it is Leeds' defeat to Sunderland that is most well remembered as David killing Goliath.

The following season, Leeds were eliminated by another Second Division side in Bristol City, losing 1–0 in a replay at Elland Road. It would be the club's last FA Cup tie under Revie. That meant that since losing the 1970 final to Chelsea, Leeds had won eight ties in a row against fellow top-flight sides but lost three out of ten against sides from outside the First Division. In the same era (1964–65 to 1973–74), Arsenal lost twice as many FA Cup ties against sides from outside the top-flight as Leeds did, but it is the defeats to Colchester and Sunderland that stick in the minds of many.

Non-league ties

Leeds managed to avoid any potential banana skins against non-league teams in their first eighty-one FA Cup ties, which is the second longest run of any league team without facing a side from the non-league for the first time. Only Portsmouth – whose first tie with a non-league side came in their ninety-fourth in the competition – have had a longer run.

Date	Team	Opponent	Tie No.
15/01/1972	Portsmouth	Boston United	94
24/01/1970	Leeds United	Sutton United	82
11/01/1947	Swansea City	Gillingham	40
28/11/1931	Cardiff City	Enfield	38
07/01/1939	Southampton	Chelmsford City	36

When Leeds did face a non-league opponent for the first time in January 1970, they were top of the First Division and became the first table-topping team to face a non-league side since Newcastle United in 1927 (who beat Corinthians, presumably with a lot of spirit, 3–1). Sutton United were Leeds' opponents in the fourth round in 1969–70 and Leeds dispatched them 6–0, with Allan Clarke on the scoresheet four times. None of Sutton's team had, at that stage, featured in the Football League but two players got their moves on the back of it – Mick Mellows joined Reading in the 1970–71 season, while centre-half John Faulkner impressed Don Revie so much that he signed him for Leeds. Just seventy days after the Sutton match, Faulkner was lining up against Burnley in the First Division; he scored an own goal, but luckily for him the game is much better remembered for Eddie Gray's two superb goals. Faulkner only played three more games for Leeds before joining Luton.

Having avoided non-league teams until 1970, in 1975 Leeds faced Wimbledon who had just knocked First Division side Burnley out in the third round at Turf Moor, becoming the first non-league team to beat a top flight side away from home since 1920. Wimbledon's winner was scored by Mick Mahon, who had been part of Colchester's side against Leeds in 1971. Although Mahon wasn't in the team at Elland Road in 1975, Leeds failed to get past Wimbledon, drawing 0–0, with Peter Lorimer's penalty saved by Dickie Guy. In the replay, Leeds prevailed away from home 1–0 thanks to an own goal scored by Dave Bassett (later Wimbledon manager and Leeds assistant to Dennis Wise in the 2007–08 League One campaign).

Leeds progressed from their next two FA Cup ties against non-league teams. They beat Telford United 2–1 at the Hawthorns in 1987 thanks to an Ian Baird brace and, after a replay, knocked out Rushden & Diamonds in the third round in 1999. Leeds picked a strong team for both games against Rushden, although they had Jonathan Woodgate sent off in the initial game and went 1–0 down in the replay at Elland Road. A brace from Alan Smith – at eighteen years old, the youngest Leeds player to score two goals in an FA Cup game – and a Jimmy Floyd Hasselbaink goal gave Leeds a 3–1 win, with much-loved title-winning central defender Chris Whyte making a late appearance for Rushden at Elland Road. If that game was a bit of a scare, Leeds' next tie against a non-league team would be a full-blown nightmare.

Histon in 2008 is seen by many as the lowest point in the club's long history, knocked out of the FA Cup by a side from a tiny Cambridgeshire village with a population of fewer than 5,000. The winning goal, delivered in the first half by postman Matt Langston, saw Leeds lose to a non-league team for the first time in the club's history.

By now in League One, Leeds had gone past Northampton in a replay in the first round – their first FA Cup victory since 2003 – but probably wished they'd allowed the Cobblers to make the shorter journey to Histon's Glassworld Stadium. It was the start of a poor run of form for Leeds, who lost five games in a row as Gary McAllister was sacked and replaced by Simon Grayson. Histon will always have the memories of knocking Leeds out, but the club only played one more game in the FA Cup proper, losing in the first round the following season to Swansea. By 2010–11, they'd been relegated from the Conference and now play in the United Counties League Premier Division South alongside the likes of Godmanchester Rovers and Leicester Nirvana.

The following season, Leeds were once again drawn away at

non-league opponents in the second round, this time at Kettering Town. Leeds were in exceptional form going into the game, winning eighteen of their first twenty-three games in all competitions before the trip to Rockingham Road. Histon had been second in the Conference when Leeds faced them and Kettering were going similarly well and sat third. Leeds picked a strong team again (only Lubo Michalik and Robert Snodgrass survived from the Histon defeat) but despite many attempts and clattering the woodwork, found themselves 1–0 down to a goal by Ian Roper, who'd played against Leeds at Elland Road only eighteen months earlier for Walsall in League One. Another upset was on the cards until Jermaine Beckford – who'd missed the Histon game with an injury – turned home a Snodgrass cross to take the game to a replay. After the game, it was announced the winner of the tie would face Manchester United at Old Trafford in the third round. In the replay, Luciano Becchio gave Leeds the lead before an equaliser from former striker Anthony Elding took the game beyond ninety minutes. After a goalless first half in extra-time, Leeds finally broke down the Kettering resistance with four goals, two from Mike Grella and one each from Tresor Kandol and Beckford to win 5–1.

Sutton United, the first non-league side Leeds faced in 1970, are the club's most recent non-league opponents too. In 2016–17, Sutton reached the fourth round for just the third time in their history – and they'd lost the first two by an aggregate score of 14–0. Leeds were going well under Garry Monk, winning seven of their previous nine games, but made ten changes to their line-up for the Sutton game at Gander Green Lane, with only Stuart Dallas retaining his place from a midweek win over Nottingham Forest. It was the most changes Leeds made for an FA Cup tie since the 1973 final against Sunderland, and just as they had then they lost 1–0, with Liam Cooper sent off late on to pile on further misery.

> The 2017 defeat at Sutton saw seven different Leeds players make their final appearances for the club, while three of those made their one and only appearances (Mallik Wilks, Paul McKay and Billy Whitehouse). It is the only game in the club's entire history to see three different players play their only game for the club.

January 3rd, remember the date

Although the 1–0 win at Old Trafford in the FA Cup in January 2010 may have lost some of its lustre in recent years, having played Manchester United seven times since then without winning, in the context of its time the achievement was extraordinary.

In the history of the FA Cup, only two teams from outside the top two divisions have ever won away from home against the reigning league champions. They are Norwich against Arsenal in 1953–54 and Leeds against Manchester United in 2009–10. Since the war, it's only happened four times at home or away.

Round	Date	Match
Fourth Round	30/01/1954	Arsenal 1–2 Norwich City
Third Round	04/01/1992	Wrexham 2–1 Arsenal
Third Round	03/01/2010	Manchester United 0–1 Leeds United
Fifth Round	18/02/2017	Millwall 1–0 Leicester City

3 January 2010 was the only time Manchester United lost in the FA Cup third round under Alex Ferguson, and the only time they lost in twenty-nine FA Cup ties under him against a side from outside of the top-flight. Going into the game against Leeds, at home they were unbeaten in their last twenty-nine FA Cup games against teams from outside the top division, since losing to Second Division Norwich in 1967. Against teams from the third tier or below, they hadn't lost at Old Trafford since 1930 against Swindon. Ahead of playing Leeds, Man Utd were second in the Premier League and it's one of only seven occasions a side in the top two of the top-flight has lost at home against a side from the third tier or below. One of the other seven was Leeds in 1976 against Crystal Palace.

Date	Match	Top-Flight Team – Position
11/02/1903	West Bromwich Albion 0–2 Tottenham Hotspur	1
12/01/1907	Newcastle United 0–1 Crystal Palace	2
10/01/1948	Burnley 0–2 Swindon Town	2
24/01/1976	Leeds United 0–1 Crystal Palace	2
23/01/1999	Aston Villa 0–2 Fulham	2
03/01/2010	Manchester United 0–1 Leeds United	2
24/01/2015	Chelsea 2–4 Bradford City	1

On the day, each Leeds United player produced an exceptional performance. Perhaps most surprising of all is that this XI of Leeds FA Cup heroes – Ankergren, Crowe, Naylor, Kisnorbo, Hughes, Howson, Kilkenny, Doyle, Johnson, Beckford, Becchio – only ever started this one match alongside one another.

Leeds went on to win promotion from League One, although only after a wobble in the second half of the season. The victory at Old Trafford was sandwiched directly into the centre of the league season, with Leeds having played twenty-three League One games before that FA Cup third round tie, winning seventeen and losing just once. After the victory at Man Utd, Leeds actually lost more league games (nine) than they won (eight). All worked out okay in the end . . .

Form Position	League One 2009–10	P	W	D	L	GF	GA	GD	Pts
1	First 23 Games	23	17	5	1	45	13	32	56
10	Second 23 Games	23	8	6	9	32	31	1	30

Leeds haven't played on 3 January since then but even when they do, the date will always be associated with that great victory against their biggest rivals.

Rochdale, Newport, Crawley . . .

Leeds United's recent FA Cup history has been one of struggle. They haven't reached a semi-final since 1987, losing 3–2 to Coventry despite going 1–0 up. Since reaching the quarter-final in 2002–03 under Terry Venables, Leeds have not gone past the fifth round once, only reaching that stage four times in the last twenty-two seasons. Forty-five different teams have played an FA Cup quarter-final since Leeds last got there, with the likes of Bristol Rovers, Lincoln City and Grimsby Town all featuring in one since 2003–04. Reading have played in four quarter-finals in that time.

Between 2017–18 and 2021–22, Leeds were knocked out in the third round in all five seasons, including defeats to League Two sides Newport County (whose side featured a certain Ben White) and Crawley Town, the latter of whom substituted on TV personality Mark Wright for a brief cameo late in the game at 3–0 up. It was one of four FA Cup matches presided over by Marcelo Bielsa, with Leeds losing all four.

Between that 2003 quarter-final against Sheffield United and the Crawley defeat, Leeds played in nine FA Cup ties against sides from a lower division. They lost seven of them.

Season	Round	Opponent	Result
2002–03	Quarter-Final	Sheffield United	Eliminated
2007–08	First Round	Hereford United	Eliminated
2008–09	Second Round	Histon	Eliminated
2009–10	Second Round	Kettering Town	Progressed
2013–14	Third Round	Rochdale	Eliminated
2016–17	Third Round	Cambridge United	Progressed
2016–17	Fourth Round	Sutton United	Eliminated
2017–18	Third Round	Newport County	Eliminated
2020–21	Third Round	Crawley Town	Eliminated

In more recent seasons, the FA Cup has at least produced some victories and some goals. After a six-game losing run between 2017 and 2022 – the club's worst run since losing seven on the bounce between 1955 and 1961 – Leeds reached the fifth round in both 2022–23 and 2023–24, the first time they'd achieved that in consecutive seasons this century. A 5–2 third round replay victory in January 2023 against Cardiff saw two players – Willy Gnonto and Patrick Bamford – score braces, a first in an FA Cup match since 1972 against Bristol Rovers when Peter Lorimer and Johnny Giles did so. That victory helped Leeds on their way to the final, though their route in 2023 would be blocked at the fifth round stage by Fulham. Bamford was once again on the scoresheet in the third round in 2023–24, this time scoring a phenomenal goal from outside the box against Peterborough which won him the club's goal of the season award. After dispatching Plymouth after a replay in the fourth round, Mateo Joseph's brace was not enough to knock out Chelsea in the fifth round, who beat Leeds 3–2, but it was no great surprise – Leeds have played nine games against Chelsea in the FA Cup and never won a single one. The ghosts of 1970 linger on.

Since Leeds won the 1972 FA Cup, 256 players have been born and played for Leeds in the FA Cup, with forty-four of those on the scoresheet for the club. The player born closest to the victory over Arsenal on 8 May 1972 to then play for Leeds in the competition is Frank Strandli, born eight days later on 16 May 1972. Fittingly, his last appearance for the club was in an FA Cup defeat in February 1994 against Oxford United.

6

THE WILDERNESS YEARS
2004 - 2018:
THE DAYS BEFORE BIELSA

To fully appreciate the impact Marcelo Bielsa had on Leeds United, it is important to look at what came before. By the time he arrived in the summer of 2018, Leeds had spent as many seasons out of the top-flight as they had within it since Howard Wilkinson had led them back in 1990, up to the relegation in 2004 amid financial implosion.

2004 - 2007

Dropping down to the Championship in 2004 saw the biggest turn-over in players in the club's history. From those glorious European nights, out went Viduka, Smith, Robinson, Harte, Matteo and many more, and in came the likes of Ricketts, Joachim, Wright, Butler and Sullivan, all of whom had Premier League experience but were not – with respect – marquee signings. Twenty-six different players (among them Steve Guppy, John Oster, Gylfi Einarsson and Leandre Griffit) made their debuts in 2004–05, the most in a single season in the club's history. It wasn't quite 'only me and Gary Kelly' as manager Kevin Blackwell insisted, with Lucas Radebe still there, alongside players like Michael Duberry, Frazer Richardson, Aaron Lennon and Matthew Kilgallon, but seven new faces made their debut on the opening day against Derby County, the most since the first game after the Second World War in 1946. Richardson was the first scorer in the newly named Coca-Cola Championship and that result left Leeds in fifth but that was their highest position all season, ending Christmas Day in nineteenth and only six points above the relegation zone. The high point of the first half of the season had been a 36-year-old Brian Deane, in his second spell, scoring four times against QPR in November and becoming the club's oldest ever hat-trick scorer – breaking his former teammate Gordon Strachan's record by 227 days.

The club's debutants slowed down in the second half of the season; from February onwards only five players made their first appearances, and two of those would play a key role in a much better campaign in 2005–06. Midfielder Shaun Derry signed from Crystal Palace and scored in each of his first two home games (then scored in none of his next thirty-four at Elland Road), while Rob Hulse signed initially on loan from West Brom and became the first player since Charlie Keetley in 1928 to score as many as five goals in his opening five games for Leeds. With this impact it was little surprise when he was made a permanent addition, especially given goals had been hard to come by – David Healy, who joined in October, had been top scorer on seven goals, only one ahead of Hulse's six. The club's initial front two, Joachim and Ricketts, had managed two between them, both of which were scored by Joachim as Ricketts failed to find the net at all in twenty-one league appearances. It remains the most league games by any Leeds player in the number 10 shirt without scoring.

Leeds United No. 10s	League Games without Scoring
Michael Ricketts	21
Noel Hunt	20
Tom Hindle	13
Don Revie	13
Gwyn Thomas	12

After a fourteenth-place finish in 2004–05, Leeds made big improvements in 2005–06. With Hulse taking over the 10 shirt from Ricketts (who had been demoted to number 30 for his last few games) and new signings Eddie Lewis, Robbie Blake and Richard Cresswell all having a positive impact, Leeds spent 227 days in the play off spots. They even harboured hopes of pipping Neil Warnock's Sheffield United to second place, as Reading ran away with the league on 106 points.

The most memorable day of the season came at St Mary's on 19 November, when Leeds found themselves 3–0 down to Southampton only to come back and win 4–3, with all four goals scored after the 70th minute, the latest any side has ever recovered from 3–0 down to win in Championship history. Liam Miller's winner – his only goal for Leeds – in the 86th minute gave Leeds victory from three goals down at half-time for the first time in the club's history, while it was the first time since the 4–3 win over Derby back in November 1997 that Leeds had come from 3–0 down to win.

That win kick-started a good run of form for Leeds; between then and victory over Crystal Palace on 4 March they won forty-two points, only six fewer than Reading and eleven more than Sheffield United had in that time, cutting the gap to the Blades to six points with a game in hand. Sadly, Leeds only won one of their final ten games, scoring just six goals, ending the season fifth and in the play-offs. The opponents were Preston who, in the same time Leeds had won one out of ten games, had picked up twenty-four points and were the Championship's form side going into the semi-finals. Leeds knocked Preston out 3–1 on aggregate, as goals from Hulse (his last for the club) and Richardson gave Leeds a 2–0 win in the second leg at Deepdale. Late in the game, both Stephen Crainey and Richard Cresswell had been sent off, only the sixth time two players had been red carded in the same game for Leeds and it remains the last time Leeds won a game despite going down to nine men (the other two wins were against 1860 Munich in August 2000 and Arsenal in August 2001).

Spooked by pre-match fireworks in Cardiff, Leeds lost the final 3–0 against a Watford side whose manager Aidy Boothroyd had been coach at Leeds in 2004–05, while their XI featured Matthew Spring and Marlon King, who had both played for Leeds the previous season too. We probably don't need to dwell on that game any further.

Leeds made a dismal start to the following season, and manager Kevin Blackwell was sacked early in 2006–07, with the club twenty-third in the table, and replaced by Dennis Wise. Wise was keen to improve the players' fitness, with Leeds dropping points to late goals against QPR (90th minute, 2–2), Crystal Palace (90th, 1–0), Cardiff (83rd, 1–0) and Wolves (90th, 1–0) within the opening eight games alone. The squad had a distinctly senior feel to it, with 261 appearances in total by players over the age of thirty (the second most in one season ever), while debutants included Geoff Horsfield (thirty-two), Alan Wright (thirty-five), Ugo Ehiogu (thirty-four), Robbie Elliott (thirty-three), Tore Andre Flo (thirty-three), Alan Thompson (thirty-three) and Radostin Kishishev (thirty-two). Four of the club's six oldest starting line-ups ever were named that season, including the oldest of all time against West Brom in January 2007, with every player born in the 1970s and an average age of 31 years and 167 days.

Line-up vs WBA, 20 January 2007	Age
Neil Sullivan	36 years, 330 days
Armando Sa	31 years, 126 days
Hayden Foxe	29 years, 211 days
Rui Marques	29 years, 139 days
Robbie Elliott	33 years, 26 days
Robbie Blake	30 years, 322 days
Kevin Nicholls	28 years, 18 days
Alan Thompson	33 years, 29 days
Eddie Lewis	32 years, 248 days
Tore Andre Flo	33 years, 219 days
David Healy	27 years, 168 days

If the season had only counted from when Wise took over, then Leeds would have picked up enough points to secure safety and finished twentieth. Sadly, from Christmas until the end of the campaign, Leeds only emerged briefly from the relegation places once after a 2–1 win over Plymouth in April via a late Lubo Michalik winner. Leeds were relegated after failing to beat Ipswich in their final home game of the season and, unthinkably, were relegated to League One. For the first time in the club's history, in 2007–08 they would be playing outside the top two divisions.

2007 – 2010

Wise remained in charge for the following season in League One, despite the fifteen-point deduction imposed (at that stage, the second-biggest ever deduction in the EFL, behind Peterborough's nineteen points in 1967–68) and Leeds made the best start to a league season in their history, winning twelve of their first fifteen games. Having been on the receiving end of late goals early in the previous season, many of those scored during the opening weeks in 2007–08 were late winners; against Tranmere (Kandol eighty-ninth), Southend (Flo eighty-fifth, Marques eighty-eighth and Beckford ninetieth, the latter two of which I missed as my dad wanted to 'beat the traffic'), Nottingham Forest (Beckford eighty-ninth), Yeovil (De Vries eighty-ninth) and Oldham (Westlake ninetieth). By the turn of the year Leeds were third, but Wise left in late January to join Newcastle as director of football. However, many fans felt it was the departure of his assistant, Gus Poyet, in October that had been the reason for the club's downturn in form, which was the best in League One up to 27 October, but only fifth best from then until Wise's final game against Luton on 26 January. It was unlikely Leeds were going to maintain that early season form, but a drop of 1.09 points per game tells its own story.

Form	Team	P	W	D	L	Actual Pts	Points per Game
1st	Wise/Poyet	13	11	2	0	35	2.69
5th	Wise without Poyet	15	7	3	5	24	1.60

Replacing Wise was club legend Gary McAllister, an ever-present in the 1991–92 title-winning campaign. It was a slightly rocky start, as two wins in eight and a squandered two-goal lead at Port Vale left Leeds tenth. But from 22 March until the end of the campaign, Leeds enjoyed the best record in the division, as twenty-two points from nine games carried them into the play-offs against Carlisle United – the team who'd ended Leeds' unbeaten start to the season in November.

THE WILDERNESS YEARS 2004 - 2018

The late season signing of a 33-year-old Dougie Freedman proved an inspired choice, with McAllister pairing the Scot up front with Jermaine Beckford in place of Tresor Kandol. Freedman was on hand with five league goals in the run-in, including two in a 3–2 win over Carlisle in April, and he was involved in all three goals across both legs in the play-offs. After netting a last-minute goal in the first leg to crucially halve the deficit to 2–1, he assisted both of Jonny Howson's goals in the second leg as Leeds made it to Wembley with a 3–2 aggregate win. Howson, who became the club's youngest ever captain when he was given the armband away at Millwall in April 2008 aged 19 years and 334 days, was the club's youngest scorer of a brace since Alan Smith in 2000. Unfortunately, neither Freedman (on his thirty-fourth birthday), Howson or twenty-goal Beckford could find the net at Wembley against Doncaster, with Leeds going down 1–0 on the eve of my fourteenth birthday. It wasn't a fun bus journey home.

The following season Leeds were expected to win the League One title and the season started well, with thirty goals scored before the end of September. There were big wins in the League Cup against Chester City (5–2) and Crystal Palace (4–0) and a 5–2 demolition of Crewe in the league with five different players on the scoresheet – including, for the first time in a Leeds shirt, Fabian Delph. At the end of September Leeds were third and only a point off the top, but by the time a 3–1 defeat to MK Dons came around on 20 December they were fifteen points behind league leaders Leicester City and had lost five in a row, including a 1–0 defeat to non-league Histon in the FA Cup. McAllister was sacked after the MK Dons defeat – which featured Mansour Assoumani's one appearance – and replaced by Simon Grayson.

Robert Snodgrass scored the final goal of McAllister's reign and the first of Grayson's, in a 1–1 draw with Leicester on Boxing Day. Although Snodgrass only scored five goals up to the end of that season, his assists were mounting up, assisting eleven goals in the final fourteen games of the season, enjoying the most creative season by a Leeds player since Strachan in 1989–90. Leeds recovered from tenth in mid-January to finish fourth; after a disappointing defeat to Carlisle in January, Leeds won more points than any other side in the division in that time. This run included an eleven-game winning streak at Elland Road – the best since 1969 – with Beckford in great form, scoring fourteen goals in those wins.

Grayson had tightened up the defence too, never conceding more than twice in any of the season's twenty-five league games under him. The signing of centre-back Richard Naylor in January was the catalyst, as Leeds won fifteen of their twenty-two games with Naylor in the XI and only conceded sixteen goals with him on the pitch. Sam Sodje ended the season as Naylor's defensive partner with Leeds only conceding two goals in the 420 minutes he was on the pitch (one of which was a spectacular headed Sodje own goal against Tranmere) as Leeds secured a play-off spot. It was heartbreak yet again though as Leeds failed to get past Millwall in the semis, losing 2–1 on aggregate despite Luciano Becchio's goal in the second leg nearly taking the roof off Elland Road.

The 2009–10 season was, thankfully, Leeds United's last in League One. Despite losing the talented Delph in the summer, Leeds started the season with a run of eight wins in all competitions, their best ever run from the start of the season. By the turn of 2009, Leeds had only lost two games all season (a 1–0 defeat to Liverpool in the League Cup and a 2–1 defeat, naturally, at Millwall) and were eight points clear at the top of the league. In 2009, Leeds won thirty-two league games, a total that has been bettered by just three teams in the entire history of the Football League in one year.

Year	Team	Wins
2021	Manchester City	36
1982	Liverpool	33
2011	Southampton	33
1948	Rotherham United	32
1964	Tranmere Rovers	32
2005	Chelsea	32
2009	Leeds United	32

2010 started pretty well too, with a 1–0 win over Manchester United in the FA Cup – the first win at Old Trafford since 1981. But from the best form in the country in 2009, Leeds started slipping and dropping points, with a 2–2 draw with Spurs in the FA Cup fourth round sandwiched between a 2–0 defeat at Exeter and 3–0 defeat at Swindon in League One. By the end of January they'd dropped to second and wouldn't go back on top of a league table until 2017. In the first twenty-one league games of the season, Leeds only fell behind in two games. In the final twenty-five, they went behind sixteen times. Between 13 March and 3 April, Leeds lost four in a row without scoring a goal, and fell to fourth in the league.

Beckford was dropped to the bench for the run-in and replaced by Max Gradel as form improved. With four wins in six games, Leeds had their destiny in their own hands on the final day, needing a win for promotion. Gradel was sent off against Bristol Rovers and Leeds went 1–0 down early in the second half (and hadn't come back to win after conceding that late into a game at Elland Road since November 2001) but Howson, on as a sub, equalised in the 59th minute and Beckford's eighty-fifth – and final – Leeds goal in the 63rd minute won promotion. Leeds were back in the Championship and with a side containing the likes of Beckford, Becchio, Johnson, Gradel, Howson, Kilkenny and Snodgrass, the future looked bright.

2010 – 2012

Beckford was the first to depart, joining Premier League side Everton almost immediately after promotion was confirmed. His replacement in the number 9 shirt was Billy Paynter, who had scored four league goals against Leeds in 2009–10 for Swindon Town. It took him seventeen games to score his first goal, the longest ever wait for a Leeds number 9 to score, and eventually left with fewer goals for Leeds (three in twenty-eight games) than he'd scored for Swindon in those two matches in 2010. Luckily, goals were forthcoming in other areas with four players – Becchio (nineteen), Gradel (eighteen), Howson (ten) and Davide Somma (eleven) – all netting at least ten, the first time that many players had achieved that since 1973–74. Only Norwich in second scored more goals than Leeds in 2010–11, with eighty-one, but of the teams in the top half only Leicester conceded more than Leeds (seventy). Preston North End ended the season relegated but in September, despite being 4–1 down, recovered to beat Leeds 6–4 at a shellshocked Elland Road, with Jon Parkin scoring his only Championship hat-trick. It is one of only four unique results in Leeds United's history, and the club won the other three.

Date	Opponents	Competition	Score
07/04/1934	Leicester City	Division One	W 8–0
03/10/1967	Spora Luxembourg	Fairs Cup	W 9–0
17/09/1969	Lyn Oslo	European Cup	W 10–0
28/09/2010	Preston North End	Championship	L 6–4

Leeds were second on Christmas Day thanks to victory over eventual champions QPR at a frozen but happy Elland Road, which was the highest position they'd been in since dropping out of the Premier League in 2004. Between 30 October and 12 March, the only two games Leeds lost in the Championship were in Wales, losing at Cardiff in January and Swansea in February. Despite spending 174 days in the top six, Leeds finished seventh, although a 2–1 victory at QPR on the final day completed a league double over the champions.

The win at QPR was the last to feature Bradley Johnson and Neil Kilkenny, who'd made a near identical total of appearances since signing in January 2008 (Johnson 140, Kilkenny 144); both left the club after failing to agree new contracts. The League One promotion team broke up further at the start of the 2011–12 season when Max Gradel left to join Ligue 1 side St Etienne. Ross McCormack, who'd only scored two goals the previous season, took over the mantle of main goalscorer with nineteen goals, including a run of six consecutive scoring games early in the season. Club captain Howson featured in nineteen of the first twenty league games (missing the other after receiving his only Leeds red card against Middlesbrough in August) before getting injured against Millwall in December. That would be his 225th and final game for the club. He was sold to Norwich in

January, and no other player would hit 225 games for the club until Stuart Dallas in 2021. Local players are always looked upon fondly by fans and Howson, born in Morley, was a vital link between players and fans. After losing so many key names from the promotion side, it was his departure that hurt most of all.

A week after Howson's sale, another Leeds supporter was heading out of the door. Manager Simon Grayson was sacked following a 4–1 defeat to Birmingham City, with giant striker Nikola Zigic scoring all four; his only hat-trick for Birmingham. Replacing Grayson was Neil Warnock, who'd won the Championship the previous season with QPR. He said he wanted to build his team around Robert Snodgrass, who got thirteen goals and thirteen assists in 2011–12, but he also left for Norwich in the summer as Leeds finished fourteenth.

Warnock is a known promotion specialist, leading Notts County, Sheffield United, QPR and Cardiff to the top-flight in his career, but he couldn't work his magic at Leeds. The low point came in March 2012 as Leeds lost 7–3 to Nottingham Forest at Elland Road, the only time they've conceded seven in a home game, with Garath McCleary following in Zigic's footsteps by scoring four goals, also his only career hat-trick. Leeds were tenth when Warnock took over but if results only counted from his first game until the end of the season, Leeds would have finished twentieth.

2012 – 2016

After having such a young and exciting team on their return to the Championship, the average age of the team went up considerably with Warnock in charge. The starting XI age rose from 25 years and 252 days in 2011–12 to 28 years and 37 days in 2012–13. There were 266 appearances by players aged thirty or older, including forty-seven by Paddy Kenny, forty-five by El Hadji Diouf and thirty-three by Michael Brown (who managed to get booked in eleven of those games). It's a record number of appearances by players over the age of thirty in one season.

Season	Appearances by Players Aged 30+
2012–13	266
2006–07	261
2004–05	251
2005–06	249
1991–92	247
1992–93	243

Promotion never looked likely as Leeds spent just two days in the play-off positions all season. Form in the cups was better, reaching the FA Cup fifth round – losing comfortably to Man City – and the League Cup quarter-final for the first time since 1996, where they went in at half-time 1–0 ahead against European champions Chelsea thanks to a Luciano Becchio goal. Leeds then lost 5–1, one of only two times they've led at half-time then lost by four goals, along with a 5–1 loss at Shrewsbury in 1983.

Becchio was in exceptional form and had scored nineteen goals by mid-January, with his goals per game of 0.61 in 2012–13 the best since Beckford in 2008–09 (0.81). Only five players in English football had scored more times than Becchio up to his final game on 19 January but Warnock inexplicably allowed him to join Norwich (those lot again), receiving striker Steve Morison in return. Morison scored three goals in sixteen games and joined Millwall on loan for the 2013–14 season, while Warnock was sacked in early April following a 2–1 defeat to Derby on Easter Monday. Becchio didn't score a single goal for Norwich and his only two further goals in English football were on loan at Rotherham in 2014. It was a move that made no sense for anyone. Leeds ended the season thirteenth, seven points from the play-offs and seven points from relegation.

Leeds had tried the 2010–11 Championship winning manager in Warnock and now they went for the man who won the 2011–12 title in Brian McDermott, recently sacked by Reading despite winning the January 2013 Premier League manager of the month award. The season started brightly, with a last minute Luke Murphy winner on his debut against Brighton on a sunny day at Elland Road in front of 33,432 fans, the biggest crowd for a home league game since September 2010. The team was reliant on the considerable abilities of Ross McCormack, who scored twenty-eight goals and assisted another eight, the most goals and assists of any player in the Football League in 2013–14. Leeds only scored fifty-nine goals themselves, meaning McCormack had a direct hand in 61%, the highest total of any player in a Championship season since that campaign, which was the first season that Opta began recording assists for the division.

Season	Team	Player	Goals	Assists	Team Goals	%
2013/14	Leeds United	Ross McCormack	28	8	59	61.0%
2022/23	Coventry City	Viktor Gyökeres	21	10	58	53.4%
2020/21	Brentford	Ivan Toney	31	10	79	51.9%
2023/24	Blackburn Rovers	Sam Szmodics	27	4	60	51.7%
2021/22	Bristol City	Andreas Weimann	22	10	62	51.6%
2016/17	Leeds United	Chris Wood	27	4	61	50.8%
2020/21	Blackburn Rovers	Adam Armstrong	28	5	65	50.8%

Data via Opta

Leeds were sixth on Boxing Day and only ten points behind league leaders Leicester but things fizzled out and they ended the season in fifteenth, forty-five points behind the top and fifteen points behind a play-off place. Between defeats to Nottingham Forest on 29 December and Watford on 8 April, Leeds were statistically the second-worst team in the league, ahead only of Blackpool, losing thirteen out of nineteen games and conceding thirty-nine goals, the most of any side in that time. Among those defeats was a 6–0 loss at Sheffield Wednesday, the club's heaviest league defeat since 1959, and consecutive home defeats to Bolton and Reading, lost 5–1 and 4–2 respectively. It was a grim time, with the only bright spots of the second half of that campaign coming in early February, when Leeds came from a goal down to hammer local rivals Huddersfield 5–1 via a Ross McCormack hat-trick, and beating Yeovil Town 2–1 at Huish Park, with Stephen Warnock scoring a free-kick from forty yards (the furthest distance free-kick goal scored in the Championship in 2013–14) with some help from the swirling wind. Leeds lost twenty-one league games in 2013–14, their most without getting relegated since losing twenty-three in 1936–37.

As the Massimo Cellino era truly began, McCormack departed in the summer to join Fulham, leaving huge boots to fill; as well as his goals, he had been the league's most creative player, creating over one hundred chances in 2013–14, and of Leeds' 602 shots, McCormack was involved in 42% of them (143 shots, 108 chances created). McDermott also departed to be replaced by – and I still can't believe I'm typing this – Dave Hockaday, whose only previous managerial experience was at non-league Forest Green Rovers, where he'd only avoided relegation to the Conference South in his first season due to Salisbury being expelled from the league instead. He lasted six games – at that point the shortest Leeds managerial reign in games – and was sacked by Cellino after losing 2–1 to Bradford City in the League Cup, despite having gone 1–0 up in the 82nd minute via Matt Smith. Smith was also sold in August to Fulham on the night of the club's infamous 'don't go to bed just yet' tweet, as fans who waited up for a new signing were instead treated to news of the departures of Smith and young striker Dominic Poleon. The Hockaday reign was a disaster; Luke Murphy had been sent off in the first half of the Bradford defeat, the fourth red card under Hockaday and as many as they'd had in fifty-four games under McDermott, and the team managed just twenty-eight shots in four league games under him – the fewest of any Championship side.

After four games under caretaker Neil Redfearn, in which Leeds had the best form in the division with ten points, Darko Milanic was appointed and lasted thirty-two days and six winless games, breaking Brian Clough and Jock Stein's unwanted record for shortest spell in charge in days (both managed forty-four days in 1974 and 1978 respectively). Leeds twice scored first under Milanic through a Mirco Antenucci goal and lost both games 2–1 to Rotherham and Wolves, seemingly frightened to attack after going ahead; they only mustered sixteen shots on target in six games under the Slovenian, compared to facing forty-two shots on target of their own, the second most in the division. Redfearn stepped up again as caretaker, but Leeds were twenty-first in mid-January with relegation back to League One a distinct possibility. They then put together a run of eight wins in twelve games to shoot up the table, including completing a league double over eventual champions Bournemouth and securing a 1–0 victory over top of the table Middlesbrough in February with Marco Silvestri making ten saves. Silvestri made his final appearance of the season on 14 April in a 2–0 defeat to Norwich, with six players ruling themselves out of the following game, a 2–1 away loss at Charlton which was a fifth consecutive defeat.

Since the departure of Robert Snodgrass, many Leeds fans felt the team was lacking wingers. Naturally, we were delighted with the announcement of the signings of Jimmy Kebe and Cameron Stewart the night before the away game at Sheffield Wednesday in January. Both started and were part of the side that lost 6–0 there, becoming two of six players to lose by six or more goals on their Leeds debuts. The others are Bert Worsley (1–8 vs Stoke in 1934), goalkeeper Jack Daniels (1–7 vs Chelsea in 1935) and Ken Gadsby and Gordon Hodgson (both in the 1–7 loss to Everton in 1937).

Leeds ended the 2014–15 season in fifteenth, signing off with a goalless draw against a sombrero-wearing Steve Evans and his Rotherham side. But there was cause for hope; Redfearn had given opportunities to young players, with Lewis Cook, Charlie Taylor, Alex Mowatt and Sam Byram all playing regularly, and a midfielder named Kalvin Phillips made his debut in April.

> The average age of Neil Redfearn's starting XI's for Leeds was 24 years and 309 days, the youngest line-ups of any manager in the club's history.

Uwe Rosler replaced Redfearn as manager in May 2015 and promised to play 'heavy metal' football with attack in mind, but in his eleven Championship games Leeds only managed thirty-six shots on target – the second fewest of any team – and created a league low ten big chances. Six of his first seven games were drawn (with one of those seeing Leeds knocked out of the League Cup on penalties by Doncaster), winning the other away at Derby with new striker Chris Wood brilliantly scoring his only from outside the box for the club. Rosler was the first Leeds manager to remain unbeaten in his first seven games, but he lost four of his next five and was sacked with the club in eighteenth and only three points clear of relegation.

Steve Evans, minus his sombrero, was picked as his replacement and although he had promotions on his CV, they were in Leagues One, Two and non-league, with a win ratio of just 24% in the Championship. He improved that to 34% while Leeds manager, with twelve wins in thirty-five league games, and never lost more than two in a row. But it didn't start brilliantly; Leeds were 2–0 down inside six minutes against Blackburn in his first home game, extending the winless run at Elland Road to twelve games – the longest in the club's history. Alex Mowatt ended that miserable sequence with a brilliant strike from range to beat Cardiff City 1–0, and then followed it up with a phenomenal goal at Huddersfield in a 3–0 win, his twelfth (and last) league goal for the club – eight of which came from outside the box.

Byram made the last appearance of his first spell in a 2–1 defeat at Ipswich in January, a match in which Leeds went 1–0 ahead after twelve seconds through Souleymane Doukara. Leeds lost three of five games in February, scoring just once via a brilliant Lewis Cook long-range effort against Fulham, and were beaten 4–0 by Brighton on leap year day, finding themselves 4–0 down in the first half for the first time since April 1991 against Liverpool. Evans faced former side Rotherham – now managed by Neil Warnock, who'd replaced none other than Neil Redfearn – in April and despite having twenty-six attempts lost 2–1, with centre-half Giuseppe Bellusci going in goal to face a 90th minute Greg Halford penalty after Silvestri was sent off (he didn't save it). In the next game, Bellusci conceded a late penalty against QPR – the fourth he'd conceded in his two seasons with the club, the joint most of any Championship player – spoiling nineteen-year-old debutant goalkeeper Bailey Peacock-Farrell's clean sheet in a 1–1 draw. Leeds were on course for their first top half finish since 2010–11 as they led Preston 1–0 on the final day, but a Scott Wootton mistake in his last game for the club saw North End equalise in the final seconds, knocking Leeds down into thirteenth and confirming a fifth consecutive bottom half finish. Attending games in this era was done out of love for the club rather than in any excitement.

2016 – 2018

Evans was replaced by Garry Monk, who had led Swansea to their highest Premier League finish in 2014–15 before being sacked the following season following a poor run of form. Monk had only just turned thirty-seven and Leeds was only his second job in management. He made a bad start, losing 3–0 to QPR without a shot on target in the opening game of the season – the heaviest opening day defeat since 1989–90, when Leeds were beaten 5–2 by Newcastle. Howard Wilkinson's team recovered to win the league that season, but few expected Monk to lead such a recovery after four defeats in the first six games of the season left Leeds in the relegation zone. However, the fourth of those defeats – a 1–0 loss to Huddersfield Town and a terrible match which saw just ten attempts from both sides combined – saw Swedish centre-half Pontus Jansson make his first league start for the club. Jansson's arrival helped spark a fine run of league form, and from 13 September to 13 January Leeds won the second most points in the division; forty-four from twenty games. They went third in the table after a Friday night win over Derby, their highest position since December 2010, and Leeds fans happily chanted of Jansson's desire to head bricks. While that isn't a stat Opta collect, we can say only three players made more headed clearances per ninety minutes that season than he did. Jansson was also adept with the ball at his feet, having the best pass accuracy of any Leeds player that season at 85%. He built a bond with the supporters that hadn't been seen for many years, and perhaps more than anyone was responsible for rebuilding the link between fans and players prior to the arrival of a certain Argentinian coach.

Championship – 2016–17	Headed Clearances per Ninety Minutes
Danny Batth	9.6
Marc Roberts	8.9
Richard Stearman	7.8
Pontus Jansson	7.7
Angus MacDonald	7.2

Data via Opta

Defensively Leeds improved and from just four clean sheets at Elland Road in 2015–16, they kept twelve in 2016–17, including a run of six in a row in six consecutive home victories in December and January. Joining Jansson at the back was loanee Kyle Bartley, signed from Monk's old club Swansea and he missed just one game all season, the 1-1 draw at Aston Villa in which Jansson scored. Bartley scored six goals, the most by a Leeds number 5 in a season since Chris Fairclough scored seven in 1989–90. Leeds were a huge threat from set pieces and only Newcastle with twelve scored more goals from corners than Leeds' eleven. Only one player assisted more goals from set plays than creative new signing Pablo Hernández (seven), which included a run of four corner assists in the space of five matches in early 2017, assisting Bartley, Chris Wood twice and Jansson in games against Rotherham, Derby, Barnsley and Blackburn – the latter a 90th minute winner in front of thousands of travelling Leeds supporters at Ewood Park.

At right-back, Luke Ayling was an early season signing from Bristol City and he put in a number of impressive displays, ending the season as the second most fouled Championship defender, winning sixty fouls as the 'Ayling flop' entered the Leeds lexicon. Left-back duties were shared between Charlie Taylor and Gaetano Berardi, the latter a natural right-back who performed valiantly on the opposite side. 2016–17 was his only full season with Leeds without getting sent off, and he only received one yellow card all season. As well as singing for Jansson, the great 'Luke Ayling and Berardi, Pontus Jansson, Kyle Bartley' chant showed that it was this back four the fans liked best and for good reason – Leeds averaged 1.87 points per game when they started together, compared to 1.52 when they didn't.

Leeds were not an especially creative team under Monk and had just 151 shots on target all season, the lowest of any Championship side, and ranked sixteenth for touches in the opposition box. But they didn't need to have many shots on target to score with Chris Wood in the team, who ended the season as the Championship's leading scorer with twenty-seven from just forty-four shots on target. Wood scored thirty in all competitions, becoming only the sixth player in the club's history to hit that number in a season. Two of them came in a superb 2–0 home win over Brighton in March, a result which put Leeds fourth, eight points behind the Seagulls in second and eight points clear of Fulham in seventh with just eight games to play. The play-offs looked a certainty, but this is Leeds United of course. The Whites' form hit the rocks and across April and May only two teams picked up fewer points (six), with the only win in an eight-game run coming against Preston at Elland Road. In the penultimate game of the season at home to Norwich, Leeds found themselves 3–0 down in the first half, conceding as many goals that afternoon as they had in the first half of the other twenty-two games at Elland Road combined that season. Leeds recovered to draw 3–3 – the first time they'd avoided defeat when three down since the 4–3 win at Southampton in 2005 – but the point left Leeds in seventh, three points behind Fulham in sixth but trailing by thirteen on goal difference. A 1–1 draw on the final day at Wigan confirmed Leeds' seventh-place finish. This ended their five-season streak of bottom-half finishes, but after spending 156 days in the top six — ninety five more than Fulham – it was a disappointing end to a season of real promise.

Despite the setback, Leeds wanted Monk to stay but he opted to join

Middlesbrough in the summer. Thomas Christiansen – who'd played twice for Barcelona in the early 1990s and been joint top scorer in the Bundesliga in 2002–03 when playing for VfL Bochum – was chosen as his successor after leading APOEL to the 2016–17 Cypriot title. He could hardly have made a better start, remaining unbeaten in his first nine matches (the best ever unbeaten start by a Leeds manager) and even allowing for two goalless draws in August against Preston and Fulham, Leeds scored twenty-three goals in their first nine matches.

Christiansen kept hold of most of the Monk team, as well as adding Spanish attacking midfielder Samuel Sáiz, who scored a hat-trick on his debut against Port Vale and had five goals in his first five games – a total only Charlie Keetley has beaten (six in 1927–28). Chris Wood left to join Premier League side Burnley in August and was replaced up front by burly loan striker Pierre-Michel Lasogga from Hamburg, and he fired in a brace on his debut in a 5–0 win over Burton Albion. This was the biggest Leeds win since 2004's 6–1 hammering of QPR, and a game in which Leeds had thirty shots, 69% possession and faced just one shot – all season bests for the club. The following game was a 2–0 home win over Birmingham, sending Leeds top of the Championship for the very first time since relegation in 2004, after spending 2,757th days in the division. At this stage, Leeds had the third most shots and faced the fewest shots on target in the Championship, but unfortunately this was Christiansen's peak and the wheels soon came off.

In the next game away at Millwall – who'd faced thirty-one shots in their previous game at QPR, the most by a team all season – Leeds managed just one shot and fell to a limp 1–0 defeat. From that defeat until Christiansen's last game in charge, a 4–1 loss to Cardiff in early February, Leeds ranked twenty-second for shots and twenty-fourth for touches in the opposition box across the Championship, and Leeds were tenth in the table, twenty-four points off the top. Red cards also became the norm, with four in the last five games under Christiansen as Samuel Sáiz, Eunan O'Kane, Liam Cooper and Gaetano Berardi were all given their marching orders in defeats to Newport, Ipswich, Millwall and Cardiff.

Christiansen's replacement was Paul Heckingbottom, manager of a Barnsley side who were twenty-first in the Championship and, since beating Leeds the previous January, had the fewest points of any ever-present side in the division, and had lost nine of their previous fourteen matches. Leeds didn't win any of his first three games, though Lasogga found the net in all three to give him a respectable return of ten goals in seventeen starts. After a season that began with six clean sheets in seven games, Leeds managed just two in their sixteen matches under Heckingbottom, facing the fifth most shots, and only relegated Sunderland kept fewer clean sheets than Leeds. They were seven points behind a play-off spot before Heckingbottom's first game but they ended the season, once again, in the bottom half in thirteenth, fifteen points behind sixth. Leeds had the nineteenth worst form in the league from 10 February to the end of the campaign, losing as many games in that time as Heckingbottom's former side Barnsley did.

Championship bottom six table – 10 February – 6 May 2018

Team	P	W	D	L	GF	GA	Pts
Leeds United	16	4	4	8	18	27	16
Birmingham City	16	5	1	10	16	27	16
Barnsley	16	3	5	8	19	28	14
Bolton Wanderers	17	3	5	9	12	28	14
Sunderland	16	2	6	8	21	28	12
Reading	16	2	6	8	15	31	12

Despite a 2–0 victory over QPR in the final game of the season, it's fair to say things never clicked under Heckingbottom's leadership and most fans expected further managerial – and squad – change. Heckingbottom was indeed sacked in June, but few could have predicted that eight of that final day's starting XI would play crucial roles as the club was reborn the following season. Even fewer could have imagined the seismic transformation that one man was about to inspire.

It was time for the Marcelo Bielsa era to begin.

7

THE BIELSA ERA

'It will be incredible for English football to have him in the Premier League next season. Winning titles helps to have a job next season but at the end of your life, what you remember is not the titles you have won, what you remember is the memories you have and whether the manager taught you a lot. What we remember are the experiences and the memories, the players you have had, the managers you have had. Marcelo is at the top of the list. Absolutely at the top of the list.'

These were the words of Pep Guardiola in July 2020, just after Marcelo Bielsa had completed what he set out to achieve when he took the Leeds job in June 2018 – leading the club back to the Premier League. Seeing Bielsa celebrate with the players at Elland Road on the night promotion was guaranteed; the video of him arriving at Thorp Arch to be serenaded by the players singing his name, him punching the air in delight; reluctantly lifting the Championship trophy, at the behest of the players, after the final game of the season at Elland Road. All wonderful memories.

The feeling of optimism in that era is certainly unrivalled in my time supporting Leeds, the belief that no matter who we were playing, we had a chance because Bielsa was in the dugout, and that stayed with me right until the end of his time at the club (aside from, maybe, a couple of punishing away games against Man City and Liverpool in the last few months of his reign).

Bielsa's attacking, possession-based philosophies were backed up in the data for the Championship in the two seasons he was there. As recently as 2014–15, Leeds ranked twenty-second in the division for shots attempted and were bottom for big chances created. In 2016–17, when they finished seventh, Leeds ranked twenty-third for shots and twenty-fourth for shots on target. The season before Bielsa arrived, in

2017–18, Leeds were eighteenth for shots, twenty-second for touches in the opposition box and fourteenth for both average possession and successful passes.

That all changed under Bielsa: Leeds ranked first for shots attempted in both 2018–19 and 2019–20. They were second for shots on target in 2018–19, then first in 2019–20, and led the way for touches in the opposition box in both seasons.

Leeds United – Championship	Total Shots	Championship Rank
2013–14	602	17
2014–15	520	23
2015–16	571	15
2016–17	521	22
2017–18	548	18
2018–19	791	1
2019–20	755	1

Leeds United – Championship	Shots on Target	Championship Rank
2013–14	179	19
2014–15	157	22
2015–16	155	23
2016–17	151	24
2017–18	170	18
2018–19	242	2
2019–20	251	1

Data via Opta

Leeds began controlling Championship games under Bielsa – in 2018–19, Leeds' average possession (first in the division) was 64.5%, a 15% improvement on the previous season, while they completed 47%

more passes in the first season under Bielsa than they had in 2017–18. With patterns of play drummed into them in training, the accuracy of passing also improved hugely, going from 72.8% in 2017–18 up to 79.4% in 2018–19, with another slight increase in 2019–20 to 80.2%.

Leeds United – Championship	Average Possession	Championship Rank
2013–14	49.1%	12
2014–15	48.1%	17
2015–16	51.0%	10
2016–17	50.6%	10
2017–18	49.6%	14
2018–19	64.5%	1
2019–20	64.3%	1

Leeds United – Championship	Completed Passes	Championship Rank
2013–14	11,809	16
2014–15	12,972	14
2015–16	13,612	11
2016–17	14,106	11
2017–18	12,982	14
2018–19	19,042	2
2019–20	18,504	2

The 3–1 victory over Stoke on the opening day of 2018–19 – which Bielsa had predicted to his players pre-match would be won by two clear goals due to the heat – set a few common trends of Leeds under their new Argentinian coach.

The first was that, while their shot count of twelve was nothing spectacular, they'd only allowed nine shots on their own goal. Across their two Bielsa seasons in the Championship, Leeds would have more shots than their opponent in 83% of games (seventy-eight of ninety-four); in the two previous seasons, this percentage was down at 36% of games (sixteen in 2016–17, seventeen in 2017–18). The greatest shot deficit Leeds suffered in a Bielsa Championship game was seven (5 vs 12), which came away at Millwall in October 2019 in a game they saw Leeds reduced to ten men after just fourteen minutes when Gaetano Berardi was sent off (incorrectly; this red was later rescinded). Even in the Millwall defeat, facing seventy-six minutes with a man disadvantage, Leeds enjoyed an incredible total of 68% possession and completed almost 300 more passes than the Lions. It remains the highest possession and most completed passes (461) by a team with a red card as early as the 14th minute that Opta has on record for the Championship.

The second trend of the Stoke match was having a higher share of possession; similar to the shot total, the 51% of possession in that match was nothing out of the ordinary (Leeds' second lowest of the entire season) but it was one of forty-seven Championship games that campaign where Leeds had the control of possession. The only exception came away at Sheffield United in a 1–0 win in December, when the Whites had 44% possession. Their overall average possession (including play-offs) in 2018–19 of 64.2% was, at that time, the most by a Championship team Opta had on record in one season. Leeds in 2019–20 then overtook it (by 0.1%), enjoying more possession in forty-three of forty-six games in their promotion season. Perhaps the starkest shift from one game to the next against an opponent was between games against Bolton in 2018 – in March at Elland Road, Leeds enjoyed just 43.6% possession and completed 191 passes; in their next meeting in December, Leeds had a 26.8% increase in possession, up to 70.4%, and completed 164% more passes (191 in March, 504 in December). There were only twenty-eight games between those meetings, and four players started both games. Leeds won both, but while the 2–1 success in March against Bolton was one of just two wins across a run of twenty games, the 1 0 away victory in December was the fifth in a run of seven consecutive wins. The Bielsa style revolution was in full swing.

Leeds scored the opening goal in each of Bielsa's first four matches – wins over Stoke, Derby, Bolton and Rotherham – to give the Argentinian the best ever winning start to a Leeds managerial reign. The previous season, Leeds had lost five matches when scoring first, but under Bielsa its importance couldn't be overstated – they won their first twenty-one games when they scored the opener, longer than even the best winning run Leeds had when taking the lead under Don Revie (nineteen in a row from December 1971 to August 1972). The run came to an emphatic (and traumatic) end in April and May 2019, with defeats to Wigan and Derby, but those were exceptions rather than the rule for Bielsa's Leeds. In fifty-three Championship games when scoring first, Leeds won forty-seven, a win percentage of 88.7% that was better than any other Championship side in 2018–19 and 2019–20, and 23% higher than the average in those seasons for teams scoring first and going on to win (65.3%).

Championship (2018–19 – 2019–20)	Scored First	Won	Drawn	Lost	Win %
Leeds United	53	47	4	2	88.7%
Fulham	26	23	3	0	88.5%
Cardiff City	23	18	3	2	78.3%
Norwich City	29	22	5	2	75.9%
Sheffield United	32	24	5	3	75.0%

Data via Opta

Merry Christmas from Kemar Roofe

After a 4–1 defeat to West Brom on 10 November – the only time Leeds lost by three goals under Bielsa in the Championship, and the only time they faced twenty shots – the following seven matches were all victories. This was the club's longest league winning run in the same season since the first seven matches of 2007–08, while it was second longest winning streak of Bielsa's club career (behind the eight games in a row Marseille won in the 2014–15 campaign). Four of the first

196

five wins in the Leeds sequence were won without conceding, with the other seeing Leeds come from 1–0 down to beat QPR 2–1. What followed in wins six and seven were two of the most memorable victories of the season. They fell either side of Christmas, and both were won 3–2. Both were won with a 90th minute winner. Both times Kemar Roofe scored that decisive winner.

Leeds were 2–0 down after seventeen minutes against Aston Villa on 23 December, only the third time all season they'd trailed by two goals in the Championship. It had been almost seven years since Leeds had recovered a two-goal deficit and come back to win, against Doncaster Rovers in February 2012, and Leeds had lost sixty-nine of seventy-three games since that Doncaster comeback when two goals behind. It looked bleak based on history, but this was a new era and a new team. Rather than crumbling, Leeds just continued to play their normal game, and after Villa's two goals they didn't have another shot on target, while Leeds had seven. Leeds introduced eighteen-year-old Jack Clarke at half-time and he halved the deficit in the 56th minute, his first goal for the club, becoming the third-youngest player to score a goal under Bielsa in his managerial career.

Date	Player	Team	Opponent	Age
01/03/1998	Lucas Castromán	Vélez Sarsfield	Boca Juniors	17 years, 150 days
03/09/1997	Juan Darío Battala	Vélez Sarsfield	São Paulo	17 years, 350 days
23/12/2018	Jack Clarke	Leeds United	Aston Villa	18 years, 30 days
24/09/1994	Pavel Pardo	Atlas	Tampico Madero	18 years, 60 days
23/09/1990	Mauricio Pochettino	Newell's Old Boys	Chaco For Ever	18 years, 205 days

Pablo Hernández, fifteen years Clarke's senior, assisted his goal and five minutes later he set up the equaliser too; a Pontus Jansson header from a corner, scoring for a third consecutive game against Villa. In the 95th minute, Kemar Roofe fired into the corner of Ørjan Nyland's net to complete a magnificent – and deserved – comeback, which sent Leeds to the top of the Championship for Christmas Day, safe in the knowledge that the last ten teams top at Christmas had gone on to be automatically promoted. A Merry Christmas indeed, surely . . .

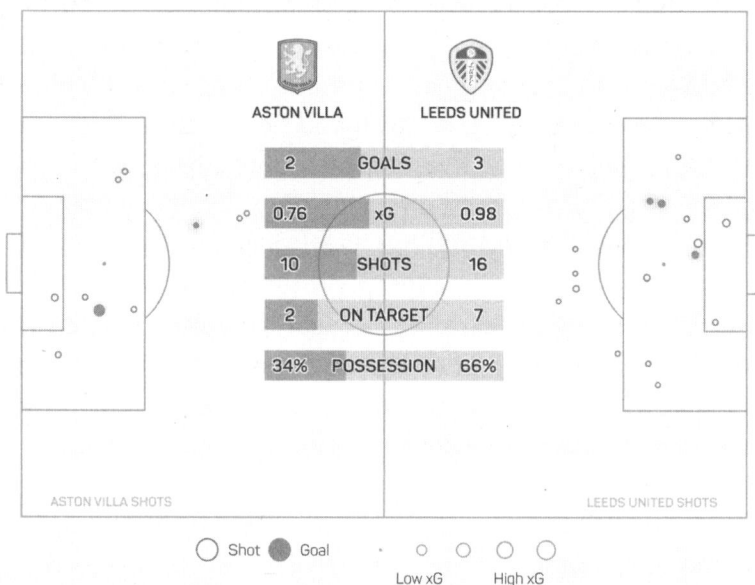

Aston Villa 2-3 Leeds United
English Championship 2018-19 | 23 December 2018

Opta

ASTON VILLA		LEEDS UNITED
2	GOALS	3
0.76	xG	0.98
10	SHOTS	16
2	ON TARGET	7
34%	POSSESSION	66%

ASTON VILLA SHOTS · LEEDS UNITED SHOTS

◯ Shot ● Goal · ◦ ◯ ◯ ◯ Low xG High xG

Three days later on Boxing Day, Leeds took the lead against Blackburn via a Derrick Williams own goal before Charlie Mulgrew equalised with a penalty early in the second half. Leeds had ten of the next twelve shots in the game but Rovers took the lead in the 90th minute when Mulgrew's direct free-kick found its way past Bailey Peacock-Farrell in the Leeds goal; it was the twenty-second goal he'd conceded in the Championship, but the eighth from outside the box – the joint most of any goalkeeper. Roofe stepped up to spare his blushes, though. Despite Leeds failing to score with any of their first twenty-two shots in the match, Roofe scored with each of the last two, in the 91st and 94th minutes to complete a remarkable turnaround. There'd been just 4 minutes and 37 seconds between Blackburn going 2–1 ahead and Leeds winning it 3–2, roughly the same amount of time as the song

'I Will Always Love You' by Whitney Houston lasts, which was UK number one when Roofe was born in January 1993.

These goals were Roofe's high point in a Leeds shirt. After scoring these two 90th minute winners he only managed two more goals for the club in fifteen appearances (both against Derby County – one after 'Spygate' in January, the other in the first leg of the play-offs). Having been joint third top scorer in the Championship up to Boxing Day, with thirteen goals and a conversion rate of 23%, this dropped to just 5% afterwards – which was the same conversion rate Leeds managed as a team against Wigan and Derby at Elland Road in April and May.

Wigan and Derby

Though the subtitle sounds like I might be moving onto an analysis of Paul Jewell's managerial career, these are in fact two of the most difficult defeats I've ever had the misfortune to attend as a Leeds fan, and both came within a month of each other. I left Elland Road on both occasions almost unable to process how we'd lost both games – particularly the latter. I'd also just failed my driving test for a second time on the same afternoon of the Derby second leg. I have had better days.

After some patchy form early in 2019, Leeds went into their game against Wigan on Good Friday in second place and on a run of eight wins in eleven, with the possibility that a win could put them six points ahead of Sheffield United if the Blades should lose to Nottingham Forest. Four games remained and the Premier League finally seemed within touching distance. Wigan were two points clear of relegation and forty points behind Leeds, and hadn't won any of their last nineteen away league games.

The game started as expected with Leeds on top, and they were awarded a penalty just fourteen minutes in after Cédric Kipré was sent off for handball on the line. Pablo Hernández stepped up and missed, but eighty-nine seconds later Patrick Bamford latched onto a Luke Ayling pass and fired in the opening goal. Leeds had won all twenty-one games under Bielsa when scoring first up to this point, and with an extra man it should really have been a foregone conclusion.

Despite Leeds having fifteen of the twenty shots in the first half, it was 1–1 at half-time due to Gavin Massey's equaliser for Wigan. In the second half Leeds had twenty-one shots to Wigan's three and yet somehow it was the Latics who found a winner, with Massey scoring his second goal of the afternoon – his two strikes that afternoon making up 40% of his total Championship goals in his career. Every outfield player who started the game for Leeds made at least one attempt on goal and Hernández ended his afternoon with eleven shots without scoring, the most by a Leeds player Opta has on record. Leeds' thirty-six shots are the joint second most on record in a Championship match and the joint most by a team to lose that game.

Date	Team	Opponent	Shots	Result
24/02/2015	Brentford	Blackpool	43	W 4–0
28/01/2014	Derby County	Yeovil Town	36	W 3–2
19/04/2019	Leeds United	Wigan Athletic	36	L 1–2
08/11/2022	Queens Park Rangers	Huddersfield Town	36	L 1–2

Data via Opta

Leeds had their most shots (thirty-six), touches in the opposition box (sixty-five) and highest possession average (77%) in a Championship match under Bielsa and somehow came away with a 2–1 defeat. Only three teams have had more touches in an opponent's box in a Championship game since 2013–14, with both Bamford (sixteen) and Hernández (twelve) having more than Wigan managed as a team (ten). An afternoon to forget, but one we'll probably always remember.

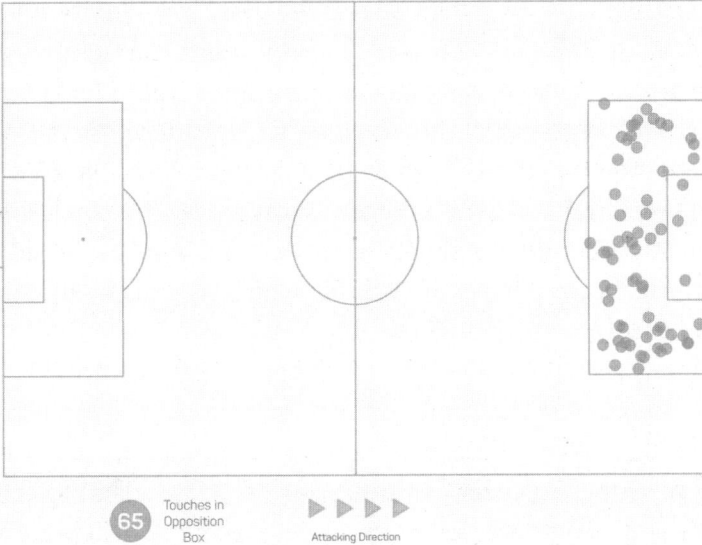

Leeds United Touches in Opposition Box
English Championship 2018-19 | Leeds United 1-2 Wigan Athletic (19 April 2019)

Opta

65 Touches in Opposition Box

Attacking Direction

> Marcelo Bielsa won seven of his ten matches as Leeds United manager against managers called Paul – the three exceptions were defeats to Paul Cook for Wigan (April 2019 and February 2020) and Paul Lambert for Ipswich (May 2019).

Across the final four matches of the 2018–19 Championship season, Leeds United – accused routinely of 'Bielsa burnout' – had the most shots (outshooting their four opponents by 108 to 39), the most touches in the opposition box and the highest share of possession of any Championship side. They only picked up one point out of twelve though, in a hotly contested match at Elland Road at the end of April, with Bielsa's instructions to allow Aston Villa to score after Mateusz Klich had put Leeds 1–0 ahead – with Jonathan Kodjia down injured at the time – eventually earning Leeds a FIFA award for Fair Play (collected in Milan in September by captain Liam Cooper and fitness coach Benoit Delaval – award ceremonies were never Marcelo's scene). The result guaranteed Sheffield United were promoted in second place, and that Leeds would face Derby in the play-offs.

Leeds won the first leg 1–0 at Pride Park thanks to a Roofe winner in the second half after an exceptional assist from Jack Harrison. In three games between Bielsa and Lampard's Derby after the first leg, Leeds had won all three, scoring seven and conceding once. They'd had more shots (forty-four vs twenty-six), more shots on target (fifteen vs six), averaged more possession (57% vs 43%) and had more touches in Derby's box than they'd allowed in their own (sixty-four vs fifty-three). There were very few, if any, statistics in favour of the Rams turning it around in the second leg, and from the Leeds perspective no side who had won the first leg away from home had ever then failed to make the final.

A driving test, typically, lasts 45 minutes. For 44 minutes and 59 seconds, you can be the perfect driver, with no mistakes whatsoever. Great clutch control, excellent manoeuvring, smooth gear changes. Then, something happens to throw you off guard. That split second affects the entire outcome of the driving test – the perfect preceding 44 minutes are erased. One major fault and it's a fail. This is how I describe my afternoon on 15 May 2019 as I failed my test. What I didn't expect was that my football team would do the same later that evening.

For the first 44 minutes of the play-off second leg against Derby at a raucous Elland Road, Leeds were doing perfectly. One-nil ahead thanks to Stuart Dallas' 24th minute opening goal – and 2–0 up on aggregate – Derby needed to score three times to go through. Leeds hadn't conceded three times after scoring first all season long. As the clock hit 44 minutes, Derby hadn't had a single shot on target in either leg – their last shot on target against Leeds was in the 51st minute of the 2–0 defeat in January, and there had been three hours and three minutes of football played between the teams since then. With the game heading for half-time, one speculative long ball and a mix-up between Liam Cooper and goalkeeper Kiko Casilla allowed Jack Marriott to tap into an empty net. The entire momentum of the game – and the atmosphere inside Elland Road – shifted.

From no shots on target for 183 minutes, Derby score with three shots on target in a row and by the 58th minute were 3–1 up on the night and 3–2 ahead on aggregate, an inexplicable turn of events and the only time they led against Leeds all season. Dallas, playing like a man possessed, scored in the 62nd minute to make it level on aggregate and in this match he had his joint most shots (six), most shots on target (four) and won the most fouls (seven) in a game for the club, while the Northern Irishman led all Leeds players that day for shots, shots on target, duels, possession won, fouls won and was joint top for tackles made. No one that day did more to drag Leeds through the game than he did. Ultimately, it wasn't enough. Berardi was sent off in the 78th minute and Marriott, following in Wigan forward Gavin Massey's footsteps the previous month, scored his only Championship brace with Derby's fourth goal in the 85th minute. Leeds only made nine errors leading to opposition goals all season. Two came that evening at Elland Road.

Needing a goal, Leeds still had three more shots on target at 4–2 down, with Cooper, Dallas and substitute Jack Clarke all testing goalkeeper Kelle Roos. The last attempt of the season, though, was left to the other substitute, Izzy Brown. His only previous appearance for Leeds all season long (largely due to injury) had been at QPR in February, when he'd conceded more fouls (two) than he'd had touches (one) or passes (zero) and had also been yellow carded for his troubles. The Derby game was the eighty-sixth appearance of his career and he hadn't once taken a direct free-kick, so he was a curious choice to take this one. His effort sailed over the bar, the 825th and final shot of Leeds United's Championship season.

> Leeds spent 185 days in the top two of the Championship in the 2018–19 season, the most of any team who failed to finish in the automatic promotion spots in Championship history.

In one season, Marcelo Bielsa had transformed Leeds United into one of the most attractive teams in the country to watch. After finishing fourteenth, thirteenth, fifteenth, fifteenth, thirteenth, seventh and thirteenth in the seven prior seasons, the fact that a third-place finish was seen as a failure shows how far the club had come in such a short space of time. He had revolutionised the club from top to bottom. Everyone wanted, and craved, another season of Bielsa football and for it to end differently.

Take us home

The line-up at Ashton Gate against Bristol City for Leeds United's first game of 2019–20 contained eight players who'd started the Derby second leg play-off game. The three others from the XI on that devastating night (Ayling, Berardi and Jamie Shackleton) all remained at the club, and there was only one new signing: central defender Ben White on loan from Brighton. Leeds were going again with the same main characters from the previous season. White was a replacement for Pontus Jansson, who'd been an unused substitute in the first and last games of the 2018–19 campaign (two of only six occasions he was on the bench without getting on) and sold to Brentford in the summer. White, aged twenty-one on his Leeds debut, had made fifty-seven appearances in league football before joining but all had been in Leagues One and Two, and he'd been in the Newport line-up who'd knocked Leeds out of the FA Cup in January 2018. He was the youngest player to wear the number 5 shirt for Leeds since Peter Swan in 1988 and some fans were concerned about his inexperience. They needn't have worried – he took to the role like a duck to water and led the Championship that season for interceptions (118), completed the fourth most passes and carried the ball 6,638 metres, the third most of any central defender. He was signed for his composure on the ball and he had that in spades.

> Ben White was the only Leeds player to start all forty-six league games in the 2019–20 promotion-winning season, playing every single minute. He is the only outfield player to start every game in his only league season at the club.

Leeds beat Bristol City 3–1 with goals from Hernández, Bamford and Harrison which set the tone for a fantastic start to the campaign: after twenty-one matches, Leeds were top of the table and had won four more points than at the same stage the previous season (forty-six, vs forty-two in 2018–19). Not only that, but Leeds had also managed to improve in all the metrics where they'd led the way the previous season; after twenty-one games, they'd had 110 more touches in the opposition box, created fourteen more big chances and completed over one hundred more passes. Leeds' pressing also showed an uptick, winning possession in the final third ten more times, while defensively Leeds had faced twenty-one fewer shots and ten fewer shots on target and only conceded ten goals, the joint fewest in a season after ten games along with the ten they conceded in 2009–10. The only possible concern for Bielsa is that despite having the extra shots, Leeds had scored three fewer goals than at the same stage previously; they may have led the way for shots, but they were sixteenth for shot conversion.

Though three fewer goals had been scored, there'd been some exquisite goals across the opening twenty-one games in 2019–20, perhaps none more so than Stuart Dallas' opening goal away at Stoke City in the August sunshine, set up beautifully by Hernández by a first-time pass – his fourteenth assist in forty-six Championship games under Bielsa at that point.

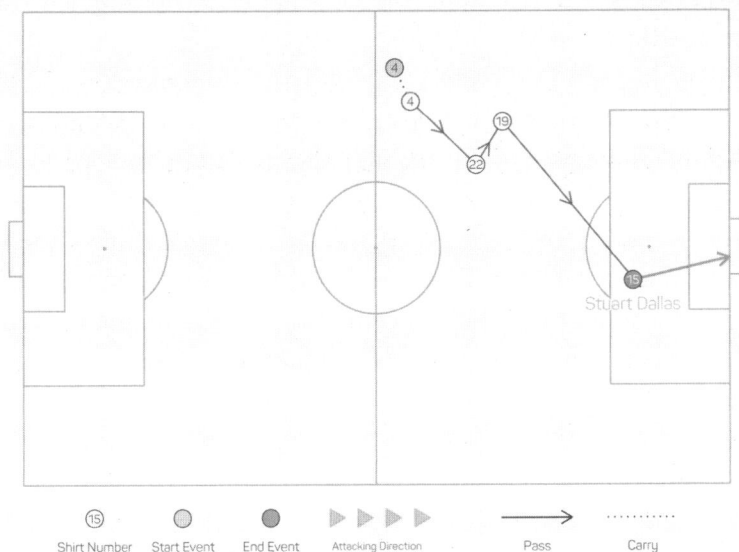

Stuart Dallas goal
English Championship 2019-20 | Stoke City 0-3 Leeds United (24 August 2019)

Opta

| Shirt Number | Start Event | End Event | Attacking Direction | Pass | Carry |

In the twenty-second game, Leeds were at home to Cardiff. Going into the game they were eleven points clear of third and on a run of seven wins in a row, the second seven-game winning run under Bielsa which made him the first manager since Don Revie to lead Leeds on two separate runs of seven consecutive wins.

In the first half, Leeds blew Cardiff away and went 2–0 ahead after just eight minutes through goals from Helder Costa and Bamford, the earliest Leeds had gone 2–0 ahead in a league match since March 2002 against Blackburn Rovers. They also had seven shots inside the opening fifteen minutes; their most in a Championship game under Bielsa. Since the 4–2 defeat to Derby, Leeds had won fifteen of seventeen games when scoring first and only conceded five times in those seventeen unbeaten games. Early in the second half, Bamford won a penalty and converted it to make it Leeds United 3–0 Cardiff City.

Leeds had won their previous thirty-six games when going three goals in front and there was no real danger in this game – Cardiff hadn't had a shot on target in the time Leeds had gone 3–0 up. At full-time, inexplicably, it was 3–3 with Cardiff finding the net with their three shots on target through Lee Tomlin, Sean Morrison and Robert Glatzel. This was the first time Leeds had failed to win from three goals up since September 2010, when after leading 4–1 against Preston they lost 6–4.

The winning run had come to an end and it heralded a run of two wins in twelve games in all competitions, both of which were chaotic in value: in the final game of the decade, which had begun with a 1–0 win over Manchester United on 3 January 2010, Leeds beat Birmingham City 5–4 on 29 December in a crazy game. It was the first time Leeds had won a game 5–4, their first 'new' winning result since the 10–0 victory over Lyn Oslo in 1969, and the first time Leeds had scored five in an away league game since beating Charlton Athletic 6–1 in April 2003. The scoring was as follows:

Birmingham 0–1 Leeds – 15th minute
Birmingham 0–2 Leeds – 21st minute
Birmingham 1–2 Leeds – 27th minute
Birmingham 2–2 Leeds – 61st minute
Birmingham 2–3 Leeds – 69th minute
Birmingham 3–3 Leeds – 83rd minute

Birmingham 3–4 Leeds – 84th minute
Birmingham 4–4 Leeds – 91st minute
Birmingham 4–5 Leeds – 95th minute

The decisive goal – an own goal from Birmingham's defender Wes Harding – took Leeds top of the Championship. It meant they maintained their record of ending decades top of the table, doing so in the 1980s, 1990s, 2000s and 2010s. Bring on 2029.

Division Two – 31 December 1989

Team	P	W	D	L	GF	GA	GD	Pts
Leeds United	24	14	6	4	41	24	17	48
Sheffield United	24	13	8	3	41	26	15	47

Premier League – 31 December 1999

Team	P	W	D	L	GF	GA	GD	Pts
Leeds United	20	14	2	4	34	22	12	44
Manchester United	19	13	4	2	50	25	25	43

League One – 31 December 2009

Team	P	W	D	L	GF	GA	GD	Pts
Leeds United	23	17	5	1	45	13	32	56
Charlton Athletic	24	13	9	2	46	27	19	48

Championship – 31 December 2019

Team	G	W	D	L	GF	GA	GD	Pts
Leeds United	25	15	6	4	42	20	22	51
West Bromwich Albion	25	14	9	2	47	27	20	51

Their other win in this run was at home to Millwall on 28 January. Leeds had dropped to second, were only three points clear of Fulham in third and found themselves 2–0 down after twenty-three minutes at Elland Road, only the second time all season they'd conceded two first half goals and the other was also against Millwall in October. It was an eighth consecutive league game without a clean sheet, conceding sixteen goals – in the previous eight games, Leeds had conceded just twice. Leeds went in at half-time 2–0 down and it was panic stations.

By the sixty-sixth minute, Leeds were winning 3–2. Patrick Bamford scored twice before Hernández's deflected shot gave Leeds a much-needed victory, their fifth ever at Elland Road when losing by two goals at half-time and first since September 1986 against Reading.

Opponents	Date	Competition	HT Score	FT Score
Bury	29/01/1936	FA Cup	0–2	3–2
Sunderland	04/12/1937	Division One	1–3	4–3
Leicester City	12/09/1964	Division One	0–2	3–2
Reading	13/09/1986	Division Two	0–2	3–2
Millwall	28/01/2020	Championship	0–2	3–2

Although Leeds had only won the game by one goal, they had twenty-eight shots to Millwall's eleven with Bamford having nine shots (his joint most in a match for Leeds), and these goals were Bamford's only two in a run of thirteen games in which he had forty-nine shots. There'd been a clamour from some quarters for Bamford to be replaced in the starting XI by loan striker Eddie Nketiah, who'd scored four goals in his first six appearances for the club earlier in the campaign, but injury and Bielsa's preference for Bamford to start (Nketiah only started four games, two in the League Cup and two in the Championship) meant that, immediately after starting against West Brom on New Year's Day, Arsenal recalled him. Roofe had departed in the previous summer, leaving Bamford as the senior striker at the club.

At the age of 20 years and 83 days when he netted the winner against Brentford in August 2019, Eddie Nketiah became the fourth-youngest player to score in each of his first two appearances for Leeds. The three younger than him are Alan Smith (18 years and 24 days), John Hawksby (18 years and 78 days) and Arthur Hydes (19 years and 54 days).

Leeds did try to rectify that in the January transfer window with the signing of Jean-Kévin Augustin, initially on loan. It was not, it's fair to say, a transfer that worked out. Augustin had been leading scorer with six goals at the U19 UEFA European Championship in 2016, one goal ahead of France teammate, Kylian Mbappé (also on the scoresheet at that summer's tournament was another Leeds loanee who played very few minutes, Izzy Brown). Augustin made his debut in the 2–0 defeat at Nottingham Forest in February and his three appearances all came within a week of one another. After playing just 48 minutes, having three shots and conceding one foul, Leeds fans never saw Augustin again after he sat on the bench as an unused substitute against Reading on 22 February.

The defeat at Forest, the fifth in six games in all competitions, all without scoring, is undoubtedly the lowest point of the 2019–20 campaign. After building up an eleven-point gap on third, Leeds were second and level with Fulham in third and only two points ahead of Brentford in fifth. Each of the four sides below Leeds had won that day and the side above them, West Brom, won on the Sunday against Millwall. Post-match, Luke Ayling gave an interview to LUTV in which he mentioned Leeds' failure to open scoring, saying, 'I don't think we've scored the first goal of the game in a long time now.' This highlighted the importance of doing so in the Bielsa team, and he was right: Leeds had scored the first goal in one of their previous ten games, and that had been the 5–4 win over Birmingham. The first goal had been conceded in seven in a row and Leeds had lost five.

It is interesting to note that, based on per game metrics, there was little between their attacking data in their seven match winning run and the next eleven games, which yielded two wins. Converting chances, though, was the major issue – a 5% drop in their conversion rate.

Leeds United	Winning Run (2 Nov – 10 Dec)	Next 11 Games (14 Dec – 11 Feb)
Shots	16	17
Shots on Target	6	5
Completed Passes	402	401
Touches in the Opp Box	31	35
Shot Conversion Rate	13%	8%
Possession	64.3%	67.1%

Per Game – data via Opta

Ayling also spoke of 'scrapping the thirty-one games and starting again'. He meant it figuratively, but it was the perfect quote for the remainder of the season.

Pablo Hernández, scores a goal for Leeds United

It's tough to pick a favourite moment from the last fifteen matches of the 2019–20 Championship campaign. The beautiful sweeping move that gave Leeds a 3–0 lead away at Hull, finished off by Tyler Roberts. Luke Ayling's rockstar celebration after opening the scoring against Huddersfield in the last game before the world locked down. Ezgjan Alioski, after scoring in a 3–0 win over Fulham in the first game in front of an 'empty' Elland Road in June, applauding the cardboard cut-outs of fans. Hammering Stoke 5–0, with five different scorers, with Hernández sweeping in the fourth goal following a thirty-pass move. Hernández, scoring a goal for Leeds United (as commentator Bryn Law informed us) away at Swansea in the 89th minute. Emile Smith Rowe, scoring a goal for Huddersfield Town against West Brom that clinched Leeds' promotion. Leeds beating Derby, the previous season's antagonists, in the penultimate game 3–1 and receiving a guard of honour after promotion. It could be any of those.

Ultimately, though, the image of Marcelo Bielsa lifting the Championship trophy after the final game, having had to be cajoled into it by his players, was my favourite. The man who made it happen, and made us all dream again, with a big grin on his face as he lifted it. Leeds United were going back to the Premier League.

It wasn't all as easy as it sounds, nor was it devoid of any nerves, but the statistics speak for themselves. In the final fifteen matches of the Championship season, Leeds United picked up thirty-eight points, winning twelve, drawing two and losing one.

After losing to Forest, Bielsa forewent his usual lengthy video sessions and instead gave the team a motivational speech, for which he received a round of applause. In the following game, a Kiko Casilla mistake gave Brentford the lead but Leeds responded with an equaliser from Liam Cooper, and Fulham's failure to beat Millwall the following day left Leeds still in second.

The next five games were all won without conceding and Ayling, who'd spoken of the lack of opening goals, gave Leeds the 1–0 lead in three of those wins against Bristol City (1–0), Hull (4–0) and Huddersfield (2–0). Leeds restricted their opponents to just nine shots on target across all five and, in the 4–0 win at Hull, goalkeeper Casilla was replaced by nineteen-year-old Illan Meslier. The Frenchman started all but one of the remaining eleven games and was the youngest player (19 years and 364 days) to wear the number 1 shirt for Leeds in a league game since Phil Hughes in 1983.

Then the world, and football, stopped. Some said that the pandemic, and the games behind closed doors, helped Leeds get over the line, but in the final five games before the pandemic forced a three-month hiatus (at least for Premier League and Championship clubs), Leeds were one of only two sides in England's top four tiers who'd won their previous five games, and they were the only club who'd kept five consecutive clean sheets.

England's top four tiers – best form in last five games pre-pandemic

Top Four Tiers	Won	Drawn	Lost	GF	GA	Pts
Leeds United	5	0	0	9	0	15
Oxford United	5	0	0	14	3	15
Cheltenham Town	4	1	0	7	2	13
Coventry City	4	1	0	7	2	13
Liverpool	4	0	1	10	6	12

When football resumed in June – only the second time Leeds had played a game in that month, having drawn 2–2 in the second leg of the Fairs Cup against Juventus in June 1971 – Leeds picked up four points in three games, their one win in this sequence coming in a 3–0 victory over Fulham (Bielsa's fiftieth as Leeds manager in ninety-three games) which probably flattered Leeds; it was a rare game without the majority of possession (42.6%, the lowest in a Championship game under Bielsa) and it was the fewest successful passes Leeds managed in a Championship game across their two seasons in it under Bielsa. Not having a lot of possession wasn't necessarily a bad thing; Leeds won the six games in which they had their lowest possession figure under him, while on the flip side, Leeds had 70% or more possession in twenty games across those two seasons and lost ten of them.

July was perfect. It is one of two months in the club's history where they played six league games and won all six, and the other, in April 1956, also saw Leeds gain promotion to the top-flight. The six games were won by an aggregate score of 17–2. Ten different players found the net, a record at that time that was equalled in February 2025. Some 736 league games since their last top-flight match in May 2004, Leeds were back.

Scoring first remained the order of the day and even in the game they didn't, away at Derby, they trailed for all of 114 seconds before

Hernández equalised. Hernández missed the first game back against Cardiff, but Leeds won seven of the eight games he appeared in. His minutes were carefully managed by Bielsa, coming on as a sub in six consecutive games (and being subbed off in two of them with his work done) and despite playing just 389 minutes in those June and July matches, only three players had more goals and assists combined in the Championship behind closed doors.

Player	Minutes	Goals	Assists	Goals + Assists	Mins/Goal or Assist
Saïd Benrahma	783	7	1	8	98
Jamal Lowe	751	3	4	7	107
Jacob Murphy	615	4	3	7	88
Pablo Hernández	389	3	3	6	65

Data via Opta

Leeds were winning 1–0 at half-time against Stoke City when Hernández was substituted on and twelve minutes after the break he produced a superb assist; ghosting across the pitch after taking a short corner and switching the play, he pulled the ball back for Liam Cooper to score and make it 3–0. Fifteen minutes later, he scored one of the goals of the season, finishing off a thirty-pass move – the most passes before a Championship goal scored all season. The move lasted all of seventy-eight seconds and only Harrison and Bamford (who does a lovely dummy before it reaches Hernández) don't touch it in the build-up. It is a superb goal.

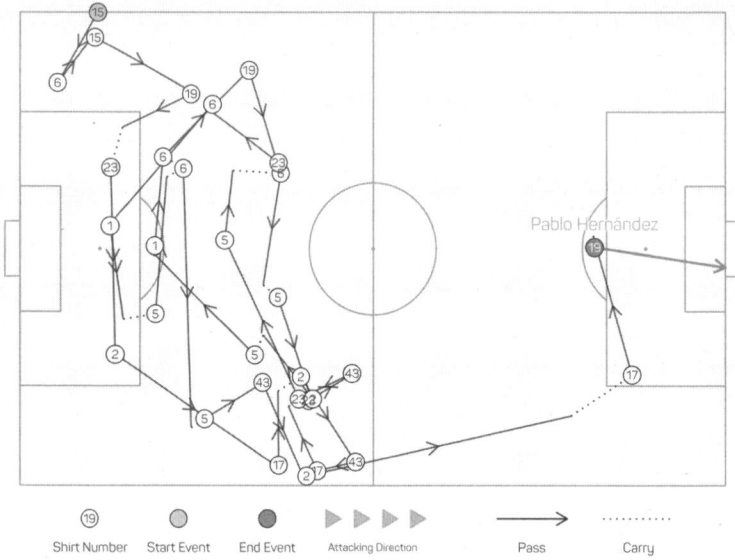

Pablo Hernández goal
English Championship 2019-20 | Leeds United 5-0 Stoke City (09 July 2020)

Opta

Pablo Hernández

Shirt Number · Start Event · End Event · Attacking Direction · Pass · Carry

The next game, away at Swansea, possibly defined Hernández's time at Leeds. It was certainly the case for the Duck and Drake pub in Leeds city centre, on the side of which is a mural of Hernández celebrating his 89th minute winning goal in the game, his shirt off, for which he received a yellow card for excessive celebration – the only card shown for celebrating in the Championship in June and July's behind-closed-doors games. It was worth it. Hernández was the fourth-oldest Leeds player to score the winner in a 1–0 victory, behind Peter Lorimer, Gordon Strachan and Jack Charlton, who had sadly passed away two days before the Swansea win. Not bad company to be in.

Oldest scorers in 1–0 Leeds wins

Date	Player	Opponent	Age
12/10/1985	Peter Lorimer	Middlesbrough	38 years, 302 days
23/02/1985	Peter Lorimer	Charlton Athletic	38 years, 71 days
15/02/1984	Peter Lorimer	Swansea City	37 years, 63 days
11/03/1972	Jack Charlton	Coventry City	36 years, 308 days
30/08/1993	Gordon Strachan	Oldham Athletic	36 years, 202 days
26/04/1971	Jack Charlton	Arsenal	35 years, 353 days
19/12/1970	Jack Charlton	Everton	35 years, 225 days
12/07/2020	Pablo Hernández	Swansea City	35 years, 92 days

Gaetano Berardi's red card away at Millwall – though later rescinded – was his eighth Leeds United sending off, overtaking the record of seven by Alan Smith between 1999 and 2003. Between his first and final Championship games for Leeds, Berardi actually conceded fewer fouls (112) than Lewis Cook (116), who played sixty-eight fewer games than Berardi did in that time.

Although Leeds had strung together three wins in a row at the start of July, it hadn't offered up much of a gap in the league table. Leeds played later than their promotion rivals in both the wins over Stoke and Swansea, which ramped up the nerves for supporters, especially as Brentford in third spot kept winning. Ahead of the 16 July game against a rock bottom Barnsley side, Leeds were top but only two points ahead of West Brom and three ahead of Brentford. It was the only Championship game of the day and it was a fraught (to say the least) experience, even after Michael Sollbauer put through his own net in the 28th minute to give Leeds a 1–0 lead. Neither side had a shot on target in the first half, though Leeds controlled possession at 64%. In the second half, Leeds managed just two attempts as Barnsley took the initiative and the Tykes ended the game as losers but having outshot Leeds by twelve to six, the biggest differential in a Championship game under Bielsa in which both sides had eleven men for the full game. The six shots Leeds had was the only time under Bielsa they didn't reach double figures for attempts in a home Championship match.

The result put Leeds five points clear at the top – the first time all season they'd been that far ahead – and a day later Emile Smith Rowe's goal for Huddersfield in a 2–1 victory over West Brom ensured promotion for Leeds; he had eighteen shots at the John Smith's Stadium, but only this one went in. Brentford's defeat at Stoke the day after meant that Leeds were champions and – after a huge celebration and some very sore heads – had two stress-free games to look forward to away at Derby and home to Charlton.

The Damned United are back

The game at Derby was unique in the Championship under Marcelo Bielsa for one reason: the starting XI did not feature Mateusz Klich. His story had been remarkable, discarded by previous manager Thomas Christiansen after 131 league minutes in 2017–18 (fewer than Chris Wood, who made his last appearance on 15 August that season) and loaned out to FC Utrecht in the Eredivisie for the second half of the season. In one game for them, against Heracles in April 2018, Klich created eleven chances – a tally that has been bettered by just one player in an Eredivisie that Opta has on record, and matched just once since, by Cody Gakpo (who could've been a teammate of Klich's at Leeds had things worked out differently, but that's another story).

The arrival of Bielsa in the summer of 2018 didn't automatically mean a new opportunity for Klich, who played at centre-back in one friendly at Bootham Crescent against York City (the other players who started alongside him that day would make a combined total of twenty-four league starts under Bielsa, with eighteen of those coming from Jamie Shackleton), but with options in midfield dwindling he was given the opportunity to play against Las Palmas in a friendly. He never looked back. Starting with the Stoke City game in August 2018 (in which he scored the opening goal of the Bielsa era) and ending with the nail-biting 1–0 win over Barnsley in July 2020, Klich appeared in ninety-two consecutive league and play-off games for Leeds, a record run of starts for a player this century and surpassed by only seven outfield players in the club's entire history. An incredible feat even before you consider the level of intensity demanded by Bielsa.

Consecutive starts by outfield players for Leeds

Date of First Game	Date of Last Game	Player	Consecutive Starts
28/08/1920	15/12/1923	Jim Baker	145
15/01/1955	26/04/1958	Eric Kerfoot	143
30/01/1926	30/03/1929	Tom Townsley	134
21/08/1954	18/09/1957	Jimmy Dunn	134
08/09/1962	03/04/1965	Norman Hunter	113
07/03/1953	24/09/1955	Grenville Hair	104
14/08/1993	02/12/1995	Gary Kelly	99
23/02/1976	01/04/1978	Trevor Cherry	92
05/08/2018	16/07/2020	Mateusz Klich	92

Jamie Shackleton, who debuted for Leeds wearing the number 46 shirt, didn't score in any of his first forty-six games for the club. He then scored in two in a row, against Derby and Charlton in July 2020 (the latter the forty-sixth game of the season), before failing to score in any of his last forty-six games before he left the club in the summer of 2024.

He was deserving of a rest (and if his Instagram photos in the days after promotion were anything to go by, needed one) against Derby, and Leeds did the job without him, and with Klich an unused substitute they came from 1–0 down to win 3–1. This was the first time Leeds had conceded the first goal in the second half of a game and come back to win since a 2–1 win in January 2012 against Burnley, and the first time by two clear goals since November 1998 away at Liverpool in a 3–1 win on Alan Smith's goalscoring debut. The win at Derby also saw Leeds complete 87.8% of their passes – their best ratio in a Championship match under Bielsa. Given it was two days after promotion was secured, and the celebrations that followed, this accuracy is all the more impressive.

The 4–0 victory over Charlton in the final league game of the season was Leeds United's twenty-eighth league win of the season, their most in a single campaign until Daniel Farke's side broke that record in 2024–25 with twenty-nine. It left them with ninety-three points, also then a club record. It was a fourth win by four or more goals in a league game that season, the most since 1972–73. It won Leeds the title by ten points, the biggest margin since Newcastle won it by eleven points in the 2009–10 season. Why were we all panicking?

Championship winners – most points ahead of second

Season	Team	Points	Points Ahead of 2nd
2005–06	Reading	106	16
2009–10	Newcastle United	102	11
2019–20	Leeds United	93	10
2022–23	Burnley	101	10

353 days after the start of the season and 5,912 days since they last played a top-flight game, Leeds United were back. Marcelo Bielsa had made us all dream, and now those dreams were becoming a reality.

Next stop – Premier League.

Leeds are falling into the top half, again

Marcelo Bielsa had transformed Leeds United from a mid-table Championship team to one of the most attacking sides in the country. In their 2019–20 Championship title-winning campaign, Leeds had the most shots of any side in the country (755) and ranked second behind Manchester City for each of shots on target (251), big chances (125) and touches in the opposition box (1,440). Leeds would now be on a level playing field with Guardiola's side, albeit the Premier League was a completely different prospect, especially for promoted teams. In the previous ten seasons, the average finish for promoted clubs was fifteenth, and 37% had gone straight back down.

Bielsa simply stuck to the same principles and Leeds reaped the rewards. Leeds averaged 57.8% possession, the second most by a Premier League promoted team Opta has on record since 2003–04, and had the fifth most shots, fifth most shots on target, fourth best expected goals total and their possession average was the fourth highest, ranking ahead of Arsenal, Man Utd and Spurs. Leeds took the Premier League by storm and were the neutral's favourite team to watch, while offering fans hope during the pandemic lockdown; often, watching Bielsa's Leeds go toe-to-toe with the country's best sides was the highlight of the week. The club's eventual ninth-place finish was nothing short of what they deserved for some of the best football – particularly relative to the quality of opponent – seen at Elland Road, certainly in my lifetime.

Premier League – 2020–21	Leeds United	Premier League Rank
Total Shots	522	5
Shots on Target	199	5
Touches in the Opp Box	928	8
Passes Played into the Box	1,244	3

Completed Passes	15,079	8
Possession Average	57.8%	4
Big Chances	76	9
Expected Goals	56.6	5
Expected Goals (Excl. Pens)	53.4	4

Data via Opta

Ranked alongside other promoted teams that Opta has on record, Bielsa's Leeds had the most shots on target (199), most touches in the opposition box (928), completed the second most passes (15,079) and had the third best passing accuracy (80.8%).

Season	Team	Shots on Target
2020–21	Leeds United	199
2010–11	West Bromwich Albion	184
2003–04	Wolverhampton Wanderers	170

Data via Opta (since 2003–04)

Season	Team	Touches in the Opp Box
2020–21	Leeds United	928
2012–13	West Ham United	923
2012–13	Southampton	912

Data via Opta (since 2008–09)

Season	Team	Completed Passes
2011–12	Swansea City	18,038
2020–21	Leeds United	15,079
2020–21	Fulham	14,458

Data via Opta (since 2003–04)

Games involving Leeds were unmissable, with only two teams' games seeing more goals scored than Leeds (116), while Leeds' matches had the most shots (1,080). Eight of their thirty-eight games had five or more goals (Leeds won three, lost five). The opening game against Liverpool set the tone (the line-up of which contained four players who'd started against Stoke in August 2018: Ayling, Klich, Phillips and Hernández) with Leeds losing 4–3, but they became the first promoted team to score three at Anfield since Blackburn in 2002, while they were only the third promoted team to turn up at the reigning Premier League champions and score three (the others are Derby winning 3–2 at Man Utd in 1997 and Hull losing 4–3 at Man Utd in 2008). Jürgen Klopp's 'wow' reaction at full-time said it all. All four of Liverpool's goals had been from set pieces and they'd been restricted to 48.8% possession, their lowest in a Premier League match since the previous November.

Leeds ended the season with sixty-two Premier League goals, the most by a promoted side since Nottingham Forest in 1994–95, which was in a forty-two-game season. It was a record in a thirty-eight-game season, breaking Sunderland and Ipswich's totals from the 1999–00 and 2000–01 seasons respectively.

Most goals by promoted teams in a Premier League season

Season	Team	Games	Goals
1993–94	Newcastle United	42	82
1994–95	Nottingham Forest	42	72
1992–93	Blackburn Rovers	42	68
2020–21	Leeds United	38	62
2000–01	Ipswich Town	38	57
1999–00	Sunderland	38	57

Only five of Leeds United's Premier League games ended as draws, with only Sheffield United having fewer, but while the Blades were on the right end of only seven results, Leeds won eighteen games and fifty-nine points, the second most by any promoted club in a thirty-eight-game season, and a feat not seen since Ipswich won sixty-six in 2000–01, when they finished fifth (one place behind David O'Leary's Leeds).

Most points won by promoted teams in a 38-game Premier League season

Season	Team	Games	Wins	Draws	Losses	GF	GA	Pts
2000–01	Ipswich Town	38	20	6	12	57	42	66
2020–21	Leeds United	38	18	5	15	62	54	59
1999–00	Sunderland	38	16	10	12	57	56	58
2018–19	Wolverhampton Wanderers	38	16	9	13	47	46	57
2005–06	West Ham United	38	16	7	15	52	55	55
2006–07	Reading	38	16	7	15	52	47	55

Historically, Leeds have always done well in their first season after promotion to the top-flight. In the 1920s, Leeds had eighteenth and thirteenth-place finishes but since then, they've finished in the top half each time, doing so in 1932–33 (eighth), 1956–57 (eighth), 1964–65 (second), 1990–91 (fourth) and 2020–21 (ninth). Among teams with five or more top-flight promotions, only Spurs (7.2) have had a higher average finish than Leeds (8.8), while no side has been promoted more often than Leeds without being relegated immediately (seven times).

England's number 9

On 5 September 2021, Patrick Bamford celebrated his twenty-eighth birthday by making his England debut at Wembley against Andorra in a FIFA World Cup qualifier, the first England player to make his debut on his birthday since Johnny Nicholls in 1954 and first Leeds striker to debut since Alan Smith in May 2001. Bamford's 62–minute appearance didn't provide a goal, and he never won another cap. Injuries meant he only played 302 more minutes in the Premier League all season, and scored five more Premier League goals for Leeds after winning his sole cap. It was undoubtedly the pinnacle of Bamford's career.

From September 2020 until August 2021, only Harry Kane scored more Premier League goals among Englishmen than Bamford, who got eighteen (and eight assists) in forty-one appearances for Leeds. Bamford had been joint fourth top scorer in the Premier League with seventeen goals in 2020–21, behind Kane, Mohamed Salah and Bruno Fernandes, and he'd had the fourth most shots and shots on target that campaign. He had more than earned his call-up to the national team.

And yet, despite being the Leeds United top scorer in the 2019–20 Championship title-winning side with sixteen goals, many fans weren't confident going into the Premier League with Bamford leading the line. Though he'd scored sixteen, he'd missed thirty-four big chances (sixteen more than anyone else) and ended the season with six goals in his final twenty-two appearances, from a total of sixty-six shots in that time. Without any real competition for his place following the departures of Roofe and loanee Nketiah, it was a given that Bamford would start, with Bielsa often defending him and praising his work rate.

Bamford had made twenty-seven Premier League appearances for four different clubs – Crystal Palace, Norwich, Burnley and Middlesbrough – before he appeared in the top-flight for Leeds but only four of those twenty-seven games had been in the starting XI and his average minutes per game was only twenty-five. He had scored once, in a defeat to Southampton for Middlesbrough, and his last game had been away at Anfield for Middlesbrough in May 2017 in a 3–0 defeat.

Fears about Bamford's top-flight pedigree were quickly allayed when he scored in each of his first three Premier League appearances for Leeds, the first player in the club's entire history to score in his first three top-flight appearances. He was also the first player to score in the first three games of a top-flight season since Mick Jones in 1968–69, the first time Leeds won the top-flight title. While Leeds weren't quite dreaming of emulating that, after the third game – won 1–0 at Sheffield United thanks to a Bamford header – they sat sixth in the table.

After two goalless games, things got even for better for Bamford and Leeds when they faced Aston Villa at Villa Park in October. Villa had made a 100% start to the season, winning their first four games and, albeit in the strange circumstances that surrounded the behind-closed-doors nature of the season, had just hammered reigning champions Liverpool 7–2 in their last home game. It was a tremendous performance by Leeds, who had their most shots in a Premier League game all season (twenty-seven) and beat the Villans 3–0, with all three goals scored by Bamford – becoming the club's first Premier League hat-trick scorer since Mark Viduka in 2003 away at Charlton. It also made him only the sixth player to score a hat-trick under Marcelo Bielsa's management, something emulated since by Jack Harrison and Darwin Núñez.

Hat-tricks scored under Marcelo Bielsa

Date	Player	Team	Opponent
13/11/1995	Luis García	América	Monterrey
28/09/1997	Patricio Camps	Vélez Sarsfield	Newell's Old Boys
30/11/1997	Patricio Camps	Vélez Sarsfield	Rosario Central
07/07/2004	Javier Saviola	Argentina	Ecuador
21/08/2004	Carlos Tevez	Argentina	Costa Rica
28/01/2012	Fernando Llorente	Athletic Club	Rayo Vallecano
23/10/2020	Patrick Bamford	Leeds United	Aston Villa
16/01/2022	Jack Harrison	Leeds United	West Ham United
05/06/2024	Darwin Núñez	Uruguay	Mexico

> Patrick Bamford's hat-trick against Aston Villa was only the
> second scored on a Friday for Leeds, along with Rod Belfitt's
> treble against Kilmarnock in May 1967. It was also Leeds'
> second all left-footed hat-trick in the Premier League, along with
> Robbie Fowler's against Bolton in December 2001. Overall, 55%
> of Premier League goals scored under Bielsa were left-footed
> (fifty out of ninety-one), the highest percentage under any
> manager in Premier League history with more than fifty games.

There was some nice symmetry in Bielsa records being broken in the
5–2 victory over Newcastle United in December 2020. The game was
the 114th overseen by Bielsa as Leeds manager, breaking the record for
games managed by Bielsa at a single club or nation (113 with Athletic
Club). Bamford's equalising goal to make it 1–1 was his thirty-fifth
goal for Leeds and therefore his thirty-fifth for Bielsa, making him the
all-time leading scorer under his management across his entire career,
overtaking Fernando Llorente's total of thirty-four while playing for
Athletic Club. Bamford eventually ended with forty-five goals under
Bielsa, a record very unlikely to be broken now.

All-time top scorers under Marcelo Bielsa

Player	Club(s)	Goals
Patrick Bamford	Leeds United	45
Fernando Llorente	Athletic Club	34
Cristian Domizzi	Newell's Old Boys, Atlas	28
Markel Susaeta	Athletic Club	24
Jack Harrison	Leeds United	24
Patricio Camps	Vélez Sarsfield	23
André-Pierre Gignac	Marseille	23

Bamford ended the season with three goals in four games against

Spurs, Southampton and West Brom to end the season with seventeen Premier League goals, the most for a newly promoted club since Charlie Austin had scored eighteen in 2014–15 for QPR. He'd played a key role in helping Leeds to their best Premier League finish since 2002 and was one of only three players to play in all thirty-eight matches, along with Stuart Dallas and Luke Ayling. For a player so often maligned by opposition fans and pundits, he'd well and truly proved the doubters wrong.

First Luke Ayling, second Lionel Messi

Released by Arsenal in 2010, Luke Ayling had played 395 matches in the Football League since then (173 in League One, 222 in the Championship) when he lined up as Leeds United captain for their first game back in the Premier League in September 2020 at Anfield. He'd put in the hard yards in the EFL and was now getting his reward.

Ayling was already a popular player before Bielsa took charge, making seventy-four appearances across the 2016–17 and 2017–18 seasons, and his injury on New Year's Day 2018 against Nottingham Forest, which put him out of action until Paul Heckingbottom's last game in charge against QPR in May, was at great detriment to the team: Leeds won 51% of their Championship games with Ayling in the starting XI across his first two seasons (thirty-five out of sixty-nine), compared to just 17% without him (four out of twenty-three).

There was far more to his game than simply winning fouls but his signature move, the 'Ayling flop', is backed up by the data – he was the second most fouled defender in the Championship under Bielsa (132 fouls won, second to Darnell Fisher) and was the most fouled full-back in the Premier League in 2020–21 (fifty-four fouls won). You can't argue with hard, scientific evidence – he knew how to win a foul.

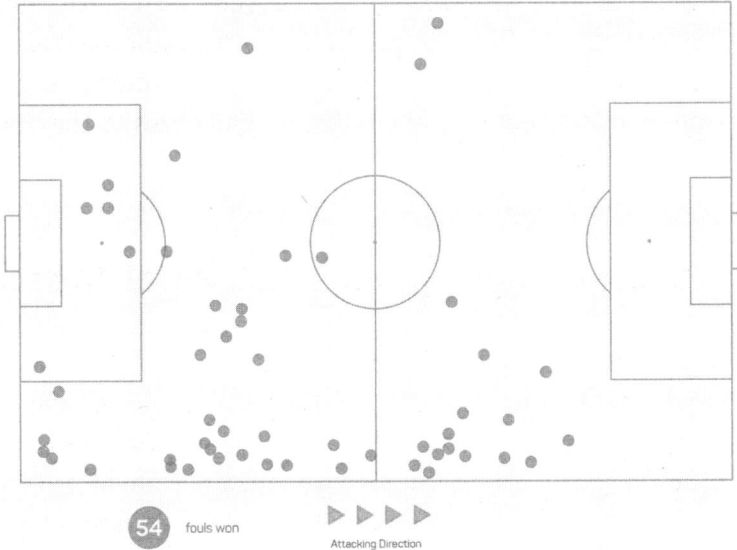

Luke Ayling Fouls Won
Leeds United | Premier League 2020-21

Opta

54 fouls won

▷ ▷ ▷ ▷
Attacking Direction

Winning free-kicks wasn't the only area in which Ayling ranked highly in the Premier League in the 2020–21 campaign. Ayling made the most tackles of any player (108), ranked fourth for possession won (279) and only eleven players completed more passes than he did (1,881). He also topped the Premier League's most unfortunate chart for goal involvements – he had the most shots (twenty-four) and created the most chances (twenty-seven) combined without scoring or assisting a goal, though he was very unlucky to have a goal ruled out for offside away at Fulham in March.

Lionel Messi was second for goals and assists combined across Europe's big-five leagues (these are: the Premier League, Ligue 1, Serie A, Bundesliga and La Liga) in the 2020–21 campaign, scoring thirty goals and assisting nine goals, and he was second for another category too: he progressed the ball upfield 5,704 metres with ball carries. The only player to progress the ball further upfield? Luke Ayling – 5,985 metres, which is just shy of four miles across the season.

Stuart Dallas, that's astonishing

The furthest distance the ball was carried during a game in the 2020–21 Premier League campaign was not by Luke Ayling, but Manchester City central defender John Stones in April 2021 against Leeds, a total of 733 metres. In the second half, with City having an extra man due to Liam Cooper's first half red card, Stones carried the ball 461 metres and 350 of those metres were upfield (that's about 31 metres further than the height of Emley Moor).

In that same half, Stuart Dallas only carried the ball twenty-four metres in total but a few of those were when he took the ball in stride in the 91st minute from a through ball from Ezgjan Alioski, shrugging off Stones before firing under Ederson to win Leeds the game at the eventual champions. It was only Leeds' second shot; Dallas has scored with the first, in the 42nd minute, and although Man City had twenty-nine of their own, the most by a team in a Premier League game all season, they only converted one. City had won thirty-six of their previous forty-three matches in all competitions and hadn't lost at home against a promoted team since February 2007 until Dallas' first brace since the Derby play-off game in May 2019 sunk them. The result also guaranteed Leeds were mathematically safe and would be spending the 2021–22 campaign in the Premier League.

Dallas was a substitute on twenty occasions in Bielsa's first season but after appearing in the XI for the Aston Villa game in April 2019, Dallas was never again a sub in a league game under Bielsa, starting 113 of his final 114 league (and play-off) games in charge. His versatility, much like Paul Madeley in the Revie era, made him so valuable to Bielsa. In the 2019–20 campaign, 61% of his league games were played at full-back, and 32% in central midfield. The following season, Dallas played 53% of his minutes in central midfield, scoring eight goals, with only Bamford bettering that with his seventeen.

In January 2022, Dallas celebrated his 250th appearance for the club – the first player to reach that total since Lucas Radebe back in 2003 – with a goal in a crucial 3–1 win over Burnley, Marcelo Bielsa's last victory at Elland Road with Leeds. He joined a stellar list of names who'd scored in their 250th games for the club and was later joined by Ayling in May 2023.

Leeds players scoring in their 250th appearance

Date	Player	Opponent
27/02/1937	Billy Furness	Bolton Wanderers
26/11/1955	John Charles	Leicester City
08/04/1966	Billy Bremner	Fulham
06/01/1973	Mick Jones	Tottenham Hotspur
14/02/1998	Rod Wallace	Birmingham City
02/01/2022	Stuart Dallas	Burnley
13/05/2023	Luke Ayling	Newcastle United

Dallas retired in April 2024 – three years to the day since his two-goal afternoon at the Etihad – and sometimes a graphic can speak for itself. He was absolutely everywhere in a Leeds shirt during his 250 appearances across the Championship and Premier League. Squint hard enough to see the second goal at Man City.

Stuart Dallas Touches
Leeds United

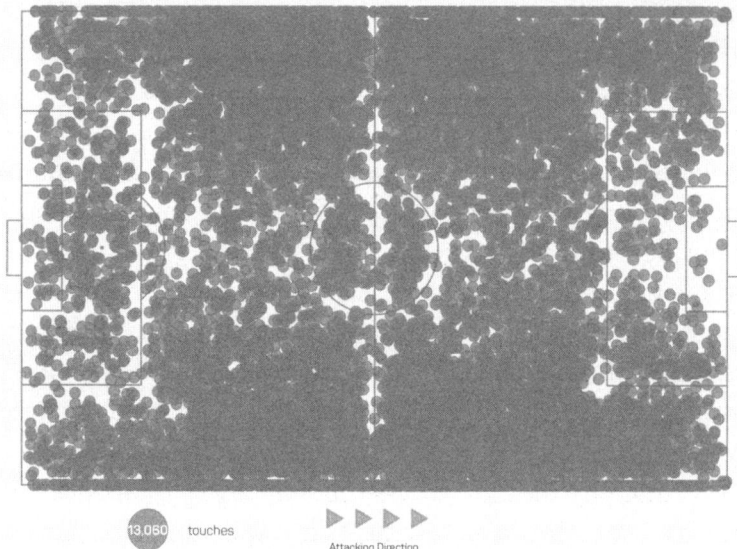

◯ Opta

13,060 touches

▷ ▷ ▷ ▷
Attacking Direction

The Yorkshire Pirlo

The player who perhaps benefitted most from Marcelo Bielsa's coaching and influence was midfielder Kalvin Phillips. In the summer of 2018, it seemed to be between Phillips and Ronaldo Vieira for the number 4 role in Bielsa's team, but with Vieira sold to Sampdoria to fund the signing of Patrick Bamford from Middlesbrough, Phillips became the choice for that position. He never looked back. In the 2017–18 season, he'd scored seven league goals (a total bettered by only Kemar Roofe and Pierre-Michel Lasogga) and had fired in the final goal of Heckingbottom's reign against QPR, but it took him thirty games to score under Bielsa as he adapted to a more withdrawn role.

Leeds fans used to chant that Ronaldo Vieira 'never gives the ball away' in acknowledgement of his excellent use of the ball. The data, sadly, showed that he did give the ball away 441 times from 2,196 pass attempts. Still, 'he only gives the ball away 20% of the time' isn't as catchy, I'll grant you.

Phillips had made his debut aged nineteen in April 2015 away at Wolves and five days later scored his first goal, a wind-assisted tap-in at home to Cardiff City. The following season he was used sparingly by both Uwe Rosler and Steve Evans, an unused sub in nineteen of the twenty-nine occasions he was in the matchday squad. Garry Monk gave Phillips more chances in 2016–17, with twenty-seven starts, though the preferred options were Vieira and captain Liam Bridcutt. Phillips became more attacking the following season, doubling his touches in the opposition to thirty-six from eighteen the previous season, while having twenty-one more shots (forty-four) and scoring seven goals compared to one the previous season. But he was still far from being a vital member of the squad.

It is the most attacking role Phillips had at Leeds as Bielsa used him 72% of the time in the Championship playing defensive midfield in a 4-1-4-1 formation. The data shows the differences in his play between the seasons. He averaged just twelve successful passes per ninety minutes in his own half in 2017–18, which rose to thirty-four per ninety in 2018–19. With Leeds controlling more of the ball, Phillips' role became central to the system – he averaged twenty-five more touches per ninety minutes in 2018–19 (seventy-nine) than he did in 2017–18 (fifty-four). He completed 2,111 passes in the Championship in forty-four games in 2018–19, up from just 962 in 2017–18 (with just under 500 minutes difference). His passing accuracy, at 72% in 2017–18, rose 10% to 82% in that first Bielsa season.

Kalvin Phillips – Championship	2017–18	2018–19
Games Played	41	44
Minutes Played	3,198	3,683
Passing Accuracy	72%	82%
Shots per ninety mins	1.2	0.9
Completed Passes per ninety mins	27	52
Touches per ninety mins	54	79
Successful Long Passes per ninety mins	2.5	4.9

During his two seasons in the Championship under Bielsa, Phillips ranked in the top five midfielders for completed passes (fourth, 3,771), long passes completed (third, 399), tackles (second, 212), interceptions (second, 113) and winning possession (fourth, 602). It was this form (most likely coupled with Leeds winning promotion) that convinced England manager Gareth Southgate to give Phillips his debut in September 2020, four days before the first game of the season against Liverpool – the first player to appear for the Three Lions before making their Premier League debut since Wilfried Zaha in 2012. Phillips was Leeds United's first England player since Alan Smith in 2004, and first to debut while at Leeds since Lee Bowyer in 2002. None of it would have been possible without the influence of Bielsa, who gifted Phillips a Newell's Old Boys shirt by way of congratulating him.

However, as Phillips' place in the Leeds team became such an influence, so was the case that, without him, Leeds were not quite the same outfit. In 2020–21, Leeds had a 54% win ratio with him in the starting XI, compared to 30% without him, while points-per-game dropped from 1.79 with, to 0.90 without (which is around thirty-four points across an entire season). Leeds lost seven of ten games without him in the XI, compared to eight in twenty-eight with him. While football is obviously a team sport, taking out a team's most central player is bound to have consequences.

The following season, it became more pronounced. Due to injury, Phillips started just twelve Premier League games under Bielsa but Leeds picked up three wins, six draws and three defeats, having a goal difference of just minus two with him on the pitch (twelve scored, fourteen conceded). In the fourteen without him in the XI, Leeds lost ten and conceded forty-six goals. There were other factors at play (including injuries to Cooper and Bamford, and a depleted squad) but Phillips' influence in the middle was greatly missed.

With Phillips on Pitch	2021–22 – PL under Bielsa	Without Phillips on Pitch
12	Games	14
3	Wins	2
6	Draws	2
3	Losses	10
12	Goals Scored	17
1	Scored/90	1
14	Goals Conceded	46
-2	Goal Difference	-29

The 2020–21 campaign saw Phillips rank in the top ten (per ninety minutes) in the Premier League among English midfielders for completed passes, long passes completed, possession won, tackles, interceptions and passing accuracy.

Stat	Kalvin Phillips	English Midfield Rank (Out of 29)
Completed Passes per ninety mins	44.1	6
Possession Won per ninety mins	7.9	2
Tackles per ninety mins	2.7	3
Interceptions per ninety mins	1.7	5
Successful Long Passes per ninety mins	5.0	2
Passing Accuracy	84.7%	9

There was no surprise when Phillips was named in the England squad for EURO 2020 at the end of that season, and his performances helped the Three Lions to the final against Italy. His seven appearances at the tournament equalled the most by a Leeds player in major tournaments for England, level with Jack Charlton. Sadly, the final did not end the same way as 1966.

Player	Major tournament apps	Tournament(s)
Jack Charlton	7	1966 & 1970 FIFA World Cups
Kalvin Phillips	7	EURO 2020
Rio Ferdinand	5	2002 FIFA World Cup
Danny Mills	5	2002 FIFA World Cup
Terry Cooper	4	1970 FIFA World Cup
Norman Hunter	3	EURO 1968 & 1970 FIFA World Cup
David Batty	2	EURO 1992
Trevor Cherry	1	EURO 1980
Allan Clarke	1	1970 FIFA World Cup
Robbie Fowler	1	2002 FIFA World Cup
Nigel Martyn	1	EURO 2000

End of season form to build on . . .

After a poor start to 2021 – in the first eleven games that year, Leeds lost seven, including a 3–0 loss to Mark Wright's Crawley Town in the FA Cup – Leeds' form improved after a 2–0 loss to West Ham on 8 March, a game which featured a rare Illan Meslier penalty save.

In the final ten games of the 2020–21 Premier League season, the only side who won more points than Leeds (twenty-three) were Liverpool (twenty-six), with the sides sharing a 1–1 draw in April. After securing safety with the 2–1 win at Man City, it felt like the first time under Bielsa there was absolutely no pressure on the games (aside from the final two games of 2019–20). Leeds won seven of the last ten, ending the season with a run of four consecutive victories by an aggregate score of 12–2, the club's best winning run in the top-flight in the same season since a run of six wins in March and April 2001.

PL 2020–21 – Last 10 Games	W	D	L	GF	GA	GD	Pts
Liverpool	8	2	0	21	6	15	26
Leeds United	7	2	1	19	8	11	23
Manchester City	7	0	3	27	13	14	21
Arsenal	6	2	2	18	10	8	20
Manchester United	6	2	2	18	12	6	20
Tottenham Hotspur	5	2	3	21	15	6	17
West Ham United	5	2	3	20	15	5	17
Chelsea	5	2	3	14	11	3	17

Brazilian winger Raphinha, who was signed the previous October from Rennes, where he gave up the opportunity to play in the UEFA Champions League to join Leeds, missed the three games in the run-in where Leeds failed to win, appearing in all seven wins and scoring one and assisting four goals. Raphinha was an exceptional addition to Leeds, creating sixty-four chances from his first start until the end of the season, with only three players creating more in the Premier League, and he was level with Kevin De Bruyne for assists in that time. A genuine superstar and Ballon d'Or contender (though sadly not with Leeds).

Premier League 2020–21 (22 Nov to end of season)	Chances Created
Mason Mount	73
Bruno Fernandes	69
Luke Shaw	66
Trent Alexander-Arnold	64
Raphinha	64
Premier League 2020–21 (22 Nov to end of season)	**Assists**
Raphinha	9
Kevin De Bruyne	9

Bruno Fernandes	9
Son Heung-Min	8
Jamie Vardy	8

The end of the era

The 3–1 victory over West Bromwich Albion on the final day of the 2020–21 campaign saw the final appearances of three Bielsa stalwarts, with Ezgjan Alioski, Gaetano Berardi and Pablo Hernández saying farewell. It wasn't known at the time if Alioski would remain with the club (he eventually joined Al-Ahli in Saudi Arabia in the summer), and the North Macedonian completed the full ninety. Both Berardi and Hernández, however, knew this was their last game for the club and were both substituted off with twenty minutes to go to be given a standing ovation. Berardi had made 157 appearances, and his longevity was such that he was the last remaining player at the club who'd made an appearance alongside Noel Hunt. Leeds didn't lose any of the last nineteen league games he featured in, nor did they concede a goal with him on the pitch in any of his final nine matches, totalling 457 minutes.

Both of Berardi's goals for Leeds came in the cup, scoring against Newport in the FA Cup and Salford in the League Cup, both times as captain. He is one of seven players to score more than once for Leeds but never in the league, along with Lucas Radebe (three), Jamie Forrester, Roque Junior, Michael Ricketts, Jason Crowe and Ethan Ampadu (all two).

Hernández was visibly emotional on departing Elland Road for the final time – and thank goodness there were at least 9,000 fans in the ground that day to give him an ovation – and his thirty-six goals and forty assists in 175 appearances do not do justice to his quality. He was already a sublime player before Bielsa's arrival but the pair together struck gold. Asked early in the 2018–19 campaign whether he could make Hernández a better player, Bielsa's reply was: 'I think he can make me a better coach – he is one of the best players in his position I have worked with in my career.' Either way, Hernández was the Championship's most creative player that season, creating 122 chances, scoring twelve and assisting twelve. His contribution to games as a substitute in the promotion run-in of the following season read three goals and three assists but his presence was worth many more.

He started sixty-nine league and play-off games under Bielsa, winning 62.3% of them – as of the end of the 2024–25 season, that is the second best win ratio by a player in their games in the starting XI under a manager in the club's history.

Player	Manager	Starts	Wins	Win %
Ethan Ampadu	Daniel Farke	75	47	62.7%
Pablo Hernández	Marcelo Bielsa	69	43	62.3%
Junior Firpo	Daniel Farke	52	32	61.5%
Joe Rodon	Daniel Farke	91	56	61.5%
Mick Jones	Don Revie	215	131	60.9%

The following season did not start well. A 5–1 defeat away at Manchester United was the heaviest by Leeds on the opening day of a league season since 1981, which was a 5–1 defeat at Swansea in a campaign in which Leeds would later be relegated. By Christmas, Leeds had just three wins in eighteen Premier League games, and though Raphinha was joint fourth top scorer in the league with eight goals, Leeds had only won two of the eight games he'd scored in. Bamford had been injured in September and when he returned to the team as a sub in December against Brentford, he scored a last-minute equaliser, his forty-fifth and final goal under Bielsa; he injured his hamstring celebrating and didn't reappear until March. There were a couple of possible sliding doors moments in that final season under Bielsa but the Brentford game certainly represented one – Cooper, Phillips and Bamford, seen by many as the spine of the team, were all injured in that game. Leeds had gone 1–0 ahead but it was the fifth time out of eight games Leeds had scored first and failed to win, something unheard of previously under

Bielsa. Had they held on and beaten Brentford, they'd have gone up to twelfth in the table, but they drew 2–2. After this draw, they faced Chelsea, Man City and Arsenal and lost them all by an aggregate score of 14–3, the first time they'd lost three in a row under Bielsa. The 7–0 loss at Man City was the club's joint heaviest defeat and the worst in the league since 1934.

The starting XIs, while missing key players, remained experienced enough but the substitute benches Bielsa was having to name due to injuries and coronavirus restrictions were beginning to resemble the footballing equivalent of a creche; ten of the benches he named in his final Premier League campaign had an average age of under twenty-one, with the bench against Arsenal on 18 December having an average of just 19 years and 104 days, with fifteen-year-old Archie Gray among them. Gray would've become the club's youngest ever player had he been substituted on. Leeds awarded a Premier League record eight debuts to teenagers under Bielsa in 2021–22, with Summerville, Cresswell, Gelhardt, Drameh, McKinstry, Greenwood, Hjelde and Bate all making their bows, but there was a distinct feeling it was under duress – between them, they made a combined total of just twenty-seven league appearances under Bielsa, and only Gelhardt (two), Drameh (one) and Cresswell (one) appeared in a starting XI. Gelhardt made the biggest impact in winning two penalties, scoring against Chelsea and assisting a goal against Burnley, in just 388 minutes before Bielsa's departure.

> Lewis Bate's two appearances under Bielsa were both away at West Ham, starting in the FA Cup and coming on as a sub one week later in the Premier League. He is one of two players to play under him for Leeds who has all the letters in 'Bielsa' in his name, along with Lewis Baker.

2022 started well, with league victories over Burnley and West Ham United, with Jack Harrison scoring a hat-trick in the latter in a 3–2 win – the second Sunday hat-trick for Leeds along with Lee Chapman's at Sheffield Wednesday in January 1992. After having faced twenty-seven shots on target in their last two games of 2021, defeats to Man City and Arsenal, Leeds restricted Burnley and West Ham to just seven between them. Heading into the home game against Newcastle on 22 January, Leeds were top of the form table in the Premier League for 2022 and had attempted the most shots of any side in the year so far (forty).

Newcastle had just one win and twelve points in the Premier League ahead of facing Leeds, who were ten points clear of the Magpies in fifteenth. Victory for Leeds would've pushed them eleven points clear of relegation and maintained their 100% record in 2022. Instead, a Jonjo Shelvey free-kick evaded Illan Meslier to give Newcastle a 1–0 victory and from that game until the end of the following season, Newcastle picked up fifty-one more points than Leeds. See what I meant about a sliding doors moment?

But by the end of that following season, Bielsa was long gone. After the Newcastle defeat, a miserable February followed. It started with a rousing 3–3 draw away at Aston Villa, from 3–1 down, before a dismal 3–0 defeat to Everton – one of only two Premier League games under Bielsa where Leeds didn't have a shot on target – and another defeat against Manchester United. Though Leeds did pull the game back to 2–2, from 2–0 down in the second half, Raphinha's equaliser in the 54th minute was the final goal of the Marcelo Bielsa era as Leeds lost 4–2. His last two games were 6–0 and 4–0 defeats to Liverpool and Spurs, to see Leeds break the Premier League record for goals conceded in a single month at twenty. This record would be broken – by Leeds United in April 2023, when they let in twenty-three.

On 27 February 2022, after 170 games, Leeds announced they had parted company with the Argentinian. The Bielsa era was over. But it lives on in the memories of all Leeds fans who witnessed his glorious football, and the players who made it happen.

8

2024-25 PART 1

After the stability of three and a half years of Bielsa, it didn't take long for Leeds to go back to the managerial churn that had preceded the Argentinian's reign.

His replacement was Jesse Marsch, who managed to keep the club in the Premier League in 2021–22 with four wins in ten games; three of them had been 90th minute winners, which summed up the general chaos of the games under his management. The following season started well with seven points in the opening three games, a position from which only two Premier League clubs had ever been relegated. Leeds made that three, though by that time Marsch had departed following a run of just two wins in seventeen league games. Javier Gracia replaced him but after a mere eleven games (and having broken the record - previously set by Leeds themselves – for goals conceded in a month of Premier League football in April 2023) he was replaced for the final four games by Sam Allardyce in a desperate final throw of the dice. Unsurprisingly, Leeds went down.

Amid the chaos of loan clauses and even some players refusing to play, Daniel Farke joined the club in the summer of 2023 and, after an understandably slow start, led the club on a nine-match league winning run in January and February 2024, equalling a club record. Having been seventeen points behind first place on New Year's Eve, Leeds went top of the league for Easter and an immediate return to the Premier League looked likely. But a dreadful end to the season, with a Championship low of four points collected in the final six games, saw Leeds finish third on ninety points, the first side to win that many without getting automatic promotion in the second tier since 1998.

The season ended with the club's sixth unsuccessful play-off campaign, losing 1–0 to Southampton (on, of all days, my thirtieth birthday) in the final at Wembley – yet another bad day out in the capital. It had been a painful few years for Leeds and their fans, but the 2024–25 season was when things were about to become fun again.

But it wasn't going to be easy, with another summer of squad churn to contend with. Missing out on the Premier League after defeat to Southampton meant that player departures were inevitable. Even as a Premier League club, Leeds were powerless to stop Raphinha and Kalvin Phillips depart in 2022 for Barcelona and Manchester City respectively. With another season of Championship football looming, the club's top talents were always likely to be snapped up – though some departures hurt more than others.

Cooper and Ayling

Heroes of the 2019–20 promotion team – and mainstays in the side that finished in the top-half of the Premier League – both Liam Cooper and Luke Ayling departed the club in the summer of 2024. While sad to see them go, they weren't surprise departures; both had seen their minutes decrease under Daniel Farke, with each averaging just fifty-three minutes per appearance in the Championship in 2023–24 – their lowest in a league season at Leeds. Cooper scored the first goal of the Farke reign, a header against Cardiff, and in doing so injured himself and was substituted off. Ayling also started the Cardiff match – which was the last of 131 games they started alongside each other – and in the third league game of the season against West Brom he scored his eleventh and final goal for the club. It meant that his last five goals for the club were all scored under a different manager, becoming the first player in the club's history to score five goals in a row under a different manager each time.

Date	Opponents	Manager
14/08/2021	Manchester United	Marcelo Bielsa
18/03/2022	Wolverhampton Wanderers	Jesse Marsch
18/03/2023	Wolverhampton Wanderers	Javier Gracia
13/05/2023	Newcastle United	Sam Allardyce
18/08/2023	West Bromwich Albion	Daniel Farke

Playing (and scoring) under different managers was something Cooper also got used to. Three of his first four league starts in 2014 were under a different manager (two under Dave Hockaday, one each under Darko Milanic and Neil Redfearn) and in total Cooper made an appearance under thirteen different managers (including caretakers), a club record and three more than the next most, Gary Kelly on ten. His goal against Cardiff also meant Farke was the sixth of those thirteen he'd scored under, equalling the Leeds United club record.

Player	Managers Scored Under (Including Caretakers)
Peter Lorimer	Revie, Clough, Lindley, Armfield, Gray, Gunby
Trevor Cherry	Revie, Clough, Lindley, Armfield, Adamson, Clarke
Frank Gray	Revie, Armfield, Stein, Lindley, Adamson, Gray
Arthur Graham	Armfield, Stein, Lindley, Adamson, Clarke, Gray
Liam Cooper	Redfearn, Rosler, Heckingbottom, Bielsa, Marsch, Farke

In total, Cooper started a match alongside 123 different players at Leeds United, a tally that only Gary Kelly can better (136). Cooper spanned such a long era that the list of players is not so much a who's who but a 'who's that'? One game started alongside the likes of Aapo Halme, Brian Montenegro, Granddi Ngoyi, Dario Del Fabro and Ross Turnbull. Two alongside Lee Erwin, Jordan Botaka, Laurens De Bock and Tyler Denton. Five alongside Pawel Cibicki and Caleb Ekuban, eight with Adryan. Fourteen alongside the midfield trio of Rudy Austin, Tom Adeyemi and Marc Roca. Outside of the promotion team, his most starts were with Marco Silvestri (sixty-seven) in the days before

Bielsa's arrival. Ayling's 131 games starting alongside Cooper were bettered only by the 136 times both Kalvin Phillips and Stuart Dallas were named in the XI alongside the centre-back.

Cooper made his last appearance as a substitute in the second leg of the play-offs against Norwich, his 284th game for the club. Only twenty-eight players have made more appearances for Leeds. He started 222 games as captain, the first in January 2015 at Sunderland in the FA Cup and the final time in March 2024 at Watford (this 222nd game as captain ended 2–2). Only Billy Bremner (489) and Trevor Cherry (224) have started more games with the armband, and only Norman Hunter has worn the number 6 shirt more often. As for Ayling, he ranks joint thirty-first in the club's all-time appearance holders, with only three players wearing the number 2 shirt on more occasions. He also captained the club eighty times and under seven different managers – only Cooper was skipper under more (eleven).

Between them, Cooper and Ayling made 552 appearances in total; to give an idea of their longevity in the face of the tumultuous nature of the club when they joined, that's significantly more than the combined appearances of the starting XIs in their debut games – 359 for the XI against Middlesbrough on Cooper's debut in August 2014, and 296 for the XI against Birmingham on Ayling's debut in August 2016.

vs Middlesbrough – 16 August 2014	App Number	vs Birmingham – 13 August 2016	App Number
Marco Silvestri	2	Robert Green	3
Sam Byram	82	Luke Ayling	1
Stephen Warnock	47	Sol Bamba	55
Rodolph Austin	83	Kyle Bartley	3
Jason Pearce	93	Chris Wood	40
Luke Murphy	42	Marcus Antonsson	3
Billy Sharp	1	Pablo Hernández	2
Tommaso Bianchi	2	Charlie Taylor	75
Nicky Ajose	3	Hadi Sacko	3

Souleymane Doukara	3	Ronaldo Vieira	4
Liam Cooper	1	Alex Mowatt	107

Leaving with the best wishes of everyone connected with Leeds, Cooper eventually joined Bulgarian side CSKA Sofia in September 2024, while Ayling had joined Middlesbrough on loan at the end of the 2023–24 season (later made permanent), where from February until the end of the season he had the most open play assists (eight) of any player in the entire division. It was two more than even Georginio Rutter managed.

Rutter and Summerville

It was a tough start for Georginio Rutter at Leeds. A club record signing in January 2023 with Leeds perilously close to the foot of the Premier League, in eleven league games that season he appeared under four different managers (Marsch once, Skubala three times, Gracia six and Allardyce once). Given a meagre twenty-four minutes per appearance Leeds lost eight of his eleven games as their season descended into a soap opera, and relegation duly followed. There was one sign of life in the last game of 2022–23, however – the club's last Premier League goal may have been scored by Jack Harrison, but it was assisted by Georginio Rutter. Goals by Harrison wouldn't feature again, but assists by Rutter were about to become a very familiar sight.

Rutter ended the 2023–24 Championship campaign with fifteen open play assists, three more than any other player, and only Emiliano Buendia in 2020–21 for Farke's Norwich side (sixteen) has more in a season that Opta has on record since 2013–14. Only Finn Azaz created more open play chances than Rutter's eighty-five and his quality saw him targeted by Championship defenders – he was the most fouled player in the division, winning 119 free kicks, the most since Jack Grealish for Aston Villa in 2018–19. Thirty-nine of those fouls were won in the final third of the pitch, also the most of any player.

He was a terrific dribbler and played with a freedom of spirit (and often a smile on his face), with a total of 309 dribbles across the Championship season – the third most in one season on record. Sixteen of these were in the 3–1 victory over Leicester City in February when, despite some failed attempts in the second half, it was Rutter's powerful run into the Leicester area that eventually led to the ball dropping for Connor Roberts to equalise, which gave Leeds the impetus to go on and win the game.

It's for all of these qualities that it wasn't a surprise when he was the subject of bids from Premier League clubs over the summer. He did stick around for the start of the 2024–25 campaign, featuring against Portsmouth on the opening day (and assisting Wilfried Gnonto's goal) and coming on as a substitute in the League Cup defeat to Middlesbrough, before signing for Premier League side Brighton and Hove Albion.

Rutter's performances saw him make the 2023–24 Championship Team of the Year, and alongside him was teammate Crysencio Summerville, who also won the league's Player of the Year. Between them, they'd created sixty-two chances for one another in the Championship (thirty-one apiece, in a neat piece of symmetry for how well they linked up), which was twenty-two more than any other duo in the division. Rutter assisted six of Summerville's twenty Championship goals, the most assists by a Leeds player to another in a season since Robert Snodgrass assisted six of Jermaine Beckford's goals in League One in 2008–09.

It wasn't just with Rutter that Summerville excelled in 2023–24, with the Dutchman creating 120 chances in the Championship, which has been bettered by a Leeds player on record just once, when Pablo Hernández (of course) created 122 in 2018–19. Summerville scored twenty Championship goals, with only two players scoring more, while in all competitions he was the first Leeds player to score twenty goals and assist ten goals (twenty-one goals, ten assists) in a season since Jimmy Floyd Hasselbaink in 1998–99.

In early August 2024, Summerville departed to join West Ham United. While few fans were surprised to see him go, with Rutter leaving a fortnight later it meant the club had lost players who had managed a combined twenty-nine goals and twenty-six assists the previous season (in the Championship in 2023–24, forty-four of the eighty-five goals Leeds had scored had either been scored or assisted by Summerville or Rutter, amounting to 52% of the total output). That creativity would be hard to replace, but a month earlier they'd lost something even more valuable than goals, assists or mazy dribbles – a modern-day link to the club's vast history.

Gray matter

Between them, members of the Gray family have made 1,077 appearances for Leeds United – so far. Starting on New Year's Day 1966, when Eddie Gray made his goalscoring debut against Sheffield Wednesday as a seventeen-year-old, the Gray name runs through Leeds like a stick of Blackpool rock (Eddie's second and third appearances for Leeds were against Blackpool, incidentally).

At least one member of the Gray family has made an appearance in just under 17% of the club's games in its entire history, while since 1966 that accounts for just over 27% of the games played in that time. From Boxing Day 1974 until May 1979, at least one member of the Gray family played in 227 out of 228 games, the exception in this run coming on 12 April 1975 in a 2–1 win over Arsenal. After this game, there was a 201 game streak with either Eddie or his brother Frank making an appearance, while both brothers played in 140 of those 201 games.

Eddie made his last appearance in the final game of 1983–84, when he was player-manager, and Frank played his last game on the final day of the following season. Eddie remained in charge of the first team until October 1985 and later returned for a second spell in an attempt to save the club from relegation in the 2003–04 Premier League season. Though he was unable to prevent relegation, it did mean that at Leeds he'd managed both Peter Lorimer (club debut September 1962) and also James Milner, who was still playing in the Premier League in 2024–25.

Ten years after Frank's final appearance, his son Andy made his Leeds United debut as a seventeen-year-old against Notts County in the League Cup in September 1995. He eventually broke into the first team towards the end of the season, starting the final twelve Premier League games of 1995–96 and playing against Aston Villa in the League Cup final. The following season, however, two of his three starts were against Darlington in the League Cup, and he left the club in 1998. Returning aged thirty-four on a free transfer under Neil Warnock in the summer of 2012, he made his first Leeds appearance for 15 years and 206 days in a 3–2 win at Peterborough in August, breaking the club record for gap between appearances by eight years, previously held by John Lukic (7 years and 173 days between 1983 and 1990). Lukic had been in goal when Andy Gray made his first debut in 1995, and had made 127 appearances alongside Eddie Gray and seventy-six alongside Andy's father Frank in the 1980s.

Playing alongside Andy in the first and last games of his second spell in 2012–13 was full-back Sam Byram, who in 2023 would re-join Leeds after leaving in January 2016. His 7 years and 206 days put him in second place for gap between appearances, behind Andy Gray's fifteen-year record. And when Byram came on as a substitute for his second debut in August 2023 against Cardiff, he was playing alongside a seventeen-year-old Archie Gray, son of Andy, making his Leeds United debut. The Grays really are everywhere at this club.

At 17 years and 147 days, Archie was the youngest member of his family to debut for the club, breaking his dad's record by 161 days. Family bragging rights were assured . . . until younger brother Harry came along and featured in April 2025 aged 16 years and 195 days.

Date	Player	Opponent	Age on Debut
21/04/2025	Harry Gray	Stoke City	16 years, 195 days
06/08/2023	Archie Gray	Cardiff City	17 years, 147 days
19/09/1995	Andy Gray	Notts County	17 years, 308 days
01/01/1966	Eddie Gray	Sheffield Wednesday	17 years, 349 days
10/02/1973	Frank Gray	Leicester City	18 years, 106 days

Seeing any young player break into the first team is always nice, but when it's someone from a family with the history of the Grays it makes it extra special. Archie ended up featuring in fifty-two of the fifty-five games in 2023–24, the second most appearances by a teenager in a season for Leeds – behind the fifty-three matches played by Byram in his breakout season in 2012–13.

Season	Player	Teenager Games
2012–13	Sam Byram	53
2023–24	Archie Gray	52
2008–09	Fabian Delph	51
1949–50	John Charles	47
1963–64	Gary Sprake	47
1993–94	Gary Kelly	47
2015–16	Lewis Cook	47

The first leg of the Championship play-offs saw Gray make his fiftieth appearance for Leeds United to break the club record for youngest to fifty games for the club, aged just 18 years and 61 days – Terry Connor had been the previous youngest in 1981 aged 18 years and 90 days, playing alongside Eddie Gray. The third youngest to do so is James Milner in 2004 against Arsenal; his manager that day was – you guessed it – Eddie Gray.

Date	Player	Opponent	Age on Fiftieth Game
12/05/2024	Archie Gray	Norwich City	18 years, 61 days
07/02/1981	Terry Connor	Tottenham Hotspur	18 years, 90 days
16/04/2004	James Milner	Arsenal	18 years, 103 days
29/04/1950	John Charles	Bury	18 years, 123 days
01/10/1963	Gary Sprake	Northampton Town	18 years, 181 days

With Luke Ayling's powers on the wane, Gray was the preferred option at right-back, only playing 30% of his minutes in central midfield compared to 64% at full-back. He did get a run-out in midfield away at Chelsea in the FA Cup, however, winning ITV's man of the match from commentator Lee Dixon. He misplaced just three of his forty-three passes and, proving it was in the blood, made six dribbles – the most of any player on either side. His performance that night proved that he had what it took to play in the top-flight, and Leeds fans hoped it would be with the Whites.

It wasn't to be, and Gray's July departure to Spurs was a major disappointment. Leeds had sold plenty of other young, talented players to Premier League sides over the years, but losing one with such a link with the club's storied past particularly hurt. He's one of only four players to play fifty times for the club but only ever as a teenager. Two of the other three went on to play for the England senior side, and it's surely only a matter of time before Archie joins them.

Player	Every Leeds Game as a Teenager
Lewis Cook	85
Ronaldo Vieira	71
James Milner	54
Archie Gray	52

And you never know – with Harry making his debut in the club's promotion campaign (a promotion he certainly enjoyed celebrating) and with Leeds back in the Premier League, could he be the next Gray playing regularly in the Leeds first team, breaking yet more records?

Leeds Fringe

Others to leave the club in the summer of 2024 included goalkeeper Kristoffer Klaesson, who was an unused sub on seventy-one occasions but made three appearances for Leeds and ended on the winning side in all three. He was the first Leeds player to debut after the departure of Marcelo Bielsa, coming on for an injured Illan Meslier at 2–0 down at Molineux in March 2022. At full-time, Leeds had won 3–2 and Klaesson made four saves without conceding. He was back on the bench for the next game and eventually made his next appearance on New Year's Day 2024, with Meslier banned and Karl Darlow injured, featuring in a 3–0 win over Birmingham. His next game was in the FA Cup the following week, another 3–0 victory over Peterborough. Despite this exceptional win ratio – and having gone 215 minutes without conceding, making eight saves – it was his last game for Leeds. He left the club as the only player to play as many as three games and win every single time.

Also departing were Jamie Shackleton and Ian Poveda, who'd combined for the seventy-seventh and final Championship goal of the 2019–20 promotion season, Poveda assisting Shackleton in the 4–0 win over Charlton. Between them, they made 124 appearances for Leeds but eighty of those were coming on as a substitute, with Shackleton's total of fifty-five behind only Patrick Bamford, John Pearson and Mateo Joseph in the list of sub appearances since they were introduced in 1965. 92% of Poveda's league games were as a sub, the third-most behind Jay-Roy Grot (95%) and Jaidon Anthony (94%), and his two starts were separated by 1,119 days – a record across a Leeds player's first two starts (they also turned out to be Poveda's only two appearances in a Leeds starting XI).

Date	Player	Days between First Two Starts
12/08/2023	Ian Poveda	1,119
20/04/1965	Peter Lorimer	934
23/10/1948	Len Browning	759
01/04/1975	Gary Liddell	701
07/03/2018	Bailey Peacock-Farrell	701

Charlie Cresswell was given the number 5 shirt at the start of the 2023–24 season but the form of Rodon, Struijk and Ampadu – plus having experienced backup in Liam Cooper – kept him confined to the bench. After featuring in three of the first four league games of the season, he played only seven Championship minutes for the remainder of the season. Cody Drameh was another player who spent more time sat on the bench (seventeen times) than on the pitch (ten games) for Leeds, though when he did feature it tended to be in high-scoring games; his ten games saw forty-four goals scored, the highest ratio of any player in the club's history. Pure drama.

Leeds	Games	Goals	Goals Against	Total	Goals per Game
Cody Drameh	10	16	28	44	4.40
Simon Johnson	12	20	28	48	4.00
Harry Roberts	87	165	174	339	3.90
Colin Grainger	37	67	77	144	3.89
Billy Jackson	39	67	82	149	3.82
Alan Humphreys	44	75	92	167	3.80

By the end of August, eight of the twenty players in the squad for May's play-off final defeat had departed. Thankfully, new heroes arrived and those still at the club were ready to go again for another crack at promotion. A remarkable season was ready to begin.

2024–25

Opening day

Between 1990 and 2009, Leeds United did not lose a single one of their opening league games of the season, a Football League record run for unbeaten openers. Starting with the 3–2 victory over Everton in August 1990 and ending with the 2–1 win over Exeter City in August 2009, Leeds went twenty in a row without losing. The run had gone on for so long that when Derby ended it with a 2–1 win at Elland Road in 2010, two of Leeds' players that day – Aidan White and Sanchez

Watt – weren't even born when Leeds had last lost an opener in 1989 away at Newcastle.

It's fair to say no players in either XI for the 2024–25 opener were born when Leeds and Portsmouth had last faced each other on the opening day of a league season (a 2–2 draw in the First Division in 1930). Facing Pompey at all was a pretty rare occurrence – February 2012 was the last meeting, a goalless draw in Neil Warnock's first official game in charge. At the end of the game, he approached the away end and gave them a fist pump; Portsmouth were second bottom and only named four substitutes, two of which Warnock signed the following season in Jamie Ashdown and David Norris. Hardly classic memories.

This time around, Leeds made a fast start and within the opening seven minutes they'd hit the woodwork three times through efforts from Gnonto, Ampadu and Gruev – the only team Opta has on record to hit the woodwork three times in the first ten minutes of a Championship match. It brought back memories of Clarke Carlisle away at Rotherham United in November 2004 who managed to, almost improbably, hit the woodwork with three efforts from corners within the first thirteen minutes of the game. He rolled his ankle after the third attempt and was substituted off; Leeds then lost 1–0, which ended Rotherham's twenty-one-game winless run.

The luck appeared to be turning, though, as Pascal Struijk converted a penalty, just the third time this century the opening goal of the season came from the spot, along with David Healy against Norwich in 2006–07 and Max Gradel against Southampton in 2011–12. Struijk also emulated the great Jack Charlton in two ways: firstly, his penalty was the first scored by a Leeds player wearing number 5 since Charlton had scored against Derby in March 1963; second, having scored against Ipswich and Preston in his last two games the previous season, Struijk was the first central defender to score in three games in a row for Leeds since Charlton in March 1972 – one of which was in the famous 7–0 hammering of Southampton.

Scoring first had been critical the previous campaign, never once conceding more than one goal after netting the opener, and it usually heralded a victory. At half-time, though, it was Leeds 1–2 Portsmouth, the first time Leeds had scored first and gone in behind at the break in a Championship game since April 2016 away at Hull. This was not an ordinary game.

Leeds equalised fifty-four seconds into the second half through Gnonto, and it remained 2–2 until the final minute of the game when, with their third touch in Leeds' box in the second half and first shot from inside the box of the half, Portsmouth made it 3–2 with a Callum Lang penalty. Despite dominating the game, Leeds were staring at their first Championship defeat after scoring first since the Derby play-off game in 2019.

Step forward Brenden Aaronson. On as a 72nd minute substitute for his first Leeds appearance since May 2023, having spent 2023–24 on loan at Union Berlin, he equalised 176 seconds after Leeds had gone 3–2 down to make it 3–3 and recover Leeds a point. In doing so, he also equalled his goal tally from the entire 2022–23 season. But he almost doubled it; in the 98th minute, he was put through one-on-one with goalkeeper Will Norris, for the twenty-seventh and final shot of a topsy-turvy game. From almost the identical spot he'd equalised, this time he put it narrowly past the post, scuppering an instant redemption story.

The twenty-two shots Leeds had in this match were their most in a Championship game since the first match of 2023–24 against Cardiff (twenty-five). In their two opening Championship games of the season under Farke, Leeds had forty-seven shots to their opponents' twelve but drew both games 2–2 and 3–3 – not the ideal start to the season but given the circumstances of the ending of the Portsmouth game, it was a point gained.

It was only the second time Leeds have drawn 3–3 in the opening game of a season; the other was in 1996 against Derby County. Less than a month later, Howard Wilkinson – who'd lost at Wembley a few months earlier – was sacked and Leeds later finished eleventh, scoring only twenty-eight league goals all season and drawing nine games 0–0. At least this time around it would be different, and certainly more entertaining . . .

Carabao loses its fizz

Before this season, Leeds had featured in the League Cup first round on eighteen occasions and progressed in seventeen of those, with sixteen wins and one penalty shootout triumph over Fleetwood in 2016 after a 2–2 draw. The other game had also been a draw, 1–1 against Doncaster in 2015, with Rovers going through 4–2 in the shootout. But the first round of the League Cup was, usually, a safe haven and nothing to worry about.

Promotion was top of the list in 2024–25, not winning a cup competition, but in any case, Leeds didn't have a particularly fine history in the League Cup, despite it becoming the club's first major trophy when they won it in 1968. Since then, Leeds had made the semi-finals just four times – in 1978, 1979, 1991 and 1996 – and only in the latter did they make the final again, losing 3–0 to Aston Villa. From 1996–97 onwards, even a quarter-final appearance was rare, just two in 2012–13 and 2016–17, losing to Chelsea and Liverpool. Two of the club's four heaviest defeats also came in the League Cup, losing 7–0 to West Ham in 1966 and 7–0 to Arsenal in 1979, both of which remain the only two times a top-flight side has won by that big a margin against a fellow top-flight team in the competition.

In 2024–25, Leeds were drawn at home to Middlesbrough, whose side featured Luke Ayling, and though it didn't end 7–0, the 3–0 loss at Elland Road was the club's heaviest home defeat in the League Cup against a side from outside the top-flight. After having four of the first seven attempts in this match, by the time Leeds had another in the 69th minute it was 3–0 to Middlesbrough and the game was out of sight. It was the first time Leeds had conceded three goals in each of their first two games of a season since 1959 and they had now conceded sixteen goals across the previous eight games. What Leeds really needed now was a clean sheet.

The defeat to Middlesbrough marked the final appearance of Georginio Rutter. He became the fourteenth player to play his last game for Leeds in the League Cup first round, joining the likes of Steve Guppy, Eirik Bakke, Ben Parker, Zac Thompson and Liam Bridcutt.

End of August

After conceding six in two games, Leeds then kept three consecutive clean sheets. The first came in a goalless draw against West Brom, which was not a game for the footballing purists; just days after the club announced Rutter's departure, the game lacked any of the spark that he may have provided, and Leeds mustered just six touches in West Brom's penalty area, and there were only nineteen touches in either box all game – a Championship low for 2024–25. Following this came consecutive 2–0 victories in Yorkshire derbies, against Sheffield Wednesday at Hillsborough and Hull at Elland Road. The win in Sheffield was Daniel Farke's 100th victory as a Championship manager in just his 190th match at this level, the quickest any manager has reached 100 wins in the Championship era (2004–05 onwards) and the quickest in the second tier overall since Harry Bradshaw of Arsenal in 1903. Farke's top-flight record may have been questioned (continually), but at this level his ability to create winning teams cannot be disputed.

Date of 100th Win	Manager	Games to 100 Championship Wins
23/08/2024	Daniel Farke	190
01/12/2012	Mick McCarthy	193
21/11/2017	Steve Bruce	194
18/02/2017	Chris Hughton	196
25/09/2010	Billy Davies	217

The victory over Hull at the end of August saw three Leeds players make their debuts, the most in the same league game that wasn't the opening day of a season since Darren Kenton, Peter Sweeney and Bradley Johnson all made their bows in a 1–0 win at Crewe in January 2008. Manor Solomon, who'd scored against Real Madrid in a UEFA Champions League game as recently as 2020, joined on loan from Spurs and made an immediate impression, assisting Mateo Joseph's opener and in doing so became the first Leeds player to assist on their debut since Barry Douglas in Bielsa's first game against Stoke in August 2018. With sixteen minutes remaining, Largie Ramazani was introduced for his first game, and Japanese midfielder Ao Tanaka followed twelve minutes later. In the time he was on the pitch, Tanaka gave the Leeds crowd a taste of his passing ability – he completed eighteen passes, only thirteen fewer than Hull managed as a team in that time.

It thankfully wasn't the case with Solomon, but assisting on your Leeds debut doesn't always guarantee a successful stint at the club. Others to do it are Lamine Sakho against Newcastle (nineteen games in the club's 2003–04 relegation season), Michael Ricketts (his only assist in twenty-nine games) and Peter Sweeney (only started five more games for the club afterwards).

Solomon was the first Israeli player to play for Leeds, while Tanaka was the first Japanese player. Japan have steadily risen in the FIFA world rankings in recent years, from as low as fifty-seventh in 2017 to ending in the top twenty at the end of each year since 2022. In alignment with their success, Japanese players have started appearing with far more regularity in the English game. Between 2004–05 and 2021–22, only three (Junichi Inamoto, Yuki Abe and Tadanari Lee) played in the Championship but in the last three seasons alone that's risen to ten players. Few have had quite the impact Tanaka would in his debut season, though.

What's in a name?

Ao Tanaka's name contains the letter 'a' four times, making up 50% of it. In Leeds United's entire history, only Bobby Webb has played for the club with a higher percentage of one letter in his name, which was 56% with the letter 'b'.

Player	Name Length	Letter	Letter total	% of that letter
Bobby Webb	9	B	5	55.6%
Ao Tanaka	8	A	4	50.0%
Roy Wood	7	O	3	42.9%
Bob Abel	7	B	3	42.9%
Peter Sweeney	12	E	5	41.7%
Bobby Sibbald	12	B	5	41.7%

With four 'a's' and one 'o' out of eight letters, Tanaka's name is made up of 62.5% vowels, which is the joint second highest percentage in the club's history along with Ian Moore. Only 2006 loanee defender Ugo Ehiogu, whose name is 66.7% vowels, can beat Tanaka. The fifth highest percentage on the list is Toumani Diagouraga, who is the only player in the club's history with ten vowels in his name to make an appearance. Rivalling him later in the season was new signing Josuha Guilavogui (nine vowels). On the flip side of that, the most consonants in a name is Cameron Borthwick-Jackson (seventeen), followed by Jimmy Floyd Hasselbaink (sixteen). Another shout-out for Borthwick-Jackson here, who is one of two players whose name is spelled with at least five letters on each row of a keyboard, along with striker Marcus Antonsson, whose name neatly fits five letters on each row.

Player	Length	Vowels	% Vowels
Ugo Ehiogu	9	6	66.7%
Ian Moore	8	5	62.5%
Ao Tanaka	8	5	62.5%
Tomi Ameobi	10	6	60.0%
Toumani Diagouraga	17	10	58.8%

The only player in the club's history whose name you can spell without using a single letter on the top row of a QWERTY keyboard is goalkeeper Jamal Blackman.

And so we go from Ao to Z. On his first start for Leeds on 21 September away at Cardiff, Largie Ramazani scored his first goal for the club, the first Belgian scorer in the club's history. He was also the fifteenth player with the letter 'z' in his name to score a goal for Leeds and first since Mateusz Klich had scored a penalty against Barnsley in the League Cup in August 2022.

First Leeds goal by Z players

Date	Player	Opponent	Goals
04/02/1922	Bill Poyntz	Bury	1
11/12/1926	Bill Menzies	West Ham United	1
05/10/1974	Duncan McKenzie	Arsenal	2
09/11/1988	Mark Aizlewood	Shrewsbury Town	1
03/10/1995	Andy Couzens	Notts County	1
30/08/2003	Zoumana Camara	Middlesbrough	1
07/08/2004	Frazer Richardson	Derby County	1
15/01/2011	Sanchez Watt	Scunthorpe United	1
09/08/2011	Ramon Nunez	Bradford City	2
17/09/2016	Pablo Hernández	Cardiff City	1
03/03/2017	Alfonso Pedraza	Birmingham City	1
09/08/2017	Samuel Saiz	Port Vale	3
26/08/2017	Ezgjan Alioski	Nottingham Forest	1
05/08/2018	Mateusz Klich	Stoke City	1
21/09/2024	Largie Ramazani	Cardiff City	1

That 2–0 win against Cardiff with Ramazani on the scoresheet was a welcome three points and took Leeds back into the top six, and they were never again outside of it for the remainder of the season. Leeds had dropped to ninth after their first league defeat of the season the week before, losing 1–0 at home to Burnley. It was a fourth home defeat in the space of seven games – having started twenty-three

games unbeaten at Elland Road under Farke – and perhaps even more worryingly was the eighth time in fourteen games Leeds had failed to score. Leeds had seventeen shots against Burnley – and didn't face a single shot after the 32nd minute – but the final attempt came in the 70th minute from Joe Rodon, marking the first time Leeds had not had a shot after the 70th minute under Farke.

Leeds go global

October started with a trip to Norwich City, the first meeting with them since the 4–0 victory in the second leg of the play-off semi-final in May. On that night, two Dutchmen (Piroe and Summerville), a Bulgarian (Gruev) and a Frenchman (Rutter) were on the scoresheet; only one Belgian (Ramazani) scored this time around in a 1–1 draw but there was a big significance in Farke's team – it was the first Leeds line-up to ever feature players of eleven different nationalities.

Player	Nationality
Illan Meslier	France
Jayden Bogle	England
Pascal Struijk	Netherlands
Joe Rodon	Wales
Junior Firpo	Dominican Republic
Ilia Gruev	Bulgaria
Ao Tanaka	Japan
Wilfried Gnonto	Italy
Brenden Aaronson	USA
Largie Ramazani	Belgium
Mateo Joseph	Spain

Leeds had come close to naming this on a few occasions before finally doing it at Carrow Road. The first time they'd had ten in an XI had been back in February 2011 away at Swansea when Simon Grayson named

Kasper Schmeichel (Denmark), Eric Lichaj (USA), Andy O'Brien (Republic of Ireland), Robert Snodgrass (Scotland), Jonny Howson (England), Neil Kilkenny (Australia), Max Gradel (Cote d'Ivoire), Luciano Becchio (Argentina), Davide Somma (South Africa), as well as George McCartney and Alex Bruce (Northern Ireland), though Bruce had also won two caps for the Republic of Ireland.

Leeds never named more than three Englishmen in their line-ups for a Championship game in 2024–25, and all-English XIs have actually been incredibly rare. There have been just eighty-one in total in the club's history, starting with the first ever game against Port Vale in 1920. The most recent instance came on the final day of 1992–93 against Coventry, consisting of Beeney, (Ray) Wallace, Dorigo, Batty, Newsome, Whyte, Shutt, (Rod) Wallace, Chapman, Hodge and Tinkler. Since that Coventry game, the closest Leeds have come to a full English was in October 2007 against Darlington (Dutchman Mark De Vries the odd man out) and April 2014 versus Charlton (Ross McCormack starting and missing a last-minute penalty).

Across the 2023–24 and 2024–25 campaigns there has been a strong Welsh contingent in the Leeds team. Against Chelsea in a February 2024 FA Cup tie, four Welshmen (Joe Rodon, Ethan Ampadu, Dan James, Connor Roberts) started a game for Leeds for the first time since September 1981 when Brian Flynn, Byron Stevenson, Carl Harris and Gwyn Thomas lined up against Man Utd. It was also the first time four non-English players of the same nationality had started alongside one another since December 2014, when the Italian quartet of Silvestri, Bellusci, Bianchi and Antenucci faced Derby in a 2–0 defeat. The record for this, unsurprisingly given Leeds' many links to this country, is seven Scotsmen in fourteen starting XIs between 1975 and 1984. Eddie Gray featured in thirteen of those and even in the one he didn't, his brother Frank was in it.

In the 1–1 draw with Norwich in October 2024, Ramazani had scored Leeds' equaliser and he now had two goals and an assist in his three league starts, becoming the first Leeds player to score or assist in his first three since Robbie Keane in early 2001. Keane's six-game streak came to an end on 7 February, which was twenty days before Ramazani was born.

Though Ramazani had scored the goal against Norwich, the stand-out player on the night had been Willy Gnonto, who supplied the assist for the goal. Of the fourteen shots Leeds had, the Italian had either taken the shot himself (four) or created it (five), while he had eleven of the thirty-six touches in Norwich's box. Gnonto had burst onto the scene at the age of nineteen in Leeds' relegation season of 2022–23 but found himself behind Rutter and Summerville in the pecking order in 2023–24 and started just twenty-two times, playing the full ninety minutes in only three. But with those two gone, it appeared he was taking on the mantle of main man in the Leeds attack, and in the next game away at Sunderland he was on hand to assist both goals in the 2–2 draw – his third consecutive game with an assist, becoming the youngest Leeds player this century with an assist in three games in a row.

When	Player	Age on Date of Third Game
September/October 2024	Wilfried Gnonto	20 years, 334 days
February/March 2009	Robert Snodgrass	21 years, 181 days
March 2024	Georginio Rutter	21 years, 332 days
August/September 2000	Michael Bridges	22 years, 31 days

The game at table-topping Sunderland is better remembered for the inexplicable mistake by goalkeeper Illan Meslier in the 97th minute to gift the Black Cats an equaliser which, somewhat unfairly, went down as a Junior Firpo own goal. It began the first of many serious discussions over the course of the season about replacing the Frenchman and, frustratingly, had come at a point when Meslier had started to look a safer pair of hands; after letting in three of four shots on target on the opening day against Portsmouth, Meslier had saved fourteen of the next seventeen shots he'd faced going into the final seconds at the Stadium of Light. Nobody remembered those saves when the ball hobbled through his grasp to drop two valuable points, though.

Leeds score a goal . . . from a corner?!

There are very few things that elicit bigger groans at football matches than a player failing to beat the first man at a corner. That roar when a team wins a corner, the anticipation as the corner-taker steps up . . . only for the ball to end up with our own goalkeeper five seconds later after it's been headed out comfortably. Whether it's been Alan Thompson, Ian Harte or El Hadji Diouf taking the corner, whatever the era, we've seen it countless times down the years at Elland Road.

Is it really worth getting excited for every corner, though? Statistically, probably not. Looking at the ten seasons of the Championship before 2024–25, only 3.4% of corners saw a goal scored on average. In the seven seasons Leeds spent in the Championship in that time, they scored from exactly 3% of their corners, very marginally below the average for the entire division in that time. Some sides are exceptions to this; Cardiff in 2023–24 took 198 corners and scored from eighteen of them, a conversion rate of 9%. By contrast, Marcelo Bielsa's Leeds had 355 corners in 2019–20 (the most on record) and scored a measly eight corner goals (a 2.2% conversion).

That being said, Leeds' lack of potency from corners was becoming something of a talking point going into the home game with Sheffield United. At that stage, Leeds had taken fifty-three corners without scoring in 2024–25, but the Blades had been similarly blunt, with fifty-six corners and zero goals. Leeds' run without a corner goal stretched back to 13 February against Swansea but finally, after twenty-eight games without one, Pascal Struijk's excellent finish from a Joe Rothwell corner ended the streak of 178 goalless corners (in that time, Crysencio Summerville and Ilia Gruev had taken 110 corners between them without any success). One of Rothwell's great strengths was his set piece delivery; he'd ranked third for chances created from set plays in his last season with any meaningful Championship minutes in 2021–22 for Blackburn Rovers and it was a similar story in 2024–25 – Rothwell topped the leaderboard for that metric (forty-three).

> Joe Rothwell became the first Leeds United player to share his surname with a place in Leeds since Simon Walton in 2006, with Walton just a mile from the club's training ground at Thorp Arch. Leeds also had a Jimmy Walton in their first ever game in 1920. This is Leeds United heritage.

Sheffield United had failed to have a shot on target in the 2–0 defeat at Elland Road, the first time that had ever happened in the Championship on record for the Blades. After ten Championship games, Leeds had only faced twenty-one shots on target and seventy-three shots overall, the second lowest on record since 2013–14 by a side in the first ten games of a Championship season. Leeds were also giving away far fewer chances than the previous season.

After ten matches

Leeds in Championship	Shots Faced	Shots on Target Faced
2023–24	95	29
2024–25	73	21

Data via Opta

The second goal against Sheffield United had been scored by Mateo Joseph on the eve of his twenty-first birthday, and a few days later Brenden Aaronson went one better with a goal on his twenty-fourth birthday to send Leeds 2–0 ahead against Watford in just the 7th minute. He was the first Leeds birthday scorer since Pontus Jansson in February 2019 against Swansea; also in the XI with Aaronson was Joe Rodon, celebrating his own twenty-seventh birthday. This was just the second time in the club's history two players celebrating their birthdays started the same match, along with John Sheridan and Brendon Ormsby in a Full Members' Cup match in October 1986 against Bradford.

In the victory over Watford, Leeds were treated to the very best of new signing Ao Tanaka. His quality on the ball was unquestionable (at this stage, he'd only misplaced 26 out of 334 pass attempts) but the keenness with which he enjoyed the other side of the game – getting stuck in and winning the ball back – was in evidence. Tanaka became the first player in a Championship match in 2024–25 to win possession of the ball ten or more times, complete fifty or more passes and also make five or more tackles. Come the end of the season the Japanese international was in the top ten for each of these categories among Championship midfielders.

> The night after Leeds beat Watford 2–1, Raphinha scored his first ever Champions League hat-trick in Barcelona's 4–1 win over Bayern Munich. In doing so, he became only the third player to have scored a European Cup hat-trick and also played for Leeds, along with Mick Jones (scored his hat-trick for Leeds vs Lyn Oslo in 1969) and Ian Rush (hat-trick for Liverpool in 1984 vs Benfica, played for Leeds in 1996–97).

October ended with the club's first goalless draw against Bristol City since 1979, and for the second time in three games Leeds hadn't faced a single shot on target, with Illan Meslier not having to make a single save. He'd be even more of a spectator in the next game.

Plymouth forget to attack

Bearing in mind Plymouth were managed by Wayne Rooney, a man who was once the all-time record England scorer with 53 goals, and with over 200 Premier League goals to his name, Argyle's lack of attacking ambition at Elland Road was almost impressive. Opta has analysed nearly 7,000 Championship matches since the 2013–14 season, and at Elland Road on 2 November Plymouth became only the second side to fail to have a single shot in a game, and the first since Millwall against Blackburn in March 2022. They successfully completed just twelve passes in the final third of the pitch, also a Championship low since 2013, and only completed thirty-two passes in the Leeds half, the latter the third lowest on record and amazingly not the fewest completed by a team in the Leeds half all season (Stoke managed just thirty-one in the fog on Boxing Day).

At the other end, Leeds did remember to score goals; three in the space of eight first-half minutes secured a 3–0 victory. It was a performance of complete dominance and the 78.5% possession figure – the biggest by a Leeds team on record since 2013–14 at Elland Road – told its own story, as did the fact that Tanaka's 106 successful passes were only sixteen fewer than Plymouth had managed as an entire team. Rooney had been to Elland Road twice in 2024 and was twice sent packing 3–0, also losing on New Year's Day with Birmingham, which was his final game in charge. He lasted another ten at Plymouth after the chastening loss at Leeds, before being given his marching orders on New Year's Eve with the club in twenty-fourth and with a goal difference of minus twenty-nine.

Making their Leeds debuts against Plymouth were midfielders Josuha Guilavogui, Sam Chambers and Charlie Crew, with Guilavogui the oldest outfield debutant (34 years and 44 days) since Michael Brown in 2011, and Chambers becoming the first player born after Leeds started their League One campaign in 2007–08 to play for the club. Guilavogui's addition added considerable experience, and in debuting alongside Chambers and Crew it was the third and fourth largest gaps in ages for players making their debuts in the same game.

Date	Older Player	Younger Player	Opponent	Age Gap
26/08/2008	Paul Telfer	Aidan White	Crystal Palace	19 years, 354 days
07/08/2004	Neil Sullivan	Simon Walton	Derby County	17 years, 201 days
02/11/2024	Josuha Guilavogui	Sam Chambers	Plymouth Argyle	16 years, 333 days
02/11/2024	Josuha Guilavogui	Charlie Crew	Plymouth Argyle	15 years, 269 days
07/08/2016	Robert Green	Matt Grimes	Queens Park Rangers	15 years, 178 days

We're in London, aren't we?

November saw Leeds' first trip to London since the play-off final defeat to Southampton as they faced Millwall. Across the 2022–23 and 2023–24 seasons, Leeds played eleven games in the capital city and lost ten of them. Their one victory was against Millwall at the Den in September 2023, a 3–0 win which was the biggest in London since March 2015, when Fulham were beaten 3–0 at Craven Cottage.

The game at Millwall in November 2024 was the club's fiftieth game in London since that Fulham win in 2015 – their all-competitions record in the capital in the meantime reads like the name of a Welsh railway station:

L D L D D L L D L L L W L D L L L L L L L L D L L L L L W D L L L L W D L-
W L L L L L L L L W L L L D

Between 2015–16 and 2023–24, no side in England's top four tiers lost more away league games in London than Leeds did (twenty-eight). Marcelo Bielsa was able to transform the football club in many ways but even he couldn't improve the record in London, taking him fourteen games to record a London victory behind closed doors away at Fulham. Perhaps most ironically of all is that after this terrible record, his last win as Leeds United head coach came in a 3–2 win away at West Ham in January 2022.

London teams would probably say the same about playing in Leeds, however. At Elland Road, Leeds have won each of their last eleven Championship matches against London teams stretching back to a 2–1 win over QPR late in 2018. Compare and contrast these results across the club's last four Championship seasons against London teams, one at Elland Road, the other in the capital – they can beat these teams, just not when they go south down the M1.

Record vs London Teams – Champ (2018–19 – 2024–25)	At Elland Road	In London
Won	11	1
Drawn	1	3
Lost	0	8
GF	26	9
GA	6	18
GD	20	-9
Points	34	6

6 November: Millwall 1–0 Leeds United. Possibly the most obvious defeat of the season.

End of November

Not for the last time during the season, Leeds followed a defeat to Millwall with three consecutive wins. Two were fairly routine home victories in which Leeds outshot their opponents by forty-one to twelve and had eighty-one touches in their opponents' boxes across the two games. QPR were sent packing – for a fifth consecutive defeat at Elland Road – thanks to goals from Jayden Bogle and Joel Piroe (the latter scoring his sixth substitute goal in 2024, a new record by a Leeds player in a single calendar year, breaking super-sub Keith Edwards' total of five in 1987 – whose memorable goals that year included scoring home and away in the play-offs against Oldham and in the FA Cup semi-final defeat to Coventry).

Luton Town were beaten 3–0 on 27 November with Leeds becoming just the fifth team on record to have more than ten shots on target (eleven) and complete more than 700 passes (714) in a Championship match since 2013–14. Struijk (116), Rodon (113) and Tanaka (113) all completed more than one hundred passes and Leeds enjoyed a near-perfect evening of control against a Hatters side who'd been in the Premier League the previous campaign.

In between these wins over QPR and Luton was a 4–3 win in south

Wales away at Swansea City, the first Championship game of the season to see Leeds face more shots on target (five) than they had themselves (four). Memories of losing the play-off final 1–0 to Southampton – along with other 1–0 defeats to Burnley and Millwall already in 2024–25 – left many fans feeling that once Leeds went behind there was no way back, but that wasn't necessarily backed up by the data; the win at Swansea was the third time under Farke that Leeds had conceded first in an away game and come back to score four times, something they'd only done three times in twenty-three seasons before Farke's arrival.

Conceding first away and scoring four (2000–01 – 2024–25)

Date	Match	Competition
14/11/2002	Hapoel Tel Aviv 1–4 Leeds United	UEFA Cup
19/11/2005	Southampton 3–4 Leeds United	Championship
01/12/2012	Huddersfield Town 2–4 Leeds United	Championship
26/08/2023	Ipswich Town 3–4 Leeds United	Championship
22/04/2024	Middlesbrough 3–4 Leeds United	Championship
24/11/2024	Swansea City 3–4 Leeds United	Championship

Willy Gnonto came off the bench to score a 90th minute winner at the Liberty Stadium just eighty-four seconds after Swansea had equalised. It was the first 90th minute winning goal in a 4–3 win since Lee Bowyer had scored against Derby in November 1997.

November ended with defeat away at Blackburn, with Todd Cantwell's penalty the difference between the sides. It was the eighteenth consecutive penalty Leeds had conceded since Meslier had saved a Jesse Lingard penalty against West Ham in March 2021, and even then Lingard had immediately tapped in the rebound. Meslier had let in fifteen of those eighteen penalties and, in front of supporters, the last Leeds goalkeeper to save a penalty had been Bailey Peacock-Farrell in November 2018 at home to Reading. Would we ever see a penalty save again? (Spoiler: yes, we would – although we'd still be going home complaining about our goalkeeper).

The greatest in the land (in 2024)

While Leeds would undoubtedly have swapped having the most Championship points in 2024 for getting promoted at Wembley in May, there was little argument that, as a whole, Leeds had been the best and most consistent side in the country's top-four divisions in the calendar year of 2024. The annoying blip in the middle of it – four defeats in the final six league games of the 2023–24 season – had cost Leeds automatic promotion, but the recovery for the remainder of 2024 was testament to the players and Farke and his coaching team. For just the third time in the club's history, they won the most points (96) of any side in England's top-four divisions in a single year, also doing so in 1969 (70) and 2009 (104).

Most points won in England's top-four tiers in 2024

Team	Games	Won	Drawn	Lost	Points
Leeds United	45	29	9	7	96
Wrexham	45	27	9	9	90
Wycombe Wanderers	45	25	12	8	87
Arsenal	36	26	7	3	85
Liverpool	37	26	7	4	85

Going into December's games, Leeds were third in the Championship and three points behind Sheffield United but by New Year's Eve they topped the table after five wins and a draw in December, the first time they'd gone unbeaten for the entirety of the festive month since 2015. An away victory over Derby on 29 December took them two points clear of the Blades and up to fifty-one points – the same position and same total of points they had at the end of 2019 in the last season they'd won the league. It would prove a nice omen.

It was not the first win against Derby in December 2024, bizarrely, as Leeds faced the Rams twice in the space of twenty-two days. Playing the same side twice in the same month did used to be a much more common occurrence in the Football League – between 1920 and 1969, it happened to Leeds on 160 occasions, and teams were used to meeting on consecutive days, particularly over the festive period. In perhaps the starkest example, Leeds hammered Aston Villa 6–0 on Christmas Day in 1924, then followed it up by losing 2–1 on Boxing Day.

This century it's happened just four times before the Derby double – March 2006 against Crystal Palace (won 2–1 away, lost 1–0 home), December 2016 against Aston Villa (won 2–0 home, drew 1–1 away) and February 2023 against Man Utd (drew 2–2 away, lost 2–0 home). In December 2024, the Rams were dispatched in 2–0 and 1–0 wins, and this was the first time Leeds had beaten the same team twice in the league in a month since September 1973 against Wolves.

Joe Rodon got his first Leeds goal in the 2–0 home win on 7 December, which was shortly followed by a goal from fellow defender Max Wöber, also his first for the club, with this the first time two defenders had scored their first goals for Leeds in the same game.

> Wöber's goal against Derby was notable for being scored in the 44th minute following his 21st minute introduction as a substitute. It was the first time a Leeds sub had come on and scored in the first half of a game since May 2013, when Dominic Poleon scored away at Watford.

Consecutive home wins over Middlesbrough and Oxford gave Leeds a run of nine home victories in a row for the first time since winning eleven between January and May 2009 under Simon Grayson. Elland Road was once again a fortress, and since Burnley had won 1–0 in September Leeds hadn't trailed for a single minute in a home game, scoring two or more goals in all nine victories. Scoring in wins was something

Daniel James was used to – he bagged the second goal against Middlesbrough and the opener against Oxford to extend his winning run when finding the net to seventeen matches, the longest run since Alan Smith had won twenty-one in a row between 1998 and 2001.

Another winning record went tumbling in December as the popular Guilavogui became the first player in the club's entire history to end on the winning side in his first eight league appearances; granted, he'd been substituted on in all eight and played a grand total of 84 minutes and 47 seconds in those games, and touched the ball only seventy-five times, but a record is a record. It took Guilavogui thirty-one fewer games for Leeds to win eight games than it did for both Junior Firpo and Brenden Aaronson, whose eighth wins were in their thirty-ninth games.

Date	Player	Winning League Start
29/12/2024	Josuha Guilavogui	8
09/11/2019	Leif Davis	7
22/09/2007	Andy Hughes	6
22/09/2007	David Prutton	6
05/09/2009	Jason Crowe	6
05/09/2009	Michael Doyle	6
05/09/2009	Shane Higgs	6

A victory away at Stoke City on Boxing Day put Leeds on top of the table. The game was played in such foggy conditions that at times it was hard to see what exactly was going on and that seemed to translate to the pitch, though only for the Potters; they completed just 53% of their passes compared to the 86% of Leeds, with Ethan Ampadu's ninety-four successful ones – a real feat in the conditions – only thirteen fewer than Stoke managed as a team. Piroe's two goals – not his last goals of the season against Stoke – took him to nine Championship goals for the season from only sixteen shots on target.

December's second win over Derby saw both Illan Meslier and Sam Byram make their 200th appearances for the club, the only time in the club's history that has happened in the same game. Meslier was the first goalkeeper to hit 200 games since Nigel Martyn back in 2000, while it had taken Byram two spells and over twelve years to reach his total, the longest wait between a debut and 200th game for Leeds. Brenden Aaronson was 135 games shy of 200 that night, but in his sixty-fifth game it was his winner – scored after a delightful twelve-pass move – that made the difference, the ninety-seventh and final goal of 2024. With thirty-two wins in fifty-three games in all competitions during the year, the 60.4% win ratio was the fourth-best in any year in the club's history.

Year	Games	Wins	Win Percentage
2009	57	39	68.4%
1999	52	33	63.5%
1964	47	29	61.7%
2024	53	32	60.4%
1968	65	39	60.0%

Take the lead and . . . draw?!

2024 had begun with nine straight Championship wins but there was no such luck in 2025, which began with a couple of uncharacteristic Leeds draws against Blackburn and Hull. One thing Leeds had become synonymous with under Farke had been taking the lead and very rarely relinquishing it – in the forty-six league games Leeds took the lead under him heading into 2025, they'd won forty-two and drawn four, dropping only eight points from winning positions, the fewest of any side in England's top four tiers in that timeframe.

After the first weekend in 2025, Leeds were instead leading that particular metric, having dropped four points from leading against Blackburn (drew 1–1) and Hull (drew 3–3). In the former, Leeds took the lead at Elland Road in the 88th minute via a Pascal Struijk penalty before conceding to a last minute Danny Batth equaliser. It was the first time Leeds had scored the opening goal of a game in the final five minutes and not gone on to win since November 1968 away at Chelsea, when Mike O'Grady's 86th minute opener was cancelled out by Peter

Osgood two minutes later. At the time, Hugo Montenegro's cover of *The Good, the Bad and the Ugly* was UK number one, which may be a good way to sum up the next game of 2025 away at Hull.

Blackburn were managed at the time by John Eustace and it was the fourth time Farke had failed to beat him as Leeds manager, his most games against an opposing manager in the Championship without a single win. Including two winless games against Portsmouth's John Mousinho, that put Farke winless in six games against Johns as Leeds boss. The last time Leeds beat a manager whose first name is John in a league game was when John Barnes was Tranmere manager in August 2009, with Leeds' first goal in a 3–0 win that day scored by a Johnson (Bradley).

Away at Hull, Leeds went behind early on but recovered to go 3–1 ahead by the 72nd minute, and had won each of their previous thirty-six matches when leading by two goals. A goalkeeping error by Meslier allowed Hull to make it 3–2 before a late equaliser cost Leeds two points. The Frenchman was the Championship's least busy goalkeeper, facing just fifty-five shots on target after twenty-six games, but his save ratio of 65.5% was the fourth worst of the twenty Championship goalkeepers to play twenty or more games at this stage of the season. It ensured that, rather than focusing on promotion, all the questions would once again be on the goalkeeping situation.

Farke ultimately stuck with Meslier in the Championship for the time being, but there was a fifteen-day wait for the next league game and in between was a first ever meeting with Harrogate Town in the FA Cup third round, with the local neighbours the 167th different team Leeds had faced in their history. It was the first time Leeds had faced a new side for four years, since another FA Cup third round tie against Crawley Town. That game ended in a disappointing 3–0 defeat that may have caused a meltdown in different times, but with a much changed side and the behind-closed-doors nature of the tie – plus the focus being on an exciting Premier League campaign – the result was quickly glossed over. That wouldn't have been the case had

Harrogate turned up at Elland Road and won, but thankfully a Largie Ramazani header settled the 1–0 victory, with Karl Darlow keeping his first Leeds clean sheet.

Manor Solomon's form was beginning to catch the eye and he scored early in both victories against Sheffield Wednesday (3rd minute) and Norwich City (thirty-two seconds) in January. After struggling for full fitness initially, Solomon had five goals and five assists in twelve league starts after the 2–0 win over the Canaries and was the quickest player on record from 1989–90 onwards to both score five goals and assist five goals in the league for Leeds, breaking the previous fastest held by David Healy during the 2004–05 campaign.

Since 1989-90

Date	Player	Starts to 5 Goals & 5 Assists
22/01/2025	Manor Solomon	12
15/01/2005	David Healy	15
17/10/1992	Eric Cantona	17
27/11/1993	Brian Deane	17
04/11/2018	Mateusz Klich	17
23/02/2021	Raphinha	17

Leeds ended January unbeaten to complete a fully undefeated December and January for only the second time in a season in the club's entire history, also doing so in 1964–65, winning eight of twelve games in 2024–25 to end January top of the table. The final game of the month was arguably the dullest of the season, a goalless draw at Burnley in which the first shot on target from either side wasn't until an 89th minute Dan James effort, and Burnley didn't have a single shot in the second half. Leeds not scoring was just about forgivable, though, as this was a seventh consecutive clean sheet in a run of twelve in a row for the Clarets. The match had produced an xG of just 0.54, the second lowest for a Championship game all season.

Luckily, the remedy for this boredom was just around the corner.

9

2024–25 PART 2

February might be the shortest month in the year but that didn't stop Leeds packing this one full of action. There was the club's biggest victory since 1972, two late comeback wins against promotion rivals, eighteen goals scored, a milestone victory for Farke and, amid this seemingly endless positivity, they still found time for the customary FA Cup defeat as well.

Leeds United 7–0 Cardiff City

For many years, Leeds struggled against Cardiff, and they were the very definition of a bogey team. In the 1983–84 season, Leeds completed a league double over the Bluebirds with two 1–0 wins and a 26-year-old George McCluskey scored the winner in both games. The next time Leeds beat Cardiff, McCluskey had just turned fifty-eight years of age, and the year was 2015, with Alex Mowatt's spectacular long-range effort in a 1–0 win ending a run of seventeen matches without a victory against them. Only eleven goals were scored in this winless streak, and Leeds never managed more than one goal in a single match.

Things couldn't have been more different at Elland Road on 1 February as Leeds recorded their biggest victory since the famous 7–0 hammering of Southampton in March 1972. It was only the tenth time in the club's entire history that Leeds had managed a victory by seven or more goals – and six of those were achieved by the club's greatest manager, Don Revie. Outside of his outstanding era, the last win by such a margin was way back in 1934, when Dick Ray led Leeds to an 8–0 win over Leicester City in front of just shy of 12,000 supporters. They certainly got their money's worth that day.

Biggest ever Leeds wins

Date	Score	Competition	Winning Margin
17/09/1969	Leeds United 10–0 Lyn Oslo	European Cup	10
03/10/1967	Spora Luxembourg 0–9 Leeds United	Fairs Cup	9
07/04/1934	Leeds United 8–0 Leicester City	Division One	8
11/01/1930	Leeds United 8–1 Crystal Palace	FA Cup	7
25/10/1930	Leeds United 7–0 Middlesbrough	Division One	7
22/04/1961	Leeds United 7–0 Lincoln City	Division Two	7
07/10/1967	Leeds United 7–0 Chelsea	Division One	7
17/10/1967	Leeds United 7–0 Spora Luxembourg	Fairs Cup	7
04/03/1972	Leeds United 7–0 Southampton	Division One	7
01/02/2025	Leeds United 7–0 Cardiff City	Championship	7

There could be no arguments over the margin of victory as Leeds recorded twenty-nine shots – the most in a league game since the painful 2–1 defeat to Wigan in April 2019 (thirty-six that day) – and registered an expected goals total of 5.74, the biggest by a team in a Championship match in any of the last five seasons. There were also seven big chances created, forty-three touches in the Cardiff box and eleven shots on target – by contrast, Cardiff had just two shots all afternoon and posted an xG of merely 0.06. In recent history, there simply hadn't been a victory by any team in a Championship game with such dominance and one-sidedness.

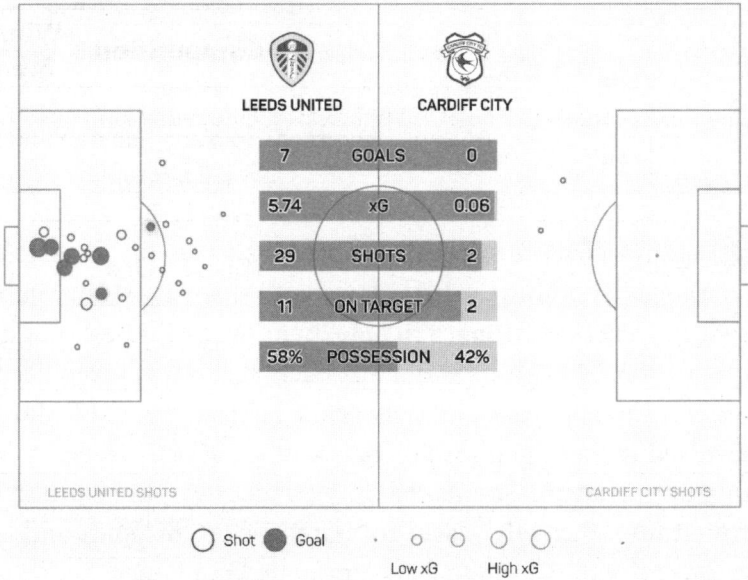

Leeds United 7-0 Cardiff City
English Championship 2024-25 | 01 February 2025

Opta

LEEDS UNITED		CARDIFF CITY
7	GOALS	0
5.74	xG	0.06
29	SHOTS	2
11	ON TARGET	2
58%	POSSESSION	42%

LEEDS UNITED SHOTS   CARDIFF CITY SHOTS

○ Shot ● Goal   · ○ ○ ○ ○
                   Low xG   High xG

Leeds had also controlled the away game at Cardiff earlier in the season and, while the scoreline only showed 2–0, the Whites had 79.3% possession and fifteen shots to Cardiff's three. With an aggregate victory of 9–0 across the season, it was the first time in the club's history they'd scored outscored their opponents by nine goals in a league season, while Cardiff were the first side to concede nine against Leeds in a season since West Ham in 1998–99.

Of the seven goals, only Joel Piroe scored a brace and was joined on the scoresheet by Brenden Aaronson, Manor Solomon, Dan James, Willy Gnonto and Mateo Joseph to give Leeds six different scorers in a game for just the third time in the club's entire history.

Year	Score	Six Different Scorers
1967	Leeds 7–0 Chelsea	Johanneson Greenhoff, Charlton, Lorimer, Gray, Hinton og, Bremner
2001	Leeds 6–1 Bradford	Viduka, Harte, Bakke, Smith, Kewell, Bowyer
2025	Leeds 7–0 Cardiff	Aaronson, Solomon, James, Piroe 2, Gnonto, Joseph

Though he didn't score himself, Junior Firpo was on hand to assist three of them, becoming the first player with three assists in a game for Leeds since Jermaine Pennant in a 3–2 win over Middlesbrough back in August 2003. Though he was a full-back, Firpo was given licence to roam down the left flank and between 1 February and 12 March, he was involved in eight goals (two goals and six assists) in eight Championship appearances – totals that any attacker would be proud of. In that timeframe, the only player to match Firpo for goals and assists across the entire division was his teammate, Dan James.

James scored Leeds' third goal in the 7–0 rout, his sixth goal across his previous eleven appearances at Elland Road and it was, perhaps surprisingly, his final home goal of the campaign (injury would rule him out of the run-in). The Welshman had also scored the third goal in Marcelo Bielsa's last victory at Elland Road as manager in a 3–1 win over Burnley back in January 2022, and this kick-started an impressive personal run of good luck when he found the net on home soil in Leeds; as of the end of the 2024–25 season, James has scored in seventeen games at Elland Road and Leeds have won every single game, including in six crucial victories in this promotion season. It is the most games scored in at home for Leeds, while winning each game, in the club's history, while the last player to enjoy a longer winning run when scoring at Elland Road was Eddie Gray between 1966 and 1978 (twenty-five wins). He's some way to go to break the record, though – Peter Lorimer won thirty-four in a row between 1970 and 1973.

The victory was also a personal milestone for Farke, who celebrated his fiftieth victory as Leeds United manager in only his eighty-seventh game in charge, equalling Simon Grayson's record for fastest to fifty wins. Grayson's eighty-seventh game was even more historic than this 7–0 hammering, though; it came in the promotion-winning roller coaster against Bristol Rovers in May 2010.

Date	Match	Manager	Game of 50th Win
01/02/2025	Leeds 7–0 Cardiff	Daniel Farke	87
08/05/2010	Leeds 2–1 Bristol Rovers	Simon Grayson	87
03/05/2000	Leeds 3–1 Watford	David O'Leary	93
27/06/2020	Leeds 3–0 Fulham	Marcelo Bielsa	93
19/10/1929	Leeds 1–0 Birmingham	Dick Ray	99

It was also Farke's second 7–0 win as a Championship coach, with his Norwich side beating Huddersfield by that scoreline in April 2021. He was the first manager to lead two second tier clubs to seven-goal victories since Tommy Docherty with Chelsea (1963 v Portsmouth) and QPR (1979 v Burnley), with Docherty quitting the Chelsea job just a day before they faced Leeds in 1967 – a game Leeds won 7–0.

> Between the 7–0 wins over Southampton in 1972 and Cardiff in 2025, sixty-five different players were born and then went on to score at least seven goals for Leeds. Of those, the three who scored exactly seven times were Luke Murphy, El Hadji Diouf and Andy Robinson.

Eighteen consecutive Leeds United goals

After annihilating Cardiff, the next game pitted Leeds against an old foe in Frank Lampard. He'd been appointed manager of Coventry City in November, his first Championship job since leaving Derby at the end of 2018–19. Lampard was in the midst of a run of nine wins in ten Championship games, but the other game in this sequence was against Leeds on 5 February as the Whites registered a 2–0 away victory.

279

In truth, it should have been more than 2–0. Leeds had twenty shots – eight on target – and posted an expected goals total of 3.64, with Piroe – scorer of the first goal – accumulating 1.48 of that on his own, well in excess of Coventry as a team on the night (0.5).

The second goal was scored by the ever-improving Jayden Bogle (who'd played under Lampard for Derby in 2018–19), his fourth of the season from right-back. It was his second goal against Coventry, also netting in the 3–0 victory in September, and he became the first defender to score at home and away against an opponent in a season for Leeds since Jason Crowe in 2009–10 against Carlisle United, with Crowe scoring at home and away against the Cumbrians in the Johnstone's Paint Trophy area final. Sticking with the Carlisle theme, the last defender to do it in a league season was Clarke Carlisle against Watford in 2004–05. Bogle would repeat this feat later in the campaign when he found the net against QPR for a second time.

With Bogle and Firpo both contributing to goals from full-back, there were also many positives at the defensive end of the pitch. Since the 3–3 draw with Hull City in January, Leeds had kept six consecutive clean sheets (one in the FA Cup, five in the league) for the first time since March and April 1981 under Allan Clarke. While hardly busy in the five Championship games in this run, with Leeds facing just eight shots on target, the clean sheet at Coventry was preserved thanks to a terrific Meslier save early in the second half from an Ellis Simms header.

Another big win followed at Vicarage Road, a 4–0 victory that was the club's biggest ever win over Watford and the second four-goal away victory under Farke, following the 4–0 win at Swansea in February 2024 (both, weirdly, were the thirty-second league games of the season). Leeds were 3–0 ahead by half-time, and following their 2–0 half-time leads against both Cardiff and Coventry this was the first time Leeds had gone in ahead at the break by two or more goals in three league games in a row since September 1971. With these fast starts – and Leeds' near imperious Championship record when scoring the first goal – opponents were already beaten by the time the second half kicked off.

Early goals haven't always been the way with Leeds. After a 12th minute Paul Green goal on Boxing Day 2012 away at Nottingham Forest, Leeds didn't score another first half league goal until May 2013, when Dom Poleon scored at Watford. This was a run of twenty-one consecutive games without a first half goal, the longest in the club's history. At Elland Road, none of the final eleven league games of 2012–13 witnessed a first half Leeds goal and only three were scored by opponents. Barely worth leaving The Peacock.

Since Abu Kamara's 89th minute equaliser for Hull on 4 January, there'd been eighteen goals scored in Championship matches involving Leeds. This run of goals reads like a chant from the Elland Road Kop: Leeds, Leeds, Leeds, Leeds, Leeds, Leeds, Leeds, Leeds, Leeds, Leeds, Leeds, Leeds, Leeds, Leeds, Leeds, Leeds, Leeds, Leeds. It was the second longest run of goals scored by a team in their games in Championship history, behind only the twenty-three-goal run produced by Fulham in October and November 2021.

This run of consecutive scoring came to an end in the next game against Sunderland when Wilson Isidor's 32nd minute goal gave them a 1–0 lead, the first time Leeds had trailed at Elland Road in the league since Burnley had won in September. It was not the night for the starting XI, who had seventeen shots between them without success; for a fourth consecutive match, Dan James had at least five attempts (he ended February with twenty-six shots in five games, only ten fewer than Preston managed as a team in four games) but this time he could not make the breakthrough, and it was left to two substitutes to provide the late magic.

Both Pascal Struijk and Joe Rothwell were introduced as 71st minute substitutes and in the 78th minute Rothwell's cross was headed home by Struijk to equalise. By this point, it was all one way traffic – Leeds had eleven of the thirteen shots in the second half, and it was the lucky thirteenth of these that won the game in the 95th minute. Once again Rothwell was the creator, and once again it was Struijk who nodded it in to send Elland Road into pandemonium. During his time on the

281

pitch, Rothwell completed all twenty-two of his passes and assisted two goals, the only player Opta has on record to maintain a 100% passing accuracy and assist two goals in a Championship match.

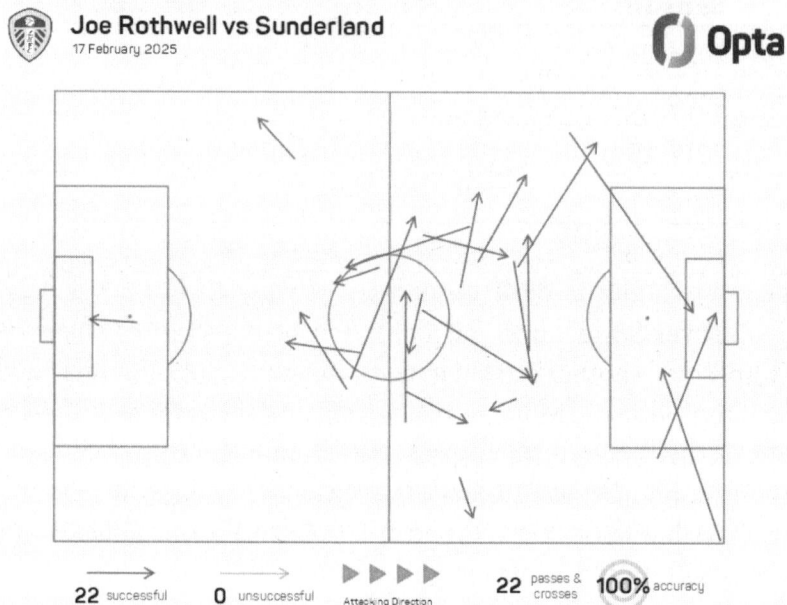

Joe Rothwell vs Sunderland
17 February 2025

Opta

22 successful · 0 unsuccessful · Attacking Direction · 22 passes & crosses · 100% accuracy

Joe Rothwell was the first Leeds player wearing the number 8 shirt to assist two goals in a game since Rodolph Austin in November 2013 against Yeovil Town. This century, he's also one of five players to assist two goals as a substitute for Leeds: the others are Lloyd Sam (October 2011 vs Peterborough), Ryan Hall (December 2012 vs Huddersfield), Pablo Hernández (December 2020 vs Newcastle) and Junior Firpo (January 2024 vs Birmingham).

Struijk, meanwhile, became the first Leeds United defender to score two goals as a substitute in a match and first player wearing number 5 to score twice since Gordon McQueen in 1977 against Middlesbrough. They were the thirteenth and fourteenth substitute goals in the Championship by Leeds players in 2024–25, setting a new club record for sub goals in a league campaign since subs were introduced in the 1965–66 season; this was later extended to seventeen goals before the end of the season.

Season	Leeds League Sub Goals
2024–25	17
2009–10	12
2019–20	11
2010–11	10
2007–08	9

The win over Sunderland put Leeds ten points clear of them in the table ahead of another crucial game against promotion rivals Sheffield United the following Monday. Leeds went into the game only two points ahead of the Blades at the top of the Championship but by full-time it was five, and Leeds also had a seven-point cushion on Burnley in third. No Championship side had ever failed to be promoted from that position with twelve games to go.

That doesn't necessarily tell the full story of the match, and for a second consecutive game Leeds went 1–0 down in the first half, this time via an own goal from Meslier. It was his second for the club, along with one away at Wolves in February 2021 as Leeds lost 1–0, but this time around his teammates spared his blushes. Goals from Firpo, Tanaka and Piroe saw Leeds score three goals at Bramall Lane for the first time since the day they won the top-flight title in April 1992, which would prove a lucky omen for later down the line.

Leeds had once again scored very late goals – Tanaka's header came in the 89th minute, while Piroe's superb long-range strike (his second from outside the box for the club) came in the 90th minute, to take Leeds to eleven goals scored in the 89th minute or later for the season. They would extend this to twelve goals in this timeframe by the end of the season, with only two sides ever scoring more in a single Championship season. From the 82nd minute onwards at Bramall Lane, Leeds had seven shots, with five on target; Sheffield United didn't have a single attempt. Many will recall the Bielsa team and their greater

283

fitness levels often making the difference in games, but the 2024–25 vintage proved themselves just as capable of late shows.

The game was Piroe's sixth match for Leeds played on a Monday but the first time he'd scored on that day of the week. This completed the seven days of the week with a goal for Piroe, becoming the fourth player to score on all seven along with Lee Bowyer, Patrick Bamford and Crysencio Summerville.

Piroe's first goals for Leeds on each day of the week

Date	Opponent	Goals	Day of Week
26/08/2023	Ipswich Town	1	Saturday
17/09/2023	Millwall	2	Sunday
29/11/2023	Swansea City	1	Wednesday
13/02/2024	Swansea City	1	Tuesday
16/05/2024	Norwich City	1	Thursday
04/10/2024	Sunderland	1	Friday
24/02/2025	Sheffield United	1	Monday

The victory at Bramall Lane was also a nineteenth consecutive league Yorkshire derby unbeaten for Leeds. Since losing 2–0 to Sheffield Wednesday in January 2020, there'd been fourteen wins and five draws against fellow Yorkshire sides, and only Sheffield United themselves between 2002 and 2007 (twenty-one in a row) have ever had a longer unbeaten streak in Yorkshire derbies in Football League history. Bragging rights in God's own county belong – for the time being at least – to Leeds United.

Among players to feature in ten or more Yorkshire league derbies for Leeds, Chris Wood has the best goals-per-game ratio, scoring twelve in fifteen games (0.8 per game). Wood was born over 11,000 miles from Yorkshire, in Auckland, New Zealand. The player with the next best is Charlie Keetley (0.78 goals per game), who was born about 30 miles from the Yorkshire border in Derby.

Tanaka's header made him the tenth different league scorer in February for Leeds – despite the shortness of the month, it was only the second time that many players had scored in a single month; the other had been in July 2020, a month and campaign when Leeds won the Championship title. More good omens, then.

Month	Scorers
July 2020	Phillips, Klich, Bamford, Cooper, Costa, Hernández, Shackleton, White, Dallas, Roberts
February 2025	Solomon, Aaronson, James, Piroe, Gnonto, Joseph, Bogle, Struijk, Firpo, Tanaka

Out of the FA Cup (again)

Having navigated their way past League Two side Harrogate in the third round, Leeds were drawn at home against fellow Championship outfit Millwall in the fourth round, with the game sandwiched between away victories over Coventry and Watford in the league. It was the first time the sides had met in the FA Cup and, outside of league football, their only two previous encounters had been in the Full Members' Cup (a short-lived competition that featured clubs from the top two divisions between 1985 and 1992, a period during which English clubs were banned from Europe) in the 1987–88 and 1988–89 seasons. Millwall knocked Leeds out in both campaigns, winning 2–0 having been 1–0 up at half-time in both victories.

Fast-forward to 2024–25, Millwall knocked Leeds out of the FA Cup via a 2–0 win and were 1–0 ahead at half-time. These things really do come in threes.

Leeds made ten changes to their starting XI, their most for an FA Cup tie since losing 1–0 to Sutton in 2017, with only captain Ethan Ampadu retaining his place. The main standout choice had been midfielder Sam Chambers starting his first match for the club at the age of only 17 years and 174 days, the third youngest player to start an FA Cup match for the club. He was unfortunate not to mark his start with a goal, too, denied by Liam Roberts in the Millwall goal.

Youngest Leeds players to start an FA Cup match

Date	Player	Opponent	Age
05/01/1980	Terry Connor	Nottingham Forest	17 years, 57 days
08/01/2005	Simon Walton	Birmingham City	17 years, 117 days
08/02/2025	Sam Chambers	Millwall	17 years, 174 days
08/01/2005	Aaron Lennon	Birmingham City	17 years, 267 days
08/01/1983	Neil Aspin	Preston North End	17 years, 271 days

Leeds had eight shots on target without success against Millwall – including seeing a Struijk penalty saved in the second half – which was the first time Leeds had that many without scoring since an August 2018 League Cup tie against Preston, also a 2–0 defeat at Elland Road. On both occasions, the opposing manager had been Alex Neil.

The result meant Leeds had lost just three of their previous twenty-eight games in all competitions but two had been against Millwall, after also losing in the league in November. Overall, it meant that in 2024–25 defeats to Millwall made up 33% of the club's overall losses for the season. Only in 1963–64 – also a promotion-winning season – have they lost a higher percentage of games against just one team, losing two of five games that season to Manchester City (in the league and League Cup).

Opponents	Season	Defeats	Defeats vs Opponent	%
Manchester City	1963–1964	5	2	40.0%
Millwall	2024–2025	6	2	33.3%
Ujpest Dozsa	1968–1969	7	2	28.6%
Manchester United	1991–1992	7	2	28.6%
Manchester City	1927–1928	11	3	27.3%
Southampton	2023–2024	12	3	25.0%

Defeat to Millwall aside, February had been a brilliant month for Leeds in their quest for promotion. Five wins in five Championship games were achieved with an impressive eighteen goals scored, the most in a month since March 1972 when they scored nineteen. March 1972 was also the last time, before February, the club had recorded a 7–0 win.

Most Leeds league goals in one month

Month	League Goals
December 1927	21
April 1956	20
April 1963	19
March 1972	19
September 1930	18
February 2025	18

Leeds ended February five points clear at the top and seven points ahead of third and, after such a prolific winning month, looked dead certs for promotion. Yet by the end of March, they'd dropped to second and were level on points with Burnley in third. It seemed to be another case of Leeds making things hard for themselves – or maybe they just really hated kicking off games before 3 o'clock . . .

The perils of the early kick-off

After the unblemished February, Leeds then faced three early kick-offs in March and failed to win any of them. Heading into the month, two of the three league defeats Leeds had suffered had kicked off before 3 p.m. (12.30 p.m. vs Burnley, 1.30 p.m. vs Blackburn) and the other had been the inevitable London defeat at Millwall kicking off at 8 p.m. Leeds added a fourth league defeat in March – the last loss of the season – and it kicked off at midday down at Portsmouth.

It was a season-long issue. Of the seven league games Leeds failed to score in, five kicked off before the traditional time of 3 p.m. Shot conversion rate dipped from 14.5% in games kicking off at 3 p.m. or later just to just 7.7% in early kick-offs. This profligacy led to a points-per-game drop of 2.53 from 3 p.m. onwards to just 1.36 in early kick-offs. Over a full season, that would have seen Leeds earn approximately 116 points had all games kicked off after 3 p.m. Had they all been early kick-offs, only sixty-two points would've been accumulated – enough to finish in eleventh spot.

After a 1–1 draw with West Brom on 1 March, the defeat at Portsmouth the following Sunday ended a seventeen-game unbeaten league run, the club's best since going thirty without defeat under Don Revie between May 1973 and February 1974. Against Pompey Leeds had thirteen shots, three big chances and accumulated an expected goal total of 2.36 (Piroe alone had 1.08 of that) without finding the net, the fourth most by a team without scoring in a Championship game all season. It was a long way to travel for a midday kick-off to see a defeat where so many chances went begging, though trips to Fratton Park have never really been successful – Leeds have a win ratio of 19% there, winning just six of thirty-one visits.

It completed a bizarre couple of winless games against Portsmouth in 2024–25. Across the two matches, Leeds had thirty-five shots to Pompey's eighteen and had accumulated a massive 5.74 xG – only having more against Cardiff across the season (8.68) – which was 4.08 more than Portsmouth. And yet, Leeds had been outscored by four to three across the two games, missing eight of their nine Opta-defined big chances and picking up just a single point. It wasn't as bad as the 6–1 defeat against them in 2003–04, but Portsmouth could probably be classed as the bogey team of the season.

All six of Leeds United's defeats in 2024–25 were either against teams whose name starts with B (Burnley, Blackburn), M (Millwall x2, Middlesbrough) or P (Portsmouth). Leeds didn't lose any of the other thirty-one games against sides not starting with those letters.

Another early kick-off down south followed the next weekend as Leeds travelled to face Queens Park Rangers at Loftus Road. This was the ground where they'd suffered their worst defeat under Farke the previous April, going down 4–0 in the penultimate game of the 2023–24 season, a hugely damaging defeat in the hope of an automatic promotion spot. Leeds had been forty points ahead of QPR, ahead of the 4–0 loss, and while the gap wasn't as large this time ('only' 35 points separated the sides), defeat was unthinkable as the Hoops went into the game on a four-game losing run.

Leeds hadn't trailed by two goals in a league game since the 4–0 defeat at Loftus Road but after half an hour it was QPR 2–0 Leeds, the worrying and dangerous mixture of early kick-off and London proving the undoing, as well as some dubious defending on the pitch. Leeds had lost their previous sixty-four games in London when they'd trailed by two goals, but they rallied to avoid defeat this time around, earning a 2–2 draw with a Morgan Fox own goal and a Jayden Bogle second half equaliser. The last time Leeds had come from 2–0 down to avoid defeat in London had been in a 2–2 draw in November 1972 at Crystal Palace, with midfielder John Craven scoring two goals for Palace that day in the same year *Newsround* was first broadcast (now there's a reference that might be lost on any younger readers).

Morgan Fox's own goal for QPR was the 153rd time Leeds had benefitted from an own goal in their history. It places own goals in third on the all-time leading Leeds scorers, behind only Peter Lorimer (238) and John Charles (157).

A new Championship record

The final two home games in March saw Leeds set a new Championship record for unbeaten games when scoring the opening goal. The win over Millwall on 12 March equalled the seventy-five matches that Burnley managed without losing between 2013 and 2022, with Leeds' last defeat after netting the opener in a Championship game coming in the painful 4–2 loss to Derby in the play-offs in 2019. Since that defeat, the only time Leeds had fallen behind in a game where they went 1–0 up, had been on the opening day of 2024–25 against Portsmouth, going 2–1 and 3–2 down that day before snatching a 3–3 draw. That game aside, Leeds were virtually imperious and unstoppable when taking the lead.

The victory against Millwall was, as the cliché goes, a game of two halves. Though Leeds took the lead early on thanks to a Jake Cooper own goal, they were restricted to just four attempts and only seven touches in Millwall's box. In the second half, they had fourteen attempts to Millwall's one, while they had thirty-one touches in Millwall's penalty area, compared to facing only two in their own.

Only one of those fourteen attempts in the second half had been on target but Ao Tanaka had swept it into the back of Millwall's net. It had been a fine individual performance from Tanaka – in this game, he was the only Championship player all season long to win more than ten duels, complete more than seventy-five passes and score a goal in a single match.

Leeds broke the record for scoring first without losing in the Championship in the next game at Elland Road, though by full-time no one really felt like celebrating. Brenden Aaronson gave Leeds the lead against Swansea City after just thirty-four seconds, the second league goal scored in the opening minute by the club in 2024–25, along with Manor Solomon's against Norwich in January. It was the first time there'd been two 1st minute Leeds goals in the same league season since 2004–05, when Simon Walton and Jermaine Wright scored against Reading and Burnley respectively. Neither Walton nor Wright had won those games, and Aaronson was about to suffer the same fate.

It was an afternoon of contrasts for Illan Meslier, who saved his first Leeds penalty since March 2021 versus West Ham (this was the sixteenth he'd faced since then) and, incredibly, became the first Whites goalkeeper to save a penalty in front of supporters since a late Bailey Peacock-Farrell save against Reading in November 2018 (incidentally, this was the last time a match at Elland Road, excluding the Covid attendances, has dipped below 30,000). In the second half, though, Meslier dropped the ball at the feet of Harry Darling who equalised for the Swans, making Meslier one of only two Championship goalkeepers all season to save a penalty and be awarded an Opta-defined error leading to a goal in the same match. Wilfried Gnonto, on the pitch as a sub for all of fifty-eight seconds, rifled home to give Leeds another lead in the 86th minute, but a 96th minute equaliser by Zan Vipotnik – a shot that Meslier really should have saved – saw the points shared.

It was the second latest goal against Leeds all season, with the latest the Junior Firpo own goal against Sunderland in October. There had been calls for Meslier to be dropped after that error, but Farke stuck with his goalkeeper; this time around, he decided enough was enough and Karl Darlow was to be given the nod for the remainder of the season.

After the highs of February, Leeds had picked up just six points in five games in March, scoring only seven goals and keeping just one clean sheet.

The last time they'd earned promotion in 2019–20, in the final seven games of the season they won six, drew one, scored eighteen goals and conceded only three. Yes, something like that again would do the trick.

Leeds go back on top

Leeds had at least ten shots in forty-two of their forty-six Championship matches in 2024–25 but two of the games in which they didn't came consecutively at the beginning of April. Another early kick-off beckoned away at Luton Town, a ground where they had a good recent record, winning the last two trips – 1–0 in August 2016 in a League Cup tie and 2–1 in November 2019 thanks to a very late own-goal. The last time Leeds had trailed in a game at Kenilworth Road had been in a humiliating 5–1 loss there in October 2006 in the last of caretaker manager John Carver's five games in charge after the sacking of Kevin Blackwell.

Another 5–1 looked unlikely given that Luton were second-bottom of the league going into the game, and had scored the fewest goals of any side with thirty-five, but they made that thirty-six in the 15th minute to go 1–0 ahead. It was the fifth time in eight games that Leeds had conceded the opening goal in a league match. Daniel James equalised in the 28th minute with a lovely effort from outside the box, curled in with his left-foot – it was his thirty-seventh shot of the Championship season with his left-foot but the first time he'd scored on his weaker side. The best chance to win the game for Leeds also came via a left-footed effort, this time from Manor Solomon with eight minutes remaining, but he could only blaze his shot wide.

The 1–1 draw was described by Farke as a 'good point' which many fans disagreed with, given the lowly position of the opposition and the fact that, for the first time since 6 December, Leeds were now outside the top two positions. It was the first time Leeds had drawn three league games in a row since January 2016 and the Luton game, played in the fourth month of the year and fifth day in it, was the 405th league game since then.

Though Middlesbrough had come to Elland Road in August in the League Cup and won 3–0, there'd been eight changes to the XI from the opening game against Portsmouth and two of those – Joe Gelhardt and Patrick Bamford – made their only starts of the entire season. Gelhardt was now out on loan at Hull City but Bamford, after an injury layoff, was back for the remainder of the season and his brief cameo at Luton had shown that he could still contribute; of the four shots Leeds had with him on the pitch, he'd been involved in 75% of them, having two himself and creating another. He would be incredibly unfortunate not to score in the next game, with his fine finish at Middlesbrough ruled out incorrectly for offside.

Leeds had an excellent recent league record against Middlesbrough and the last time they'd lost there, in March 2018, Bamford had actually scored a hat-trick for Boro in a 3–0 win. Going into the April meeting, Leeds were seven unbeaten against Boro and had won each of their previous five, and they made that eight without defeat and six wins in a row thanks to a 2nd minute Daniel James goal, his last of the season. It was the earliest into a league game that Leeds had gone 1–0 ahead and then eventually won by that scoreline since February 1996 in an FA Cup match against Bolton (Rod Wallace scoring in the 1st minute). By the end of the game – with Leeds having faced seventeen shots, their most in a league match all season – most supporters' nerves were shot to pieces, not helped by the incorrectly disallowed goals scored by Tanaka and the aforementioned Bamford.

Daniel James' winner at Middlesbrough was his twenty-fifth goal scored under manager Daniel Farke. The only other Leeds United players to score twenty-five goals for a manager they share the same first name with are Frank Dudley under Frank Buckley (twenty-seven goals) and Don Weston under Don Revie (twenty-six goals).

The midweek victory at the Riverside put Leeds back on top of the Championship, as Burnley could only draw 0–0 with Derby on the same night, while Sheffield United, for the first time since October, had suffered consecutive league defeats, losing against Oxford and Millwall. The Blades' next fixture was a trip to Plymouth on Saturday, which was kicking off at the same time as Leeds' home game against Preston.

It would be the first in a string of three of the all-time best Elland Road atmospheres.

Farke breaks a club record

Preston's visit to Elland Road was the one hundredth game of Daniel Farke's Leeds United reign. The last Leeds boss to hit one hundred games had been Marcelo Bielsa in a 4–0 win over Charlton in July 2020, a month in which Leeds had earned promotion to the Premier League. It was yet another good omen and Leeds won 2–1 against the Lilywhites, securing the fifty-seventh win under Farke and setting a new record for victories in a manager's first one hundred games at Leeds; the previous most had been fifty-six by both Bielsa and Simon Grayson.

Manager	Wins in First 100 Leeds Games
Daniel Farke	57
Simon Grayson	56
Marcelo Bielsa	56
David O'Leary	54
Dick Ray	50

Manor Solomon both scored and assisted against Preston, the fourth time he'd done so in a Championship match in 2024–25 – the joint most of any player for any side all campaign long. Solomon's assist had been a brilliant cross for full-back Jayden Bogle to tap in at the back post and it had been Bogle who stood out in this match, moving Leeds constantly up the pitch on the right-hand side; he carried the ball 366 metres in this match, the most by a Leeds full-back in a game since Luke Ayling in August 2021 against Everton. Bogle's willingness to get forward would see him rank first among defenders in the Championship for touches in the opposition box across the entire 2024–25 season with 137, and another one of these touches would be crucial in the next match away at Oxford.

While Leeds were seeing off the challenge of Preston – who managed just three shots all afternoon to the twenty of Leeds – and extending their run of Championship games unbeaten when scoring first to seventy-eight, Sheffield United were doing quite the opposite. In thirty-two Championship games when going 1–0 up in 2024–25, the Blades only lost two. One was at home to Leeds in February and the other came away at Plymouth, when two late goals by the Pilgrims sunk Chris Wilder's side. Given the ambiguous nature of getting signal in Elland Road, it was left to the lucky few who infiltrated the 5G network to let others know that Plymouth had equalised and then taken the lead, leading to rapturous applause. Players warming up in front of the West Stand were asking fans for updates for the score. Elland Road felt United.

> The victory over Preston meant that Daniel Farke had ended the
> day top of the Championship for 396 nights in total, breaking
> Neil Warnock's record of 395. He would extend this to 415 by
> the end of the campaign.

Top of the table Leeds were now five points clear of Sheffield United
in third with four games remaining, a position from which no
Championship side had ever failed to go on to be promoted. The next
opponents were Oxford United at the Kassam Stadium, only Leeds'
sixth ever away game at Oxford. In yet more good omens, though,
the last time Leeds had visited Oxford for a league game had been in
March 1990 shortly before winning promotion back to the top-flight,
winning 4–2.

Solomon had assisted Bogle in the previous match and this time it
was the reverse, a Bogle cross smashed in by Solomon to give Leeds a
1–0 lead in the first half that they never relinquished, only the third 1–0
league win of the season. Much of that was thanks to the heroic efforts
of centre half Joe Rodon, who simply refused to be beaten, making
eleven clearances – seven more than any other player on either side.

Leeds were now five points clear of third with three games to go.
A win, any win, over Stoke at Elland Road on Easter Monday would
put all the pressure on Sheffield United to beat Burnley in the later
kick-off, otherwise Leeds were promoted.

Leeds United 6–0 Stoke City

Since cracking in an exceptional strike from range in the 3–1 win at
Sheffield United on 24 February, Joel Piroe had suffered a hard time in
front of goal. Going into the Easter Monday visit of Stoke, Piroe had
gone twenty shots without scoring in the Championship, with only one
player in the division – former Leeds man Sam Greenwood – having
more efforts without scoring in that time (twenty-one) At nine games,
it was the longest drought of his Championship career.

It had been even longer since a hat-trick had been scored at Elland

Road in a league game for either Leeds or their opponents; a Ross McCormack treble in a 5–1 win over Huddersfield Town in February 2014 was the last time that had happened, and this would be the 248th league game played at Elland Road since then.

After no goals from twenty efforts, Piroe then scored four goals from as many shots in the first half against Stoke, enjoying the finest first half of goalscoring in the club's entire history. It was the first time ever a Leeds player had scored four in the first forty-five minutes of a match, and the first time ever a player had achieved that in a Championship match. Piroe's third had come on twenty minutes; the last Leeds first-half hat-trick had been Jermaine Beckford away at Chester City in August 2008, while in the opening twenty minutes of a match it was Allan Clarke against Norwich in January 1973 in an FA Cup replay. McCormack had also been the last Leeds player to score four in a game, crashing in four against Charlton in November 2013 at the Valley; on home soil, it hadn't happened since Brian Deane's four goals against QPR in November 2004.

Piroe enjoyed facing Stoke in 2024–25, scoring six goals against them, making up 32% of his goal tally for the season. He's one of only three players in Leeds United's history to score six goals against one team in a season – John Charles did it three times, while Allan Clarke was Burnley's nemesis in 1970–71.

Season	Player	Opponent	Goals
1952–53	John Charles	Brentford	6
1953–54	John Charles	Rotherham United	6
1956–57	John Charles	Sheffield Wednesday	6
1970–71	Allan Clarke	Burnley	6
2024–25	Joel Piroe	Stoke City	6

City teams were not safe when Piroe was around. It wasn't just Stoke City he enjoyed scoring against – he also got three against Cardiff and two each against Coventry and Hull in 2024–25 to take his total to thirteen in fourteen games against City sides (amazingly, despite this high goal tally, he didn't even score in six games against Bristol, Norwich or

Swansea City). It's the most goals scored versus teams with a specific suffix by a Leeds United player in one season. Manchester City must surely be worried about Piroe with Leeds back in the Premier League . . .

Season	Player	Opponent's Suffix	Goals
2024–25	Joel Piroe	City	13
2008–09	Jermaine Beckford	Town	11
1953–54	John Charles	City	10
1972–73	Allan Clarke	City	10
1952–53	John Charles	City	9
1955–56	John Charles	City	9
2008–09	Jermaine Beckford	United	9

Joel Piroe's four goals against Stoke City was the first Leeds hat-trick on a Monday since Jermaine Beckford scored three against Northampton Town in an FA Cup replay in November 2008. The last Leeds league hat-trick on a Monday had been John Charles against Fulham in April 1956, which was also on Easter Monday.

It wasn't only Piroe and his four on target in the first half, as Junior Firpo netted the fourth of five first half Leeds goals. The 5–0 half-time score was the biggest margin Leeds had led by at the break since December 1970 against Sparta Prague in the Fairs Cup (also 5–0), while in the league it was the first time since the opening game of the 1956–57 season against Everton, when newly promoted Leeds were 5–0 ahead with Harold Brook notching a hat-trick that day too. It was an astonishing half of attacking football from a Leeds team who could easily have been cagey and nervous in the context of what was needed. Instead, they simply swept Stoke aside, creating seven big chances – the most by a side in the first half of a Championship game all season.

A second half Willy Gnonto goal gave Leeds a 6–0 win, their second win by six or more goals in the space of just fifteen league games following the 7–0 demolition of Cardiff; the previous two league wins by this margin beforehand came over a period of 2,439 league matches (7–0 vs Southampton in 1972, 6–0 vs Oldham in 1984). The 2024–25 season was only the second one in which Leeds had two victories by that margin in the league, and the other was in 1953–54: 6–0 vs Notts County and 7–1 vs Leicester.

Once everyone had processed what they'd just witnessed at Elland Road, it was time to cheer on Burnley for the first time all season. Their 2–1 win over Sheffield United ensured Leeds were promoted back to the Premier League, sparking jubilant scenes at Elland Road and around the city centre. As they had done in 2019–20, Leeds were promoted with two games to go thanks to a 2–1 win elsewhere (Huddersfield in 2020, Burnley in 2025). It was one of many parallels with that campaign, but the main one was simply that Leeds had returned to the promised land.

After recovering from the much deserved celebrations, Leeds had two games to break more records and win the league, starting with Bristol City the following Monday.

Harry Gray, brother of Archie, made his Leeds United debut in the 6–0 win over Stoke at the age of 16 years and 195 days, not only the youngest member of the Gray family to play for Leeds but the fourth-youngest player ever. The only other player to make his debut in a 6–0 win was Eddie Burbanks in 1953 against Notts County, who holds the distinction of being the club's oldest ever debutant (40 years and 140 days).

Leeds United 4–0 Bristol City

While some teams could be classed as bogey sides for Leeds, Bristol City were the total opposite. In the club's history, they've faced fifty-three different teams at least twenty-five times in league matches and the only side they have a win ratio of over 60% against is Bristol City, winning twenty-five out of forty league matches (62.5%). Since 2004–05 in the Championship, Leeds have won sixteen of twenty matches against the Robins, also a Championship high (80% win ratio) in that time for teams to face another twenty or more times. With a minimum of ten meetings, the best win rate is Leeds United against Plymouth Argyle (90%), a positive record which would prove handy very shortly.

Leeds Opponents – League History	Games	Wins	Win %
Bristol City	40	25	62.5%
Coventry City	84	45	53.6%
Notts County	32	17	53.1%
Swansea City	42	22	52.4%
Plymouth Argyle	42	22	52.4%

Opta began recording detailed Championship data in 2013–14 and Leeds United's 4–0 win over Bristol City was one of, if not the most, dominant performances by a team on record. Leeds are the only side in that timeframe to score four goals, have more than twenty shots, more than ten shots on target, create more than ten big chances, have more than fifty touches in the opponent's box, and complete over 700 passes in a Championship match. It was a fun night at Elland Road – already promoted, devoid of any pressure, a carnival atmosphere and with a team playing to its full potential.

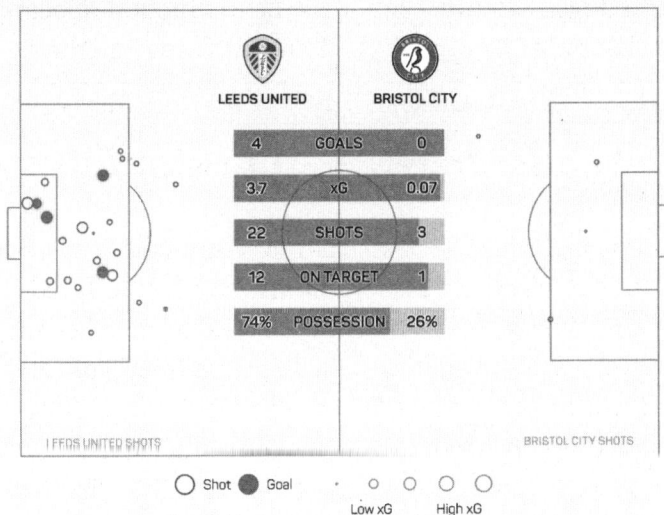

Leeds United 4-0 Bristol City
English Championship 2024-25 | 28 April 2025

Leeds completed 776 passes – their most in a league game on record since 2013–14 – while captain Ethan Ampadu was responsible for 157 of those, not too far off Bristol City's total as an entire team (226). Every single player who started the match for Leeds enjoyed a passing accuracy of at least 78%, while goalkeeper Karl Darlow didn't misplace a single one of his twenty passes. As well as creating five chances – including a lovely assist for the fourth goal – Ilia Gruev completed 108 passes, misplacing just four all evening. Leeds enjoyed 74% possession and in the first half had a move of fifty passes involving all ten outfield players which lasted 2 minutes and 32 seconds – the longest passing move in the Championship all season. It was an accomplished night all over the pitch.

Ao Tanaka gave Leeds the lead in the 21st minute and it was the thirty-third goal scored by Leeds in the opening thirty minutes of a Championship game in 2024–25, setting a new record by a team in a Championship season. Miss kick-off or go for an early half-time pint at your peril.

Season	Team Name	Goals in First 30 Mins
2024–25	Leeds United	33
2019–20	Brentford	32
2023–24	Southampton	32
2009–10	Newcastle United	31
2011–12	Southampton	31
2016–17	Norwich City	31

Data via Opta

Willy Gnonto, scoring in consecutive appearances for the first time since the previous March, made it 2–0 early in the second half. Joel Piroe – whose superb, Hernández-esque through-ball created the goal – wasn't the only one with a great record against City teams. Gnonto scored six of his nine Championship goals in 2024–25 against Coventry City, Swansea City (x2), Cardiff City, Stoke City and Bristol City. His minutes per goal against City teams was one every 106 minutes, compared to only one every 547 minutes against non-City teams. Once again, Manchester City: beware.

Putting the gloss on the victory was Largie Ramazani with two goals. He'd been substituted on in the 81st minute, making him the first player in the club's history to be subbed on that late into a game and score two goals. He ended the season with the best minutes per goal ratio – one every 130 minutes – of any player in the Championship, while he had the most shots (4.1), shots on target (1.8) and best expected goals (0.54) per ninety minutes of any player as well. When given opportunities, Ramazani was a player who made something happen and got fans off their seats, none more so than that night against Bristol City. His backflip celebration was certainly a crowd-pleaser, too.

> Over the course of the 2024–25 season, Leeds scored forty league goals against sides with City in their name. In Football League history, only Tottenham Hotspur in 1919–20 have ever scored more in one season (forty-one), which was also a season in which they won the second tier of English football.

It was the first time Leeds had won consecutive games by four or more goals since October 2009, when they enjoyed 4–0 wins against Bristol Rovers and Yeovil Town in League One. The four goals against Bristol City took Leeds to sixty-one home league goals for 2024–25, the second-most in a season in the club's history, behind the sixty-three goals they scored at Elland Road in 1927–28, and they were the first side from the second tier to exceed sixty home goals in a season since Manchester City scored sixty-three in 2001–02. It was also only the second time ever Leeds had won eighteen home league matches in a season, doing so previously in 1968–69 in their first ever top-flight title-winning season. Elland Road was a fortress.

In the final three home games against Preston, Stoke and Bristol City, Leeds had sixty shots and faced just eleven which was indicative of the entire season: their opponents managed just 121 shots at Elland Road all season long (and never once reached double figures for attempts in a match), the fewest ever faced by a team on home soil in a Championship season Opta has on record since 2013–14, while only

AS LEEDS GO MARCHING ON

four teams have ever had more shots at home in a season than Leeds in 2024–25, who ended on 427. Pure entertainment, dominance and fun at Elland Road all season long.

> Largie Ramazani scored as many Championship goals in thirty-three minutes of action in April as Sunderland managed in six games (two each).

Champions again, olé olé

If you'd asked Leeds United fans how they wanted to win the title, scoring in the 91st minute with the last shot of the season to go onto one hundred points, and above Burnley, who had just started celebrating at their own stadium, would probably be far too good to be true. But this is no ordinary football club, and this was no ordinary season.

Plymouth were the final day opponents and for a while, it looked as though this game could be a straight shootout in the Pilgrims' battle to stay up and Leeds' to gain the win they needed for promotion. As it happened, Plymouth were all but relegated and needed an enormous goal swing and other results to go in their favour to stay up. For Leeds, the task was simple: win the game and they were champions.

It was the first time the Leeds starting XI had all lined up together, but it also had another special significance – it was the first starting line-up without a player who had played at least once under Marcelo Bielsa since 21 February 2015 against Middlesbrough, with this the 498th game since then. There was one similarity with the 2015 team, though – Sam Byram was in both line-ups, the first as a 21-year-old and the most recent as a 31-year-old promotion winner.

Things didn't quite go to plan in the first half, though. Byram was involved but unfortunately for all the wrong reasons, scoring the first own goal of his 313-game career to that point, and the first in 219 games for Leeds. He wasn't alone in scoring own goals though – 13% of the goals Leeds conceded in the Championship in 2024–25 had been via their own players (four out of thirty), the highest percentage

302

of any side. At the other end, Leeds were dominating but couldn't find the net with any of their fifteen shots, the most without scoring in the first half of a league game since February 2019 against Daniel Farke's Norwich side.

It was another dominant second half, but this time Leeds did make the breakthrough. For a third consecutive match, Gnonto was on the scoresheet, becoming the first Leeds player to score in the final three league games of a campaign since Jermaine Beckford in 2008–09. Beckford had famously scored the promotion-winning goal in 2010 against Bristol Rovers and Leeds were still searching for the 2025 hero when Manor Solomon collected a pass from Gnonto in the 91st minute, dropped a shoulder and, with the 759th and final shot of the season, fired into the back of the net to write his name into the history of Leeds United.

Plymouth 1–2 Leeds. One hundred points. Champions again, olé olé.

It was fitting for Solomon to score the winner – he scored in nine league games for Leeds in 2024–25 and they won every single game, giving him the best 100% win record in league games in which a player has scored for the club. The previous best had been another Leeds promotion winner, Neil Kilkenny, who won all eight.

Leeds United – League History	Games Scored In	Games Won
Manor Solomon	9	9
Neil Kilkenny	8	8
Keith Edwards	6	6
Andy Watson	6	6
Georginio Rutter	6	6

Solomon's goal was his tenth of the season in the Championship, also registering twelve assists and becoming the first Leeds United player to hit double figures for both in the league since Pablo Hernández had twelve goals and twelve assists in 2018–19. In all, only three Championship players registered more goal involvements than Solomon in 2024–25, while his goal or assist ratio of one every 118 minutes was the best of any player to play over 1,000 minutes. His title-winning goal had capped a fine individual season.

Leeds had been used to late shows in 2024–25, scoring eighteen Championship goals from the 86th minute onwards, the most by a side in a Championship season ever. From Brenden Aaronson's 95th minute equaliser on the opening day through to Solomon's 91st minute winner on the final day, Leeds had kept everyone entertained right to the end.

Season	Team Name	Goals from 86th Min. Onwards
2024–25	Leeds United	18
2010–11	Norwich City	15
2023–24	Southampton	15
2021–22	Coventry City	14
2023–24	Ipswich Town	14

Data via Opta

Leeds had ended the season on a run of six consecutive wins for just the third time in the club's history, also doing so in 1955–56 and 2019–20, also second tier promotion seasons. In fact, the parallels with the 2020 promotion were spooky:

In 2019–20, Leeds drew with Luton in the fortieth game, then won six in a row, hammered Stoke at Elland Road and beat a relegated team on the final day of the season.

In 2024–25, Leeds drew with Luton in the fortieth game, then won six in a row, hammered Stoke at Elland Road and beat a relegated team on the final day of the season.

Leeds had won twenty-eight league games in 2019–20 but they went one better in 2024–25, with twenty-nine wins, a new club record. The ninety-five goals scored were the best since 1927–28, when ninety-eight were netted, while one hundred points set a new points record in the club's history. There were just four defeats all season – the club's fewest ever in a 46-game season and lowest since the four losses in forty-two games in 1991–92 – and not a single defeat by more than one goal for the first time in a season in the club's history. They also set a new record for clean sheets at twenty-five, a record that had stood since the twenty-four clean sheets in 1968–69 and 1970–71.

Though he had been dropped for the final seven games, it is wrong to overlook that twenty-one of those clean sheets were kept by Illan Meslier, which is the second most by a goalkeeper in a league season in the club's entire history, behind the twenty-four by Gary Sprake in 1968–69. Karl Darlow had come in and done a stellar job in the last seven games, with his four clean sheets the joint most of any Championship goalkeeper in that timeframe and only one goalkeeper to feature in all seven games had a better save ratio than he did (75%).

Meslier had featured ten times in the 2019–20 Championship promotion-winning campaign. Also playing in that season and in 2024–25 were Pascal Struijk (five games in 2019–20, thirty-five in 2024–25) and Patrick Bamford (forty-five in 2019–20, seventeen in 2024–25) and they were the first players to feature in two different promotion-winning seasons for Leeds since Grenville Hair and Jack Charlton in 1955–56 and 1963–64.

> The only two Leeds players to feature in three promotion-winning seasons are Ernie Hart and Bill Menzies, who both played in the 1923–24, 1927–28 and 1931–32 campaigns.

Central defender Joe Rodon was the only Leeds player to start all forty-six league games and became one of three central defenders to start every game of a title-winning season, along with Norman Hunter (1963–64, 1968–69 and 1973–74) and Ben White (2019–20). Rodon also completed 3,454 passes in 2024–25, the most of any player in the EFL, while his fellow Welshman and Leeds captain Ethan Ampadu ranked top for successful passes per ninety minutes in the Championship with seventy-eight. The difference with and without Ampadu was also stark – in twenty-nine league games with Ampadu, Leeds lost just once and only conceded twelve goals with him on the pitch. In the seventeen without him, they lost three and let eighteen goals in.

Looking further up the pitch, Piroe ended the campaign as leading Championship scorer with nineteen goals, while his additional seven assists gave him the most goals and assists combined. Three of the seven players with nine or more assists were Leeds players – Solomon (twelve), Junior Firpo (ten, the most of any defender) and Dan James (nine) all amongst the most creative players in the division. And while he only got two assists, the player with the most chances created for his teammates in open play was Brenden Aaronson with seventy.

> Leeds went through the entirety of the 2024–25 season without receiving a single red card for the first time since 1994–95.
> They were the third Championship champions to achieve that unblemished record, along with Reading in 2005–06 and Burnley in 2015–16.

And what of the man who picked the team? Daniel Farke became the first ever manager to win the second tier of English football on three occasions, and the first to lift the trophy with two teams since Mick McCarthy with Sunderland in 2005 and Wolves in 2009. Among managers with one hundred or more games, Farke has the best win ratio in the Championship since 2004–05 – beating Scott Parker by a very marginal amount, once again.

Championship History	Games	Wins	Win %
Daniel Farke	230	127	55.2%
Scott Parker	138	76	55.1%
Steve Coppell	139	71	51.1%
Chris Wilder	189	93	49.2%
Steve Cooper	130	63	48.5%

Farke also has the best goals-per-game ratio of any Championship manager at 1.71 per game, and it was this attacking intent that helped Leeds over the line to become champions on goal difference ahead of Burnley, the first time the second tier had been decided this way since 1989–90 – which was also Leeds winning the title. Burnley had gone thirty-three games unbeaten, only lost two games, also won one hundred points and kept thirty clean sheets and yet their goal difference was twelve worse than Leeds', with the Whites outscoring the

Clarets by twenty-six goals, enjoying the second best goal difference in Championship history (+65), second only to Reading in 2005–06 (+67). Attack had won the day – and the title.

Leeds had led the way in so many different ways – including topping the table for 116 days, over one hundred more than Burnley on fourteen – and were more than worthy champions.

Leeds United – 2024–25 – Championship	Totals	Rank
Shots	759	1
Shots on Target	261	1
Shots Faced	308	24
Shots on Target Faced	102	24
Average Possession	61.5%	1
Successful Passes	21,572	1
Passing Accuracy	86.2%	1
Successful Passes in Opposition Half	10,750	1
Touches in the Opposition Box	1,413	1

Now, with promotion and the title secured, it was time to party. The champions' parade on 5 May was a fitting way to celebrate the team that had taken the club back to the Premier League and to enjoy what we'd missed out on in 2020. It was hard to imagine then loving a promotion team more than that one, but the 2025 vintage have given us incredible moments to remember forever. They were deserved champions, and they got the ovation and acclaim they all deserved in Leeds city centre.

I was there, among the approximate 250,000 crowd – I am good at numbers, but I couldn't reliably count that amount on the day – and it was days like that which make all the lows (travelling to Wembley on your thirtieth birthday to see a play-off final defeat, that type of thing) completely worth it. The city was a sea of yellow and white, with friends, families and complete strangers all coming together to celebrate a special group of players and management – not to mention club legends Eddie Gray and Paul Reaney, on board the promotion bus celebrating with the best of them. It was one of the most remarkable days to be a part of and it left you feeling that anything really is possible for Leeds United; the potential, as always, is huge. There's simply no other club like Leeds – as you'll have gathered after reading this book.

We'll have more ups and more downs – this is Leeds, after all. But we'll always have the memories of those late wins against Sunderland and Sheffield United, the 7–0 against Cardiff, the 6–0 against Stoke, the demolition of Bristol City and the title-winning goal in the last minute at Plymouth. A special season, a special team and a lifetime of memories, adding another incredible chapter to the history of this one-of-a-kind club.

At least until the world stops going round . . .

SELECT BIBLIOGRAPHY

Books

Alexander, Duncan. *OptaJoe's Football Yearbook 2016*. London: Century, 2016.

Bagchi, Rob. *The Biography of Leeds United: The Story of the Whites*. Kingston upon Thames: Vision Sports Publishing, 2020.

Chapman, Daniel. *100 Years of Leeds United*. London: Icon Books, 2020.

Charlton, Jack. *Jack Charlton: The Autobiography*. London: Corgi, 2020.

Hay, Phil. *And It Was Beautiful: Leeds United in the Era of Marcelo Bielsa*. London: Orion Publishing Group, 2022.

Jarred, Martin and Malcolm MacDonald. *Leeds United: A Complete Record (1919–1989)*. Derby: Breedon Books Publishing, 1989.

Jarred, Martin and Malcolm MacDonald. *The Leeds United Cup Book*. Derby: Breedon Books Publishing, 1991.

Jarred, Martin and Malcolm MacDonald. *Leeds United: The Complete European Record*. Derby: Breedon Books Publishing, 2003.

Rich, Tim. *The Quality of Madness: A Life of Marcelo Bielsa*. London: Quercus Publishing, 2020.

Rothmans/Sky Sports. *Football Yearbook*. London: Headline Publishing, various years.

Saffer, David. *Champions 1991/1992: Leeds United*. Cheltenham: The History Press Ltd, 2003.

Websites

English National Football Archive. https://www.enfa.co.uk/

Oz White's Leeds United history. https://www.ozwhitelufc.net.au

Mighty Leeds, the Definitive History of Leeds United. http://www.mightyleeds.co.uk

ACKNOWLEDGEMENTS

In early January 2025, I mentioned to my girlfriend that I wanted to write a book. In turn, I mentioned it to my boss in the same week. It was a dream of mine, and I wanted to see how feasible it would be. Both were very supportive but to be honest it wasn't something I was thinking about imminently, just at some point in the future.

A few days later, after a snowy walk to Knaresborough for a quick drink, I got home and had a direct message from someone on social media. It was Tom Noble from Orion Publishing Group, asking if I'd ever thought about writing a book, and would I be interested in penning one about the stats and facts on the history of Leeds United? It was quite a strong pint I'd had, but I didn't think it was that strong. After rereading the message a few times I realised that, given the timing, I could hardly turn this chance down.

I can't thank Tom enough for his support on the book and – given he's a huge Leeds fan – his ideas and suggestions as it evolved over time. He made the whole process very straightforward – the main stress for us both was Leeds getting promoted. Jo Whitford at Orion was also an enormous help in getting the book into publishable shape, and I'm grateful to all the team there who have played a part in making this happen.

I've been at Opta for a decade now and been fortunate to work alongside a lot of immensely talented people, and many of them are now friends. For their support, particularly in the early stages of the book, I have to thank Nick Bentley and Rob Bateman for providing encouragement and their years of experience. On the legal side at Stats Perform, Meghan Nugent answered my many questions with great patience and was a huge help in getting the Opta data into the book, as were Alex Rice and Simon Smith. In the first instance of employing me, I must thank Duncan Alexander for giving me my first interview at the tender age of nineteen and then recommending me to the brilliant Matt Furniss for a job two years later. The job I'd originally applied for went to Chris Mayer, who I then worked closely with for two years and – once I'd gotten over the fact he got the job ahead of me – we got along very well and he taught me a lot, as did Jack Supple in those early days.

Within the Opta data insights team, there are so many people who contributed directly or indirectly to the book. For his Microsoft Excel formula knowledge, selflessness in passing it on and general altruism over the last ten years, a special thank you to Alan Duffy, without whom I wouldn't have been able to work out many of the stats that appear in the book. My fellow Leeds fans Jamie Kemp and Gareth Boyes have been fantastic colleagues and friends and have listened to my many nonsense Leeds stats over the years, as did Gareth's brother Alex when I worked with him, and we all celebrated promotion together in April. Mike Reid, Tom Ede and Harvey Downes have all created their own huge databases for their own teams and the facts they've crafted over the years will have inspired facts I've produced within these pages, and all have been incredible colleagues over a number of years. The Opta graphics you see in the book were the work of the very gifted duo Jonathan Whitmore and Jon Manuel, and the graphics we can now produce have been a very welcome addition to the work we do in the insights team.

I have to give a big shout-out to Dan, Michael, Oddy, Rob and all the guys at *The Square Ball* who welcomed me onto their brilliant podcast in early 2023 and have kept inviting me back ever since, and without them sending my stats and facts into the Leeds United stratosphere, I probably wouldn't have written this book.

Adam Pope also generously agreed to write a foreword for the book, for which I must say a big thank you. Popey interviewed me and my friends Ollie, Louis and James outside Stadium MK at my first away game at MK Dons in 2009 and got us onto the radio pre-match (our mums, I recall, said we 'sounded great'). Nine years later, he invited me onto his BBC Radio Leeds show to chat about the early days of Bielsa and was always so encouraging, often reading out my stats and facts on the radio before games and giving me a shout-out in the process. It was all hugely appreciated and still is. A real top man.

My amazing parents have been so supportive of my many good (or bad) decisions over the years, and this book was no different. My dad took me to my first game in 2000 and paid for my season ticket for a number of years, so celebrating promotion and then the title win with him were special moments. I also have to thank Geoff England for his many words of encouragement; I sat next to Geoff at Elland Road for ten seasons and he was often more entertaining than the football on the pitch and now, given he's fifty-five years my senior, he's continually on hand with some wise guidance on our regular pub visits.

Special thanks, too, to my wonderful partner Francesca, who has also been behind me every step of the way and probably didn't envisage that I'd be spending most evenings in the first few months in our first house together writing obscure facts about Leeds players from the 1960s. Or maybe she did.